*The Music Makers*

# The Music Makers

THE

ENGLISH MUSICAL RENAISSANCE

FROM ELGAR

TO

BRITTEN

## Michael Trend

SCHIRMER BOOKS
*A Division of Macmillan, Inc.*
NEW YORK

220515

Schirmer Books
A Division of Macmillan, Inc.
866 Third Avenue, New York, N.Y. 10022

First American Edition 1985

Library of Congress Catalog Card Number: 85-19797

Printed in the United States of America

Printing number
1  2  3  4  5  6  7  8  9  10

**Library of Congress Cataloging-in-Publication Data**

Trend, Michael.
   The music makers.

   Bibliography: p.
   Includes index.
   1. Music—England—19th century—History and criticism.   2. Music—England—20th century—History and criticism.   I. Title.
ML286.4.T74   1985        781.742        85-19797
ISBN 0-02-873090-9

*For my Parents*

We are the music makers,
    And we are the dreamers of dreams,
Wandering by lone sea-breakers,
    And sitting by desolate streams;
World-losers and world-forsakers,
    On whom the pale moon gleams:
Yet we are the movers and shakers
    Of the world for ever, it seems.

From Arthur O'Shaughnessy's
'Ode' from *Music and Moonlight*

# Contents

# Illustrations

Edward Elgar (National Portrait Gallery)
Edward Elgar boarding an aeroplane 28 May 1933 (The Associated Press Ltd)
Rutland Boughton (Royal College of Music)
Joseph Holbrooke (Mansell Collection)
Frederick Delius (Royal College of Music)
Ethel Smyth and her dog Marco (National Portrait Gallery)
Samuel Coleridge-Taylor (Royal College of Music)
William Hurlstone (Royal College of Music)
Granville Bantock (Bantock Society)
Gustav Holst and Ralph Vaughan Williams (Whittaker Centenary Fund)
Michael Tippett and Ralph Vaughan Williams (Erich Auerbach Collection)
John Ireland, Arnold Bax, Benjamin Britten and Granville Bantock (Bantock Society)
George Butterworth (Royal College of Music)
Percy Grainger with his mother Rose (British Library)
Cyril Scott (Royal College of Music)
Herbert Howells (Royal College of Music)
Ivor Gurney (Gloucestershire County Library)
Peter Warlock and E. J. Moeran, *c.* 1928 (Royal College of Music)
Arthur Bliss, 1921 (Photo: Hoppé, Mansell Collection)
Constant Lambert (National Portrait Gallery)
William Walton (Photo: Cecil Beaton, National Portrait Gallery)
Lord Berners (Photo: Bill Brandt, National Portrait Gallery)
Michael Tippett and Benjamin Britten (Erich Auerbach Collection)

# Acknowledgements

In the preparation of this book I received great assistance from John Gross, whose enthusiasm and experience ensured that I set a sound course for the undertaking, and from Elizabeth Burke, who later skilfully helped to bring it safely into harbour. I am also indebted to John Curtis and Isabella Forbes at Weidenfeld & Nicolson, to Lucy Pinney, and to David Micklethwait. Roger Wright at the British Music Information Centre in London was at all times full of helpful advice. Above all others, however, I owe a very special debt to Prue Burrows.

For permission to quote from the poetry of Ivor Gurney acknowledgement is made to Oxford University Press for material from the *Collected Poems*. I am also grateful for help with the illustrations from Dr C. Bantock, Terence Pepper at the National Portrait Gallery, Oliver Davies at the Royal College of Music, J. P. Pollitzer of the Whittaker Centenary Fund, and the Gloucestershire County Library.

# Introduction

I have tried in this book to describe the portraits which might hang in the room of a celestial gallery given to English composers born between the year after the Crimean War (Edward Elgar, 1857) and that immediately preceding the Great War for Civilization (Britten, 1913). Well-informed cynics will tell you that the walls are bare, the lighting poor and the floors unswept – indeed, that it is neglected; but a man with a careful eye will soon discern the lie. Here, rather, in a room named 'the English musical renaissance', are the images of the composers who belonged to the greatest flowering of English music since Tudor times: Elgar, Delius, Vaughan Williams, Holst, Walton, Tippett, Britten and perhaps some three score others.

It has not been my intention to write in any technical detail about the works of these composers. I have tried, instead, to provide a description of their lives and a character of their music; further, I have tried to draw in the general background against which they lived and worked. The English are very cautious about the music of their own composers and the enthusiast, trying to proselytize in the name of English music, is probably his cause's own worst enemy. My approach therefore has been to let the composers speak in their own words as far as possible. I have avoided musical quotations and have not referred the reader to specific passages in specific pieces, hoping that in a book such as this a more literary approach will be helpful.

In recent years biographies of the English composers who fall into the period of this study – individual portraits, as it were – have done much to stir up interest in the subject as a whole, and the time is ripe for a more general catalogue of the musical portrait gallery. The bibliography of this book shows the authors to which all students of recent English music are indebted. I have made much use of these and other written sources, as well as studying the music of the composers themselves.

Choosing which composers should be represented here has not

been difficult as far as the main figures go; but there is certain to be some disagreement as to which of the lesser figures should also have been included. I have been chiefly guided in my choice by the desire to include figures whose lives or music demonstrate some particular aspect of the musical renaissance as a whole that would not otherwise be covered.

The arrangement of the book is as follows: first, there is an introductory chapter which examines the main roots of the English musical renaissance in general terms; here the emphasis is on elements of continuity rather than those of change. This is followed by the parts that make up the whole – the composers themselves. Their arrangement into chapters has, in most cases, been a matter of convenience rather than a comment on their musical styles. Likewise the amount of space given to each composer is not in any way meant to be a judgement on his or her worth as an artist. To conclude the book I have appended a brief backward look at the period of musical history covered in the main chapters from the point of view of our own day – much as one might look back at a relief on the horizon – in order, especially, to see when, how, and why many of the elements that were vital to the musical renaissance fundamentally changed or died away.

One further point needs to be made before we look at the gallery of composers in greater detail. The great revival of English music from the time of Edward Elgar to that of Benjamin Britten, known by many who participated in it as the 'English musical renaissance', may be characterized in two main ways. First – following a phrase of Ernest Walker's – it was a revival of 'music, made in England'. And in this respect the story is one of sturdy and continuous growth from the 1880s onwards, a growth greatly influenced by the two world wars and the tremendous social changes and technological advances that have taken place in recent times. The areas in which 'music, made in England' may be said to have grown are numerous: the newly appearing institutions, colleges, orchestras, radio, records, music festivals, etc. Such a subject is a major study in itself and this book – although often touching on it – does not attempt to cover it. This book, rather, looks more specifically at 'English music' – the second main characteristic of the English musical renaissance – than 'music, made in England'.

There have been some writers in recent times who have regarded the use of the word 'English' in this context to be narrowly nationalistic. Such a view must, however, be resisted from a historical perspective.

The rediscovery of much English music of earlier periods, a vitally important element in the revival, was almost exclusively an English concern. This new interest encompassed folk-song, the Tudor virginalists and madrigalists, the works of Purcell, the setting of English texts and a strong feeling for the English countryside. With the areas that were not strictly English in origin – the great appeal of the world of the 'Celtic fringe' and the romantic call of the Orient – we are dealing with influences that were highly typical of many other artists in England during the period – especially in the years immediately before the First World War. In general terms many people used the words British and English interchangeably during the years covered by this book (see, for example, the Shaw quotation on page 6), but, when a specific term was sought to define the particular character of the music of the period it was always 'English'.

Finally, I should perhaps add that it has been a deliberate part of my general intention not to examine in any depth the influence of foreign composers on the subjects of this book. While it is obviously necessary to go into this matter in great detail in an individual biography – to examine or question the influence of, say, Wagner on Elgar, or Mahler and Shostakovich on Britten – my purpose here has not been to make such a study. In saying this I do not for a moment underrate the importance of such influences; I have, however, restricted myself to drawing an outline of the common characteristics of an indigenous view of music – of its place and purpose – in the years between the end of the last century and the middle years of this. In doing so I believe that the case for a real and significant renaissance of English music is clearly demonstrated.

# CHAPTER ONE

# The English Musical Renaissance

## A NEST OF SINGING BIRDS

'We must start from experience.'
(*Edward Elgar in a lecture of 1905*)

What has Benjamin Britten got to do with Edward Elgar? Surely they were worlds apart? How can we speak of a renaissance of English music that covers such different figures as Frederick Delius, Ralph Vaughan Williams, Gustav Holst, William Walton and Michael Tippett? My purpose here is to show that such questions are not as unlikely as they may at first seem, and that the elements of similarity that bind together these and other composers of the period between Elgar and Britten were strong and significant.

Like many artistic movements in English history and life the recent musical renaissance was built up of strong individuals. We can never expect to find among the composers of the period the voluntary submission to a 'school' or 'group' that has characterized the artistic history of other countries. To have addressed any of the composers of this period as a member of a group or school to their faces would have been a terrible mistake. But they shared so much common ground that to restrict oneself to thinking of them only as individuals would be equally misleading. They were considered by many of their contemporaries to be part of an 'English musical renaissance', a specific title given to the appearance of composers who in a wide variety of ways were making music which was substantially different from both the English music that had gone before and the contemporary music of the rest of the Continent. It was a remarkable period of English musical history, as those living through it were well aware.

The general image of a 'renaissance' of English music was a common one in the musical world for many years. And the nature of this renaissance was defined in one particular way. A favourite and revealing metaphor of the period was the use of a botanical image: English music was a growing thing, a plant perhaps, or a tree, and the progress of English music was judged as one would a specimen. Many musical writers used this metaphor extensively, and its widespread use tells us how the English musical renaissance was viewed by its friends: it was an organic growth which needed the right conditions in which to take. Many of the plants were humdrum enough, but there were occasions when one or other burst into the most magnificent flowers. And there was in all this also a feeling of the tenderness of plant forms, of their need for proper feeding and care. It is particularly revealing that this metaphor ceased to be used of the new English composers of the post-Second World War era. Nobody chose to apply it to the musicians emerging in that period, and the dropping of the term 'English musical renaissance' and its associated imagery at this time showed that contemporaries felt that a period of musical history should be considered to have come to an end. The phrase now became used only in an historical context.

Contemporary ideas of what made up the musical renaissance differed over the years and the wisdom of speaking out in its favour was in some part conditioned by the prevailing critical fashions of the day. The old German jibe about England being *'Das Land ohne Musik'* took far too long to die. At times writers would go to the ends of the earth in order to deny that such a 'movement' existed. This view was particularly prevalent in the 1960s. When Frank Howes's *The English Musical Renaissance* was published in 1966 it met with a mixed reception. One might have been tempted to paraphrase Malcolm Bradbury's comments on the literary movement of the 1950s, when Willoughby, in *Eating People is Wrong*, says 'Sorry, no movement. All made up by the literary editor of the *Spectator*', into 'Sorry, no English musical renaissance. All made up by the music critic of *The Times* [Frank Howes]'. From our present-day position, however, we can see that Howes was on the right lines and that there was much more to the idea of an English musical renaissance than its critics allowed.

For a start most of the composers who are the subjects of this book felt themselves that they belonged to a new, and important, tradition of English music. In looking at the individuals covered in greater detail we shall, of course, notice that many specific composers believed that their approach to the question of English music was the best one, and music writers who took their part sometimes wrote as if one particular composer's contribution was the musical renaissance itself. Overall, however, the separate composers had a much wider view as well. And the strong links between them can be seen to no better effect than in their sense of the part they played in a general progression. There was no complacency about these composers as there had been about many English musicians of previous times. As young men they expressed themselves as rebels against their immediate predecessors, while as older men they set out to guard the best part of the inheritance that they had come into. This recurring pattern between the generations was one of the surest signs of the building up of a tradition. These composers knew that while rebelling against what they took to be the dead hand of the 'establishment' figures of their day they also owed them a considerable debt; nobody expressed this better than Vaughan Williams and Holst in their talk of 'heirs and rebels', and theirs was a sentiment that can legitimately be given a much wider application. Vaughan Williams and Holst derived their idea from a statement of Gilbert Murray's: 'Every man who possesses real vitality can be seen as the resultant of two forces. He is first the child of a particular age, society, convention; of what we may call in one word a tradition. He is secondly, in one degree or another, a rebel against that tradition. And the best traditions make the best rebels.'

We tend to think nowadays that there were no *enfants terribles*, 'angry young men', or 'bright young things' on the English music scene until the years after the First World War and the emergence of such figures as William Walton and Constant Lambert; but already in the pre-war era, Cyril Scott, Joseph Holbrooke - even, in his own way, Delius - were, among others, for a while considered to be representatives of the most outrageously modern movements in music. Elgar, Vaughan Williams, Bax, Bliss, Walton, Lambert and Britten were all rebels of a sort in their times and each in their turn became part of the musical 'establishment' against which a new generation would rebel. But we should not think that the rebels/heirs, avant-garde/establishment cycle meant that there was serious personal rivalry between the composers. Rather the opposite was, in fact, the case. The composers had much in common and shared a certain 'character and mind', as Hubert Foss, a distinguished music educationalist, author and composer, once put it. They were frequently kind and helpful to each other. Together they felt that they resembled the 'nest of singing birds' that had adorned the first

Elizabeth's Court. Theirs was also a new renaissance because it too reflected a spirit of exuberance and optimism. What they lacked in an immediate tradition they made up for in their enthusiasm to create one; together they made the first substantial and sustained contribution to English music for centuries, and English music helped, in turn, make them. They were the central part of a thriving musical culture.

This group spirit manifested itself in many ways and was reflected in what music writers said at the time. It became possible to publish books about English composers, something that would have been unthinkable in the so-called 'Dark Age' of English music – the years of most of the eighteenth and nineteenth centuries. The excitement that the appearance of such a group of composers caused can be seen in many books and articles. For example, George Bernard Shaw, who first made his name as a music critic, wrote in 1922 of 'Messrs Bax, Ireland, Cyril Scott, Holst, Goossens, Vaughan Williams, Frank Bridge, Boughton, Holbrooke, Howells and the rest (imagine being able to remember offhand so many names of British composers turning out serious music in native styles of their own!!!)'.

Along with this spirit of positive enthusiasm that existed between English composers, they were drawn together by a common struggle against often strong prejudices – whatever the generally subscribed-to 'official' view of the place and purpose of music which we shall come to later in this chapter. In many houses music was not considered to be a particularly manly pursuit. In this context Shaw believed that the British were a 'people of low pleasures because we are brought up on them'. In the drawing-rooms of the wealthy and the middle classes especially the cultivation of musical talents was considered to be an essentially feminine undertaking. It was the daughters of the house who were supposed to be able to play the piano. Delius's father was insistent that his son should follow a career in the family business, finding it inconceivable that he should follow a career in music even though he himself was a great lover of the art. In families where the father was involved in the music business, like Holst's, a child might find support and encouragement for his natural talents, but in others it was likely that little support would be forthcoming. Bax, for example, portrayed his father as considering his musical talents to be an 'illness', and the individual stories of the composers in this book show again and again how the only encouragement that they really got from their families came from the female side: from their mothers, wives or daughters. This attitude to a career in music was as prevalent in the later part of the period. When the young Britten announced that he was going to be a composer he met the disheartening response, 'and what else?'

The life of a composer, as we shall see, could be very hard – especially in the early days of a career. Some composers were able to support themselves from private incomes but others had to undertake considerable amounts of drudgery or rely – often heavily – on private patronage. Payment for composers' works was also very low for much of this period and many – Elgar and Bliss, in particular – worked hard to get a proper payment for their work and that of their fellows. For these and many other reasons the composers of the time in England were further drawn together in a community of interest. That the composers of the period had this sort of particularly close relationship one to the other should not, however, suggest that they were insular in their approach to music; rather, their view of the relationship between home and abroad, in musical terms, was as central and as complicated to them as their feelings about heirs and rebels. Indeed this is another important way in which the composers of the period in England were clearly marked out as a group with a common background. It has been argued that throughout this period music in Britain dragged years behind the latest movements on the Continent. But this is a very narrow view, which seems to imply that composition should be a process of imitation rather than an act of autonomous creation. And it was, in any case, precisely those English composers who did try to be faithful followers of some contemporary European fashion who fell by the wayside. The direct English disciples of Brahms, Wagner and Schoenberg have quickly followed each other into oblivion. The tradition of the English musical renaissance was to be one of independent not insular growth: Vaughan Williams knew Ravel's music, and Bax that of Schoenberg, for example, but both knew also that they needed to find their own voices in their own way.

All composers of the period struggled against what Vaughan Williams called the 'cigar theory' of music in England. He said that music was regarded by many in England as a luxury which could not be made at home and, like cigars, had to be imported from overseas. And George Bernard Shaw made a similar point, using a different image: 'If we have to borrow tea from China ... we can at least plead that our soil will not produce tea. Now music it can produce. It has done it before and can do it again.' Following Elgar many composers stressed the need to avoid pointless imitation of foreign music. 'We must start from experience,'

said Elgar, quoting Leslie Stephen. The period was marked by a search
in the individual composers for what was 'characteristic' within themselves – a favourite word of one of the great teachers of the time, Hubert
Parry – and a search for their own voices. But the technical training
of composers in colleges of music still relied very heavily on the German
Romantic tradition and many English composers found that, while
knowing that they had something important to say, they were not easily
able to find their own way of saying it. This did not mean, however,
that English composers of the period turned their backs on the contemporary music of the Continent. There are many examples in this book
of composers learning from foreign models; but, as Vaughan Williams
once pointed out, they looked to those examples as 'an enrichment of
our native impulse and not a swamping of it'. There was also an appalling snobbery about foreign music and musicians in England. Many
composers made play with the view that they would do much better
with a foreign-sounding name. Critics also, in their labelling of various
English composers as the 'English Wagner', the 'English Debussy' and
so on, added to the feeling of national inability to take the music of
England seriously on its own terms. Against these, and many other
prejudices, the composers of the period had to contend.

One may ask a further important question: what did the achievement
of a reputation in Europe at this time actually mean? Of all the English
composers under study here one of the most successful in Germany was
Cyril Scott. What did his brief moment of fame avail him? And what
good was it that Elgar should have been considered a great composer by
Richard Strauss when both men's music was put out in the cold in the
years following the First World War? Does not the same fate await
Britten's reputation? And going to Germany for a musical training could
work two ways, both to the advantage and the disadvantage of the
pupil, as we shall see in the case of some of the members of the so-called
Frankfurt Gang.

What, then, was the remedy? In two articles in *Outlook* in 1919
Shaw gave his view: 'our composers posed as Germans as ridiculously as
our singers posed as Italians'. He saw the way forward as 'more performances, more publication and more advertisement'. 'Public opinion must
be roused to the need for providing in England the conditions in which
it will be possible for Englishmen, after a lapse of two centuries, once
more to express themselves in genuinely British music with a weight and
depth possible only in the higher forms of music.' English composers

of the period, then, did not seek out foreign models: following Elgar's advice and that of other leading figures they turned to their own country for inspiration. This came to them in many ways: from English literature, from their sense of the English countryside, and from their increased knowledge and love of English music from earlier periods of history. Each of these will have to be looked at in turn.

The close relation of music to words – Milton's 'voice and verse' – was one of the mainsprings of the whole musical renaissance. E. J. Dent, Professor of Music at Cambridge and an important national figure in the inter-war musical world in Britain, writing in *Music and Letters* in 1925, pointed out that 'our English composers have done right, notwithstanding all that foreign critics have said of our music in the past, to stick to singing as the source of their inspiration. The singing voice, directed by our own poetry, can give us varieties of rhythm perhaps more subtle than many which occur to the born fiddler.' (The last part of his remark refers to an earlier assertion that 'the German composer has had to become a slave to the fiddler'.) Another careful observer of English music, Wilfrid Mellers, made a similar point in 1941 when he noted that 'the deepest root of the [English] musical language is the verbal one'.

The search for suitable ways of setting the English language – so rich in its power to inspire – was of major importance to most of the English composers of the period. They sought in their texts not only inspiration for subject matter but also the very roots of a musical idiom. The choice of texts that these composers made is therefore often highly revealing. Of English authors only perhaps Shakespeare remained a firm favourite for setting to music over many different generations, although Housman's verse particularly dominated the middle years of the period covered by this book; his view of man and nature was one that was shared by many English composers of his day. (Housman himself is said to have detested the settings of his verse: one observer recalled him, 'as though in an extremity of controlling pain or anger', when he heard *On Wenlock Edge*, Vaughan Williams's setting of some of his poems. This was, however, in marked contrast to the close interest that many other poets showed in contemporary composers; there were many examples of close cooperation between writers and musicians.)

Along with this belief in the importance of English language and literature to English music there was a strong feeling of the importance of a sense of place in music. Many of the composers of the period sought a musical language that was associated with their feeling for the English landscape and particular parts of it. This was, to a certain extent, allied to their interest in English poetry, for much of the verse that they chose to set was pastoral in character. But, more than this, they wanted to depict their own feelings for the countryside around them in their music. The sound produced by a string orchestra was found to be particularly appropriate for creating musical pictures that had specific English connotations: there are many 'rhapsodies' and other such lyrical pieces written for strings or similar ensembles which most successfully evoke an impression of the English countryside. Many composers of the period chose, or preferred, to live in the countryside and were deeply influenced by it, some holding the view that their music could grow from the world around them. This held good throughout the period under consideration here; it was as true for Elgar and his beloved Malvern Hills as it was for Britten in Suffolk where, after a period of wandering, he put down deep roots.

In more technical musical terms the most important inspiration to English composers of the period was, however, their rediscovery of English music of earlier times. There were many ways in which this rediscovery took place. That much music previously only in manuscript form was now edited and printed was an important starting point. Musical scholars, as well as composers, began to take a real interest in the music of England's past and in certain specific figures in it, and some remarkable discoveries were made. There were substantial printed editions of the Tudor virginalists and madrigalists, of the music of the English Church, and of many hitherto obscure composers. It would be hard to overemphasize in particular the importance of Purcell in this respect and here again we can see the close relation between music and the setting of words; for it was, above all, Purcell's wonderful facility and success in setting English texts that composers of this period so admired and wished to emulate in their own work.

This admiration of English music of earlier periods, feeling for the English countryside and belief that music could grow out of words, were also important impulses leading to the revival of interest in English folk-song. The *locus classicus* of this particular view of English music was a series of university lectures that Ralph Vaughan Williams gave in 1932, published two years later as *National Music*. Nationalism and the 1930s have come to have associations – especially for Germany – that may prejudice some observers against Vaughan Williams's point of view.

There is, however, nothing narrowly chauvinistic about Vaughan Williams's use of the word 'national'. His is an intellectual argument, best compared with similar discussions of other national movements in music – such as those in Bohemia, Russia, Spain, etc. – which had begun or developed some years before. Vaughan Williams's argument ran as follows: the idea that music was an 'international language' was false. He agreed, rather, with a sentiment of Parry's that 'style is ultimately national'. Vaughan Williams expounded a Darwinian view of music, of its natural evolution; he employed the metaphor of natural growth to describe English composers needing, like a vine, to draw nurture from their native soil. Folk-music was, according to Vaughan Williams, an 'applied art' not 'art for art's sake', but folk themes, handled with integrity and love, could – and should – be used by serious composers, because folk-songs 'for generations voiced the spiritual longings of our race'; 'any school of national music must be fashioned on the basis of the raw material of its own national song'. Vaughan Williams wished to see folk-music as a contributory part of a 'spontaneous expression, first of ourselves, next of our community, then and only then of the world'. To him retreating to one's own country to seek a national musical contribution before turning towards the musical community of the rest of the world was a necessary process, for his ultimate ambition was not to foster narrow chauvinism but to prepare people for a 'United States of the World'. 'They will serve it best who bring something only they can bring to the common fund.' Thus, the view, still frequently held, that the cult of folk-music shows an insularity in English musical life, is exposed as a misunderstanding of Vaughan Williams's views. It is all too easy to misrepresent the folk-music school of composers as Arnold Bax, for instance, once did when he borrowed the music critic Ernest Newman's description of a true English atmosphere as 'solemn wassailing round the village pump', and rounded this off by remarking that 'a sympathetic Scot summed it all up very neatly in the remark, "You should make a point of trying every experience once, excepting incest and folk-dancing."' But what marks out Bax from many lesser commentators is that having had his joke he expressed his sincere respect for Vaughan Williams. And folk-song was to go on influencing English composers right down to Tippett and Britten.

We have seen that the search for an 'English inspiration' for music had many roots and the resulting character of the music written during the period under consideration had many styles; examples of music that can arouse specific 'English' associations abound. From the work of Elgar and Parry down to that of Tippett and Britten one can hear an 'Englishness' – or 'Englishry', as it came to be known in Britten's case – that is quite unmistakable. This took many forms: the nobility of Elgar's Edwardian vision, the folk-song influence in Vaughan Williams and his disciples, and the ubiquitous working-through of the revived interest in Tudor music, of English church music and that of Purcell, right down to the time of Tippett and Britten. The specific character of the music was shown in many different ways: at times it is official music for state occasions; at times it is Georgian, pastoral and elegiac; and at times it expresses the feelings of a country at war and rising from the ashes of destruction. There is in much of this music an energy, enthusiasm, optimism and sense of confidence that is not to be found outside the period. It is music that, above all, learnt not merely to imitate Continental composers. The movement that the composers were part of was as much one of musical independence as of national music. What it decidedly was not was a music of chauvinism; rather the opposite, in fact, for English composers were able to offer much more both to their own people and to the world at large when they had effectively discovered their own voices.

There were also, in much of the English music of this period, certain other qualities – rather less tangible qualities than we have hitherto looked at – held in common. Those who composed it shared a similar view of its importance and value. In order to examine this more closely we must look back at the place that music held in late Victorian Britain and what people were coming to expect of it at that time. Almost all the main roots of the musical renaissance lie in this period. One of the clearest early statements of the high expectations that were beginning to be held for English music was made in December 1881 when the Duke of Albany delivered at the Manchester Free Trade Hall one of the opening broadsides in the campaign to bring the Royal College of Music, as it was to be, into being. Speaking of the medieval piece of music 'Summer is Icumen in', the Duke said:

in a word, this little glee, which is the germ of modern music, the direct and absolute progenitor to the oratorios of Handel, the symphonies of Beethoven, the operas of Wagner, is a purely English creation, dealing with English sights and sounds, and it is animated in a very high degree by the truly English qualities of sense, fitness, proportion, and sweet, simple, domestic tunefulness.

These extravagant rhetorical flourishes, the work of George Grove, are evidently an over-exaggeration; but we must not underrate their effect – their designed effect – on the original listeners. The proposal to establish a new college of music was in some part successful because it appealed to a strong streak of national pride in the England of the 1880s. This view also reflects the contemporary feeling that, given the right institutions, England, the workshop of the world, should surely be able to produce music as well and as reliably as any other commodity. 'Music, made in England' was to be encouraged from the highest level.

But along with the narrow 'patriotic' view, one that could be found in most spheres of life in Victorian Britain, there were many other reasons for the increased position music was assuming. Members of the royal family, statesmen such as Gladstone and Rosebery, and the Archbishop of Canterbury were among those who spoke publicly on behalf of the proposal for the new college. The pursuit of music was held up as a desirable personal and national achievement. It was believed to be a civilized art: to participate in musical activity was considered to be morally and physically beneficial to the individual concerned and to the community at large. And throughout the period covered by this book this belief, although expressed in many different ways, was constantly reaffirmed.

There were, of course, still many areas of English life where music was not taken seriously, and, to a certain degree, a deeply-engrained philistinism about music persisted in England throughout the period – the path of a musician in England was never an easy one. But following the major achievement of setting up the Royal College, and the revival of the fortunes of the Royal Academy and the institution of colleges and other bodies to encourage and regulate musical life all over the country, music as a whole was given a tremendous material boost. George Grove, who was responsible for getting the Royal College going, was in many ways the very model of a successful Victorian entrepreneur. He had wide-ranging abilities and interests and was both a practical and a cultured man. But it was the next generation, that of Hubert Parry and Charles Villiers Stanford – both eminently 'respectable' men, one becoming a professor at Oxford, the other at Cambridge – which gave the seal of respectability to the idea of music as a suitable area for a career for a 'gentleman'; and the growing social respectability of music brought about in such ways was one of the vital keys of the whole renaissance.

This sense of the respectability of music was not confined to the upper classes, for although there were class divisions in the performing world, music was, on the whole, presented as a great social mixer. This may be seen in a news-report of the last public appearance in England of Prince Leopold, Duke of Albany, which took place on the platform of a village concert room: 'He sang a song to the village audience, and took his encore, with the perfect simplicity and unaffectedness that stamps the English gentleman, at the same time setting an example likely to influence smaller people as, perhaps, nothing else could.' Here we can see two suppositions at work: that music caused social distinctions to disappear and that it had a beneficial effect upon the population. An active musical life was expected to be conducive to high moral standards and a respectable existence. Participating in music was also considered to be of great educational benefit and it became an area where competition was encouraged (often, it must be said, to the detriment of the music). This idea was at the root of the – sometimes vast – competition festivals that grew up in the last quarter of the nineteenth century. (The most celebrated early example was that organized by Mary Wakefield at Kendal.) The belief that one of the chief keys to a thriving national musical life lay in education was central to the period of the musical renaissance. The growth of musical research and teaching in universities, colleges and schools was enormous. (That this was an area of lively interest can be seen in the lengthy and very intense debate that took place over what 'Musical Appreciation' should be and how it should be taught.) The number of specialist and popular journals that appeared at this time was also impressive, and in many other ways – such as the development of the didactic concert notes printed in programmes – knowledge of music spread widely.

By turning our attention to the late Victorian period we have seen how a new seriousness and sense of the purpose of music were expressed with strong confidence, in bricks and mortar and the setting up of institutions; and we have seen how the growing respectability of music was confirmed by the people who were being drawn to it as an area suitable for a career; also, music was believed to be a great link between the nation's classes and of enormous educational benefit at all levels of the country. As we go through the portraits in this book we shall see that these were central factors in the lives and work of most of the composers between the time of Elgar and that of Britten. Many of them laboured hard to increase the material and psychological position of music and some were active teachers, often because of a positive sense of wanting to take the benefits of music to as wide a number of people as possible. Many musicians had a sense of mission.

Above all, however, these composers shared a belief in the purpose of music. Parry once said to Vaughan Williams that he should write choral music 'as befits an Englishman and a democrat', and this and similar ideas persisted throughout the period. The political emphasis in some of the later composers of the period shared much of the same basic idea as Parry's: many of them believed that music had a real purpose in the shaping of political society. (If this view became too specific, however, as in the case of Rutland Boughton or Alan Bush, it could lead to a complete collapse of interest in their lives and music.) Many also believed that music had a religious or a mystical purpose that they wanted to share with their audiences, and while some distrusted what Delius called the 'Jesus element' in music there were from the period frequent examples of music with a sense of religious or spiritual purpose. Britten, no less than Elgar, believed in the power of music to bring order and understanding into a world where both were lacking, and nobody expressed this better in words than Tippett. The great humanistic and religious idea that music is above all else a form of communication – not introspection – was one that was held by almost all the composers in this study in their varying ways. (The rare exceptions to this tend to prove the rule: Lord Berners, for example, could not be said to have held such views; but his talents as a parodist are not of central concern to the period.) To say that music was believed to be, above all, a means of communication, however, is not to say that composers of the time felt they should compromise their music in any serious way for the benefit of their audiences, but simply that they felt a real respect for them. That most of the major composers of the period wrote works both of great musical power and genuine innocence, in the form of 'suites for children', most perfectly demonstrates this. And most of them also had a wide and liberal interest in the good 'light' music of their day (as exemplified by the work of, say, Edward German and Eric Coates). Such musical activities were taken as signs of good health in the body of music. Few composers, as yet, felt exclusive about their art. Most concurred with Stanford's view that without milk there could be no cream. And central to their search for a suitable artistic language was a desire to speak in a way that the general musical public could understand, the composers themselves often taking on an educational role in this respect.

Indeed, this close relationship between composers and their audiences was at the very heart of the musical renaissance, and it was the interest that the composers took in the great tradition of choral singing in Britain that was the strongest link in this relationship. The cantatas of the time of Parry, the oratorios of Elgar, the remarkable procession of song-writers, the seemingly endless search for an English operatic form – resulting in the fine operas of Michael Tippett and Benjamin Britten – were among the greatest achievements of the period. What was it about choral music that was so important to succeeding generations of English composers? In order to understand the strength of this tradition properly we must once again turn back to the nineteenth century.

Starting in the 1840s a great movement in popular singing – it has well been called a 'mania' – took off in England. In the following years there was a vast rise in musical literacy (especially through the adoption of the tonic-solfa system), and a large number of choirs were formed all over the country. The claim of Joseph Mainzer – one of the leading figures in the early days of this movement – that this was 'singing for the million' was no idle boast. This was reflected also in the appearance of cheaper editions of music. A copy of the *Messiah* in 1845 would have cost about 12s; by 1854 the price was down to 4s, and by 1859 was as low as 1s 4d. The publishing firm Novello made much of its policy of providing cheap music and a vast, and for a while unregulated, pirate industry grew up in choral music – the surest sign that the business of music was real business. There were choirs in the cathedrals, in the local churches, in village halls, in factories, in schools, and – the highest point of all – the mammoth chorus at the Crystal Palace (going up to 4,000 voices). In 1857 there is a record of the 'Hallelujah Chorus' being distinctly heard nearly half a mile from the building, the effect, 'as the sound floated on the wind, was impressive beyond description, and sounded as if a nation were at prayers', a contemporary report noted.

A nation at prayers: the English were engaged in their favourite pursuit, one that many of them took seriously indeed. It is, of course, impossible nowadays to judge the standard of performance of these choirs but the testimony of the celebrated Berlin critic Otto Lessmann in 1889 is interesting. Lessmann wrote in the *Allgemeine Musik-Zeitung*: 'I heard choral performances of greater beauty in Leeds than in any town on the Continent. The voices are so fresh; the sopranos and tenors command the high notes with astonishing facility, and the altos and basses display admirable fullness and power.' Lessmann went on to detail the financial basis of the Leeds Festival, particularly the well-subscribed guarantee fund: the committee had the sum of about £28,500 to draw on in an emergency (being the contributions of 522 individuals). 'In the face of such liberality on behalf of a musical performance, and in view of our own miserably paltry proportion, have we any occasion, or even any right, to jeer at the sincere interest of the English in music, or even to question it?', he added. Lessmann went on – and this is also highly revealing – to praise the audience.

It was natural that English composers should have produced very considerable quantities of music in response to the vast demands of the choirs. In the 1886 season, for example, it has been calculated that of the top seven composers performed Stainer, Sullivan and Stanford were included, and in the 1926-7 season, Elgar, Coleridge-Taylor, Parry, Vaughan Williams and Stanford were in the top nine. The strength of the choral tradition was extraordinary. Many thought that it could be written off as a progressive force in music after the First World War, but as a popular form it lasted well past the Second World War and enjoyed continual revivals, often at the hands of those who had shortly before tried to sound its death knell. Walton, for example, began his musical career as an arch-radical and experimentalist, but the sounds of the cathedral, the environment where he had spent his most important formative years, were deeply etched in his musical mind, and it was he who gave the tradition a new lease of life with his *Belshazzar's Feast*.

Much effort also went into looking for new ways of adding to the choral tradition, above all in the search for a suitable form of English opera, a form in which English composers had not as yet achieved much. Many composers initially tried to produce English opera that incorporated all the best features of the wide popular interest in choral singing. But this was not the way forward. Amateur English opera, although once widespread, was never a great success in artistic terms, and when a successful form was eventually developed it was really an entirely professional business. This came – with Tippett and Britten – at a time when the emphasis in English music was in any case moving quickly away from amateur participation towards performance by professionals.

During the period covered by this book, however, the active amateur tradition was the backbone of a national musical way of life. And, although choral activity was by far the most important it was not the only form of widespread amateur music making. At the local level there were many full-amateur and semi-amateur orchestras (some formed for the specific purpose of accompanying the large choral festivals that were such a feature of the time), and many other bands of instrumentalists also existed. Church bands (the descriptions of these from Hardy's stories spring to mind) were sometimes still to be found, and local gatherings of those interested in music or of groups drawn from a specific institution (like Elgar's band at a lunatic asylum) were widespread. To take one particular form of amateur music making that grew and thrived in this period we could look at brass bands. These – particularly in the North of England – became an important part of the composers' world. Holst, Vaughan Williams, Elgar, Bliss and many others wrote for brass bands, and the works that they composed have remained central to the brass-band repertoire. At the domestic level many people played the piano or a stringed instrument, often in groups or small ensembles, and there was an important revival in chamber music. That music was being made in drawing-rooms and parlours, factories and conservatories, up and down the country, was one of the greatest strengths of the renaissance.

It is essential to an understanding of the musical renaissance as a whole to recognize that much of the music written then – often in the smaller forms – was in part a response to the active musical world of the time. Like their Tudor forebears many of the best composers of the recent renaissance in English music were miniaturists. To consider the career of C.W. Orr – the composer of a handful of songs only – is to take an extreme case; yet nobody listening to his few but excellent songs will be anything but grateful for his work. Chamber and solo music also underwent a considerable revival at this time, in response to active amateur music making. The revival of the 'phantasy' form of string music, for instance, was a notable feature of the period: this form of instrumental music, such a fruitful one in the sixteenth and seventeenth centuries in England, owed much to the enthusiasm of Arnold Dolmetsch and W.W. Cobbett, and many modern English composers took to it with keen interest. The idea was that it was music for people to play. But that does not mean that the larger instrumental forms were ignored. Here too, a great deal was achieved and both composers and musical audiences learnt much. It had been Elgar's hope that a new generation of English composers should write 'big' music – symphonies, concertos and the like – and this challenge was taken up, although hardly in the exact way that Elgar intended, with considerable success. Vaughan Williams, Bax, Rubbra, Tippett and many others found that they were able to make considerable progress with the symphonic form, and many also wrote fine instrumental concertos. These were areas in which English composers had hitherto made little impression, and much was achieved in firmly establishing a tradition of English music in the larger classical forms.

But even in these major forms of music the composers and their audiences stayed close. Those interested in music in Britain tended to look for some sense of association with non-musical ideas in the large-scale music that they listened to, as they were used to doing with choral works. Most composers tried to satisfy this expectation of their audiences. The debate between so-called 'programme' music and supposedly 'absolute' music was one that went on for many years – largely without profit to anybody. In the case of the composers this was to some extent part of the cycle of rebels and heirs: the younger composers striking out with a claim that theirs was pure music untainted by the facile and obvious associations of the previous generations. Arthur Bliss, for example, began his career in the early 1920s by lauding 'absolute' music, but it was not long before he too was looking for deeper associations in his music and that of others too. Much larger-scale music had clear associations of one sort or another – Vaughan Williams's 'London' Symphony, Bliss's 'Colour' Symphony, Bax's named tone poems – and that which was not so clearly marked often had deeper associations through the personalities of the composers themselves as they emerged in their work. Audiences hear Elgar himself in his symphonies and through this are taken back to his own associations with the history, language and countryside of England. This is also the case with the numbered symphonies of Vaughan Williams and perhaps will become, in time, true as well of the symphonies of Michael Tippett. The link therefore between a composer and his audience was the very core of the English musical renaissance. Composers, performers and audiences were all music makers.

The first stirrings of the English musical renaissance were to be felt in the twenty years before the turn of the century. Starting with Hubert Parry's cantata *Scenes from Prometheus Unbound*, first performed in 1880, writers on the subject began to hail a new dawn for English music. The attachment of the onset of the revival to this event (which has now become something of a convention) happened very early on. In the years immediately following 1880 various works by Parry, and by Charles Villiers Stanford and Alexander Campbell Mackenzie, the other leading lights of the period, were greeted with similar attention and enthusiasm. As we have seen, the opening of the Royal College of Music in 1883 and the revival of the Royal Academy of Music at about the same time were also highly influential in forming the general opinion that something was at last going to happen in English music. There was considerable enthusiasm and optimism in the air.

Proof that a larger musical movement had begun was soon to be seen with the emergence of the greatest light of the period, Edward Elgar; and the first work to become a lasting monument to the living culture of English music at its liveliest moment was his *Variations on an Original Theme* ('*Enigma*') of 1899.

CHAPTER TWO

# The English Environment

## ELGAR, DELIUS

At the turn of the century the optimism of the inhabitants of the British Isles knew few bounds. In the musical world this was reflected by the publication in 1897 of James D. Brown and Stephen S. Stratton's *British Musical Biography*. Introducing their book, the authors wrote:

> In undertaking this work, [we] have been animated by the desire to present the true position of the British Empire in the world of music. A country is musical only by the music it produces for itself, not by what it takes from others. In this work, therefore, only what has been done by Britain's sons and daughters is placed on record. It is probable that in no other nation is there, at the present time, greater musical activity, creative or executive, than is to be witnessed in our own. . . .

To us it may seem to be an extravagant claim, but the authors had a point. Something new and important had happened in the musical life of the British Isles in the twenty or so years preceding the turn of the century and it had become commonplace to speak of a 'renaissance' in national musical life. *British Musical Biography* was itself a reflection of this extraordinary activity and interest. Britain's musical 'sons and daughters', occupying 462 pages of double columns, were the chief adornment of this artistic establishment, and while the biographical dictionary goes back to the earliest times the longest entries are those given to the new élite, among them Parry, Stanford, Mackenzie, Sullivan, Macfarren and Cowan. There is, however, only a short entry for the man who was to overturn this order and who was to be the greatest of the composers of the English musical renaissance. The entry on Edward Elgar was not long and concluded with the rather sad words 'ill-health compelled him to leave London in 1891, since which time he has resided at Malvern, devoting himself exclusively to composition'.

In 1897 Edward Elgar seemed anything but a pillar of the establishment. Known, if at all, as a successful 'local musician', he had enjoyed few of the benefits of the contemporary growth of musical life. Born at Broadheath near Worcester in 1857, he lived for most of his youth above the family music shop in Worcester. Elgar, who was only five years younger than Stanford and nine years younger than Parry, seems to us, however, to belong to a different world from these men.

To try and understand Elgar's life and his work as a composer one has to disentangle the 'official' image that he projected of himself from the 'unofficial' one that has been left to us by those who knew him well. Even so we will still fall short of a complete understanding of this quite enigmatic man, and that is how Elgar meant it to be.

Edward Elgar's childhood in Worcester was unremarkable; his early attempts at music were self-taught. In 1872 he was apprenticed to a solicitor, but this arrangement lasted for only a year and on leaving the solicitor's office Elgar decided to follow the life of a musician. In these early days he was a good example of an average local musician in England. He helped in his father's shop, played the organ, became known as a violinist, conducted the Worcester Glee Club, and played for the Three Choirs Festival (the popular name for the meeting of the choirs of Gloucester, Worcester and Hereford in the cathedrals of these cities by rotation). His appointment as bandmaster of the Attendants' Orchestra at the county lunatic asylum was typical of the variety of the jobs that could be held in the music trade. 'We had a festive night at the Glee Club last Tuesday', Elgar says in a characteristic letter of 1886, and while he was expected to conduct the sort of music that was customary at the time for such occasions – quadrilles, for example – he had also begun to try out his own compositions on local performers. Elgar knew, however, that he needed some sort of proper musical training and he had set his sights on going to Leipzig; but there was never sufficient money to realize this ambition. Instead he built up his teaching practice and for his own musical education used to travel to the concerts conducted by August Manns at the Crystal Palace. Elgar's journey from Worcester to central London, out to the Crystal Palace for the concert,

and then all the way home again had to be done in a day. It was, however, vital to his development as a musician. Elgar's great friend W.H.
Reed wrote many years later, 'I think it was the attendance at those
concerts that fired his ambition and turned the scales on the side of
serious composition.'

Elgar's marriage in 1889 to Caroline Alice Roberts, who had been
one of his pupils, changed the pattern of his life. Elgar and his forty-
year-old bride (he was then thirty-two) moved to London and tried to
establish themselves in the metropolis. The 'local musician' could not,
however, break into the London musical world in any successful way
and in 1891 the Elgars had to face the unhappy fact that Edward's
reputation was limited and that working in the catchment area of the
Three Choirs Festival was his best chance for the future.

So it was that the Elgars moved to Malvern. In this particular landscape, however, the social anomaly of the Elgar marriage stood out in
high relief. Alice, the daughter of a general, was thought to have married
well below her station, as Rosa Burley, headmistress of a private school
where Elgar taught, wrote: 'In those days women of the upper classes
had not formed the habit of eloping with dance-band leaders, chauffeurs
and prize-fighters.' All the evidence left by Elgar's friends and acquaintances – such as Miss Burley – has to be treated with caution: they all
had strong feelings about the composer. But on the subject of the social
stratigraphy of Malvern Rosa Burley knew what she was talking about
– her livelihood as a headmistress depended on it. Miss Burley quickly
spotted the differences in background between the couple and, in addition, noted that Alice Elgar seemed to belong to a different generation
from her husband. On being invited to dine with them Miss Burley was
surprised to find that the Elgars wore full evening dress and that she was
'taken in' to dinner in the proper way on Edward Elgar's arm. Alice
Elgar had lost a lot by marrying Edward but in their home her standards
were kept up as far as circumstances allowed. But it cannot be doubted
that Elgar's life as a successful composer owed much to his marriage,
and when his wife died, fourteen years before her husband, his work as
a composer came to an almost complete halt.

Over the next years domesticity was the leitmotif of the Elgars' life
and a series of moves, which betray a certain restlessness, mark their
route: Forli, Craeg Lea, Birchwood. Alice encouraged her husband's
composition and works of his were put on at the Worcester Festival, the
North Staffordshire Festival at Hanley, the Leeds Festival and at Bir-

mingham. Elgar was progressing in a conventional way through the
festival system of his day, but real reputations were only very slowly,
and laboriously made in this way, if at all. A young man *could* establish
himself as a notable figure of promise – as Samuel Coleridge-Taylor did,
at the age of twenty-four, in 1899 when *The Death of Minnehaha* was
first heard at the North Staffordshire Festival – but, in the main, reputations were only confirmed or underlined at the great festivals, not
made from scratch.

In 1899, however, Elgar, now forty-two, suddenly came to the attention of the wider musical public. In that year the *Enigma Variations*,
chosen for a concert at St James's Hall in London under Hans Richter,
met with immediate and immense success, and between that moment
and the death of his wife in 1920 Elgar, as a composer, never looked
back. In 1900 *The Dream of Gerontius* was performed at Birmingham
(disastrously, as it turned out); *Cockaigne* in 1901; *The Apostles* in 1902;
and in 1904 Elgar reached the high-water mark of his national acclaim.
In that year a four-day Elgar Festival was given at Covent Garden and
he was knighted. This dramatic success, coming at an age when many
of the world's greatest composers had already finished their lives' work,
and coming as suddenly as it did, was quite extraordinary. Elgar was
now, without a doubt, recognized as England's greatest composer. Parry,
with no bitterness, once said that 'the English public is curious. It can
only recognize one composer at a time – once it was Sullivan, now it is
Elgar.' In the years following the festival came the Introduction and
Allegro, *The Kingdom*, the two symphonies, the Violin Concerto, the
Cello Concerto, *The Music Makers*, *Falstaff*, *The Spirit of England*, and
the late chamber works. Elgar became for a while a professor at Birmingham University, he travelled widely both at home and abroad, he
moved back to London, living now in some style, and was clearly
recognized throughout the British Empire as the lion of music. Elgar
was the first English composer for centuries to enjoy a firm international
reputation of importance.

The wide general public of England, not usually at all interested in
musical matters, were reassured by Elgar's official image that here was
a great composer. His popularity eclipsed all other English composers
either before his time or since. But this official image of Elgar is most
deceptive: it hides many layers which, only when peeled back, begin to
reveal the man himself. Those who simply know the outer man are
often surprised by the inner. Not that Elgar was at all keen to reveal

himself to outsiders. A great part of the frustration of those who wrote memoirs of Elgar was due to their feeling that they were never able or allowed to get close to him. It is also interesting that the people who were the subject of the *Enigma Variations* did not in fact know each other at all well. Elgar's friends 'pictured within' were in no way a circle of friends; each had a separate relationship with the composer.

Elgar's hatred of talking about music was the first thing that strangers noticed about his protective carapace. He had a wonderful pose of pretending not to understand the technicalities of musical composition and would prefer instead to discuss his latest interest: golf, potato growing, chemistry, billiards, bicycling, driving, even 'pyrography' – the decorating of wood with hot pokers. His interests were legion and he was as delighted by a copy of the *Encyclopaedia Britannica* as by *Bradshaw's Railway Guide*. And music? – 'Music's off', as he wrote to his friend August Johannes Jaeger, who worked for his publisher, Novello.

Some of Elgar's interests, showing the wide curiosity of a largely self-educated man, were only passing phases. Others, however, stuck with him for life. His interest in cryptograms and codes, crosswords, puzzles and puns was well known to his friends as was his partiality for sealing rings and wax (he had a phase of sealing many unnecessary objects). In his music also – most especially in his creation of the most successful of all musical enigmas – Elgar tried to surround himself with a certain sense of mystery. One might be tempted to see in some of Elgar's whimsicality a musical Mr Pooter at work, but we should not let him fool us. Elgar was a genuinely intelligent man, as one can see, for example, in his wide knowledge of literature, demonstrated by his extensive and impressive letters to *The Times Literary Supplement*.

Elgar's friends knew much about him that he had managed to keep sealed off from the outside world – that he was subject to extreme change of mood, for instance. Black depressions dogged him throughout his life. At times he was cheerful and jocular, at others rude and offensive, especially to people he did not know. He occasionally felt close to despair and had a recurring belief that there were 'forces' acting against him. Equally, close friends also knew that when the black mood lifted he was as generous a man as one could imagine, much loved by many people, to whom he often made a gift of his music through his dedications. To the outer world, however, Elgar liked to present himself in a different light. He looked and acted like a retired military man, a man with friends and connections and with no real need to exert himself; an image curiously like that of someone who might have belonged to Alice's father's world. When Elgar posed for photographs you could tell that he was a gentleman – climbing the Malvern Hills, enjoying a round of golf, smoking his pipe at his leisure. The highest praise that Elgar gave others, as can be seen in remarks he made following the death of friends, was that they had lived their lives as 'gentlemen' and it was precisely this appellation that he strove after in his own life.

The musical generations that grew up to know Elgar as the grand old man of English music and who reacted strongly against his work were quite taken in by Elgar's public image – they had no desire to look any deeper than the surface. Beginning during the late years of his life Elgar's works entered a period of neglect and misunderstanding that persisted till the 1960s. We are now able to see how the golden glow of Edwardian England coloured a proper appreciation of Elgar's music and how his connections with German music and musicians, and his social links with Jewish financiers were later scorned by a post-First World War generation that had a fashionable anti-Romantic, anti-German and anti-Semitic bias.

But how far did Edwardian England really penetrate Elgar's music? The answer to this question is far more interesting and far more complicated than has often been allowed. That Elgar wrote some immensely popular tunes and marches was long held against him. But he answered his critics with the observation – referring to the time of the troubadours and bards – 'It was no disgrace for a man to be turned on to step in front of an army and inspire them with song.' In this respect – though these tunes and marches were only a small fraction of his work – Elgar's music was, as he once claimed, the new folk-music of Britain. But the great imperial events of the day did not, in fact, touch his music in any important way. Elgar produced formal music for coronations and other similar occasions and indeed he hit on such a successful formula for this that it has been closely copied down to the present day. But that was only one of his voices and it was by no means his most characteristic. Elgar was inspired by the figures of his native landscape – Caractacus and Falstaff, for example – but he was no jingoist. He wrote no music for the Boer War, and few compositions for the Great War. Of these one was written for Belgium, another for Poland, and for his own people he wrote *The Spirit of England*. This setting of three poems by Laurence Binyon, a sad and noble work finely matching the words, contains the lines that have so stuck in the public imagination:

They shall grow not old, as we that are left grow old:
Age shall not weary them, nor the years condemn.
At the going down of the sun and in the morning
We will remember them.

Elgar wrote in the late Romantic idiom that had come down through the German school and whose chief master in his time was Richard Strauss. Elgar and Strauss had a high regard for each other and both, of course, had been fundamentally influenced by the music of Wagner. Recognition in Germany was an important factor in Elgar's success in England. In the audience for the disastrous first performance of *Gerontius* in Birmingham was the conductor Julius Buths from Düsseldorf and he was convinced that beneath the hopelessly inadequate performance that he had just heard was a great work. Buths was instrumental in taking up the music of Elgar in Germany and at the second performance of *Gerontius* in Düsseldorf two years later, in 1902, Strauss made his celebrated but widely misunderstood remark that Elgar was the 'first English progressivist'.

It is easy to see now that as a popular musical idiom the late Romantic school was dying in the pre-war years; but that was by no means clear at the time. Compared with most of his contemporaries Elgar was rightly regarded as something of a progressive, although it might be right to define this as a 'conservative progressiveness', as Hans Keller has put it. While Elgar continued to provide works for the festival circuit he now also developed his large-scale music and established, once and for all, that English composers could write symphonies and concertos. Many of Elgar's contemporaries and many composers who came after him – in particular William Walton – realized that it was Elgar who had breathed English life into the traditional major musical forms.

Elgar himself was reluctant to talk about his music in specific terms and there were only rare moments when he let down his defences. But these are key moments to an understanding of the man and his music. In 1900 he wrote in a letter to Jaeger a quotation from the Woodland Interlude of *Caractacus* and added, 'This is what I hear all day – the trees are singing my music – or have I sung theirs?' On another occasion he told the violinist W.H. Reed to play a passage 'like something we hear down by the river'. Elgar's love of the countryside is evident in many of his compositions. This feeling in his music touched widely different people. Eric Fenby, Delius's amanuensis, once wrote, 'when I walk about the countryside of England I seldom, if ever, find myself humming anything of Delius, but always some exquisite passage from Elgar'. To

his friend Reed, Elgar also said that music is 'written on the sky', implying to Reed that the inspired composer has nothing to do but copy
it. Along with this deep love of the natural world went a strong sense
of place, and many of Elgar's most successful compositions are concerned
with specific places that he knew and loved. Above all else, however, he
was immensely skilful at delineating people in his musical texts. This can
be seen throughout his work, and anyone familiar with Elgar's works
will be well aware that this intensely personal aspect of his music is not
confined to the sections of the *Enigma Variations*.

Elgar did not compose his music in a conventionally disciplined way.
He was once pictured at work placing around his room various parts of
a work in hand which would mean nothing in terms of continuous
music to anybody except himself. He worked on various sections of the
whole composition at once, often drawing on ideas that he had had in
mind for some years. His music lived in his mind and the writing down
of it was a process of realization. He once said that 'he had musical
day-dreams in the same way that other people had day-dreams of hero-
ism and adventure, and that he could express almost any thought that
came into his head in terms of music'. Elgar was proud of his powers of
orchestration. Unlike many composers he knew from the start how the
orchestration would work.

Students of the techniques of composition are most fortunate in having at their disposal a significant correspondence between Elgar and his
friend Jaeger. In Jaeger - the Nimrod of the *Enigma Variations* - Elgar
found a friend and fellow-sufferer in the cause of music. They both felt
ill-placed in 'the vortex of jealous chicanery, fraud & falsehood', as Elgar
described the contemporary music world of England. His friendship for
Jaeger was close and his letters are full of his delight in word-play and
invention. But Elgar treated Jaeger's views quite seriously - even to the
point of making significant changes in his compositions on his friend's
advice. Neither man was in any sense well-off at the time and both
struggled for a living. As better days began for Elgar, Jaeger grew ill
and died; it was sad that he was not long able to enjoy the success of his
friend, a success to which he had contributed in a real way. Jaeger, born and
brought up in Germany, had been able to help open doors for Elgar's
music and as a friend could tell Elgar exactly what he thought of his music,
drawing comparisons which would have been unknown to many of
the more provincially-minded contemporary English composers.

Elgar's black moods are much in evidence in the Jaeger correspondence, Jaeger being a good listener. Elgar would perpetually write announcing that he had given up composition for some other 'trade' or for the delights of the countryside. But Jaeger understood Elgar and his ways of composition better than anyone except, perhaps, his wife. He also knew that while his friend's music was of the highest beauty and worth, it was likely to be misunderstood by many of his contemporaries. When studying the score of *The Apostles* Jaeger wrote to Elgar,

I'm steeped in your music just now & have no thought for aught else.... The beauty of the music moves me to tears & the longer I study the work the more & the greater beauties I find. *The Apostles* are certainly your maturest & greatest work; the certainty of touch & style displayed throughout is wonderful, & the feeling of the most touching, heart-searching kind. But it is all so original, so individual & subjective that it will take the British Public ten years to let it soak into its pachydermal mind.

Elgar's views on music in general are much more clearly expressed than his views on his own music. Elgar was not a good teacher: his young lady violin pupils in Malvern found him unsympathetic. But the lectures which he gave in 1905 as the first Peyton Professor of Music in the University of Birmingham created enormous interest when they were delivered, although much of the comment in the public press at the time was ill-informed and not a fair reflection of what he said. To have the views of a leading composer laid down in a formal setting is, however, something of great value for later generations. Elgar spoke from experience, 'experience dearly bought', as he noted. (It is known that writing these lectures was something that caused the composer the greatest agitation, and once he had delivered the first series he did his best to get out of doing any more.)

What did England's greatest composer think of 'A Future for English Music', as his inaugural lecture was called? Elgar began by stating one point of fundamental importance: 'A living art of music consists not only of composers, as some of the race seem to imagine, but also executants, and – I will dare to add – critics. Composers are in a different position from painters or literary authors.' That the whole world of music – the most social of the arts – had to be seen together was one of the central views of the period. Elgar went on to tell his audience how he and others who were young in the year 1880 – the year of Parry's *Prometheus* – felt 'that something at last was going to be done in the way of composition by the English school'. In the following twenty years 'the whole atmosphere of English music was changed', and, 'an interest hitherto unknown was taken in the work of our native composers'.

Elgar was not entirely convinced, however, that all this activity had been in the right direction. He continued, 'while we were anxious to believe all that a friendly Press told us about the new English School [we] could not help feeling that the music given us to play, was, not to put too fine a point upon it, rather "dry"'. Elgar thought that English composers were too often trying to please only their colleagues and that they should seek a larger audience. Here was the first rebel of the renaissance. In this respect George Bernard Shaw's witty comments on Stanford's *Eden* contain more than a grain of truth. In 1891 Shaw had written:

> If you doubt that Eden is a masterpiece, ask Dr Parry and Dr Mackenzie, and they will applaud it to the skies. Surely Dr Mackenzie's opinion is conclusive; for is he not the composer of Veni Creator, guaranteed as excellent music by Professor Stanford and Dr Parry? You want to know who Dr Parry is? Why, the composer of Blest Pair of Sirens, as to the merits of which you have only to consult Dr Mackenzie and Professor Stanford.

Elgar's lectures touched many a raw nerve in the teaching colleges of England, critical as he was of much of the music of the previous twenty years; with his continual emphasis on the need to guard against imitation he implied that many contemporary composers were capable of little more than this. Elgar's address made a clear plea that the young composers should look around them, to their own country, for their experience. (The young composers that Elgar had in mind on this specific occasion were Granville Bantock, Joseph Holbrooke and Walford Davies, as a marginal note in his text makes clear.) He believed that Birmingham, like another Leipzig, needed to possess all the elements that make up a musical microcosm: a proper library, orchestral concerts, choral societies and an opera house. With such conditions Elgar thought that English music could be made in England. 'I am not one of those who are continually wondering what the intelligent foreigner thinks of him. To me Britain is a world by itself; and we will pay nothing for "wearing our own noses".'

Elgar, however, had faith in the 'English school', even if, he added, he did not know what the phrase really meant. 'At the present no one who lives in the world of music in England can help feeling that something is moving,' he said, stressing the seriousness, earnestness and sincerity of the 'younger men'. Elgar was particularly keen to point out that 'the young English school ... is against mere imitation'. 'Where the Mendelssohn imitator whined, the followers of Brahms groaned, and now we seem to be threatened with shrieks transferred from the most livid pages of Richard Strauss', to say nothing of the 'decadents of the modern French School.... I plead then that the younger men should draw their inspiration more from their own country, from their own literature – and, in spite of what many would say – from their own climate. Only by drawing from any real English inspiration shall we ever arrive at having an English art.' He had his own vision of how English music should develop. 'There are many possible futures. But the one I want to see coming into being is something that shall grow out of our own soil, something broad, whole, noble, chivalrous, healthy and above all, an out-of-door sort of spirit.' Why, he enquired, had so many of the composers of the music of the past twenty years failed to live up to their earlier promise? It was not, he argued, because they had suffered from want of technical ability but from want of inspiration. He ended by exhorting the students in his audience to play no part in the small quarrels of music criticism – 'the little clique is nothing more than a kitten playing with its own tail. You students have something – or should have – a higher ideal altogether. Let your inspiration be real and high.' Elgar was urging an English inspiration on his listeners.

This was Elgar's ideal view; what was his opinion of English music as it was in practice? Despite his feeling of 1880 that something interesting was going to happen because 'the whole atmosphere of English music was changed, owing to the spread of musical education', in 1905 he found much English music was still commonplace: 'English music is white, and evades everything.' Elgar spoke of the need for good English composers prepared to take on symphonies and concertos. He spoke of the need for intelligence in singers. (In this respect a remark made by Jaeger, who was with Elgar in Düsseldorf for a performance of *Gerontius*, is interesting: 'directly Wullner opened his mouth to sing "Jesu, Maria, meine Stunde kam" we said "that man has *Brains*".') Elgar also urged a developed power of appreciation on the part of critics and audiences as a whole and the need for cheap concerts: 'Now – the English working-men are intelligent: they do not want treating sentimentally, we must give them the real thing, we must give them of the best because we want them to have it, not from mere curiosity to see how they will accept it.' Elgar had a complete vision of a working musical culture aimed at excellence and nothing else.

By expressing these opinions Elgar was bound to fall foul of the established world of music, which had so many vested interests in the status quo he was implicitly if not explicitly criticizing. When his appointment to the new chair of music became known, he received much advice from correspondents but it was, he tells us, mainly about 'millinery' – that is, gowns and hoods. The idea that one could lecture about how English music could be improved was new and largely unwelcome. Elgar's genuine concern for the future of English music led him to ask, following Reynolds, why those who were more than boys at sixteen were less than men at thirty: that is, why do British composers so often fail to live up to their early promise? Elgar implied that one of the reasons for this phenomenon was the interest shown by many for concerns that, from an artistic point of view, couldn't matter less – the politics of the music establishment and the cliques of critics. One should not, however, think from this that Elgar's relations with the 'old school' were acrimonious. He belonged to the same general musical world as Parry and Stanford. All three men understood and were part of the great choral tradition of the festivals, and although Elgar had differences with Stanford, relations between the men were good on the whole: Parry and Stanford, for example, put Elgar up for election to the Athenaeum. Elgar's chief object in his lectures was an entirely constructive one, aimed at the new, young composers of the time.

Elgar wished to see a national school of composers, drawing their inspiration from their own country and their own literature. The position at the time, as he saw it, was that a 'school' did not exist: 'we have had what I call "an egotism of several" – which is a different thing'. Despite this, it was clear that Elgar was widely regarded as the father-figure of British composers, a position that he did not really take to well, although he was always very courteous and generous to the younger composers. The new post-war generation, growing up in what they thought of as a much smarter world than Elgar's with its outdated Edwardian Court culture, knew that while they themselves had moved on in musical terms, the older man held a very considerable position in the history of music at large. For his part Elgar tried to keep in touch with the younger composers: in 1921, after the death of his wife, he moved into the centre of London and while there he gave a luncheon for musicians which included Ireland, Goossens, Bax, Boughton and O'Neill as well as Boult, Shaw and Strauss. He supported, at different times, works of Coleridge-Taylor, Davies, Holbrooke, Holst, Dunhill, Gardiner, Bliss and many others; but for all his longing for an English school taking its inspiration from England, his appeal fell on deaf ears. 'I set a high ideal for the younger men' he said; but they didn't want it. When an 'English' school did develop in the next generation its boundaries were seen to be very different from those he had marked out, and the high priest was to be Ralph Vaughan Williams not Elgar. There were worlds of difference between them. On one notable occasion Elgar was asked what he thought of the revived interest in folk-music. 'I am folk-music', was his celebrated reply. Nothing marks more clearly the difference between him and Vaughan Williams.

In the post-war years many people – not necessarily musically-minded people – came to hold a low opinion of Elgar. To a writer such as Osbert Sitwell, who championed the cause of William Walton, Elgar was an Edwardian ghost. Sitwell wrote of Elgar's music that 'in spite of its genius' it was 'obnoxious, so full of English humour and the spirit of compulsory games'. Sitwell's objection was, as we can see, more to the milieu of the music than the music itself: he was against what the music had come to stand for. And this was the pattern for some time: Elgar's music was condemned by its critics for what it had come to symbolize, and remarkable works of great beauty went largely unheard. The mistaken assumptions about Elgar encompassed both the man and his music, and the image of the retired military man writing retired military marches lasted far too long. Elgar was as passionate and as effective a composer as any of those who lived and worked at the turn of the century, but the scale of his emotions, like the size of orchestra needed to express them, did not find favour in the newer world. His choral work *The Music Makers* of 1912, set to Arthur O'Shaughnessy's text, 'We are the music makers,/And we are the dreamers of dreams ...' was very popular for a while but sat uneasily in the post-war world where the dreams of the dreamers had become shattered illusions.

Following the death of his wife at the age of seventy-one, Elgar's life as a working composer ended: he lived for another fourteen years and only in the very last period of his life did he turn again briefly to composition. 'My active creative period began under the most tender care and it ended with that care.' His relationship with his wife had been a very private one and we shall always remain largely in the dark about it. Alice Roberts was devoted to 'the arts' and wrote indifferent poetry

of a type all too familiar from the period. But that is not to denigrate
her. Near the end of her life she regretted that she had not written more
for herself; but she was, as she put it, 'consoled by wise dictum – "the
care of a genius is enough of a life work for any woman"'. Alice had
decided at the start of their marriage that much of her own life would
be sacrificed for the genius of her husband, and she supported him in his
life of composition both materially and spiritually. When one thinks of
Elgar's great friendships, one tends to think first of the rather light-
weight memoirs of Dora Powell – 'Dorabella' of the *Enigma Variations*
– or Rosa Burley, but infinitely more important than these friendships
was the iron link that bound him to Alice. These other friendships were
not at all unwelcome to Alice as long as they promoted her husband's
musical life. Alice followed an empirical rule in these matters: if a person
was beneficial to Elgar's musical invention then he or she was encouraged
to visit, otherwise they were not. It was, however, her 'most tender care'
above all else that Elgar needed.

In his later years many changes took place in Elgar's life. His earlier
intense interest in religion declined, he transferred much of his affection
from people to animals, particularly dogs and horses, and he allowed
himself considerable nostalgia for the past. A curious incident which
took place in 1924 reveals his changed opinions. Elgar discovered that
the position of Master of the King's Music was to be abolished and he
wrote to the King's private secretary urging that the position be retained:
'its suppression wd. have a very bad effect abroad where the effacement
of the last shred of connection of the Court with the Art wd. not be
understood'. Elgar, both in this situation and in other similar ones,
longed for the days when music was valued at the very highest level of
society. In his old age Elgar came to believe that he was not properly
valued. One of the reasons why this had come about, he felt, was because
'everything seems so hopelessly & irredeemably *vulgar* at Court'. He had
written in 1924 a new piece, the 'Empire March', for the Wembley
Exhibition. The King, however, insisted instead on 'Land of Hope and
Glory', not the composer's favourite piece.

Elgar looked back with great nostalgia to the pre-war world, to the
splendour and majesty of the Victorian and Edwardian Courts. He had
an abhorrence of many of the new movements that had flourished after
the war, and, in part, he lived on in the memory of the noble days of
his prime. To Elgar the new world was vulgar; ironically, the spirit of
the new age itself thought the same of Elgar and his music. In the words

of Professor E.J. Dent, words which were to cause considerable controversy, Elgar's music was felt to be 'too emotional and not quite free from vulgarity'.

Near the end of his life Elgar said, 'I have had some satisfaction & even pleasure in my life but have no pleasant memories connected with music.' Was this at all true? Much of what Elgar said or wrote has to be taken with reservations. Elgar lived all his adult life pretending not to be interested in music but he knew where he stood. Music was everything to him, and to his fellow-countrymen he *was* music. During his main period of composition he became popular in a way that no other composer either before or since has ever been popular in Great Britain. His greatest tunes stirred his countrymen to a most extraordinary degree and even his more 'serious' music had a widespread appeal. G.B. Shaw was right when he wrote, 'of all English composers Elgar is alone for Westminster Abbey'; but as it turned out, after his death Elgar's remains stayed at home in the west of England and he is to be found buried in the graveyard of Little Malvern next to his wife. The 'outsider' returned to the place he had come from. He had returned both from the musical world of the metropolis which he had dominated but where he had never really belonged, and from a new world which he had seen and had found unwelcoming. Throughout his music one can hear the age in which he lived, but more importantly, one also hears the nobility and generosity of Elgar's character. Nobody got closer to understanding Elgar than his friend Jaeger, and his judgement of the composer was the most acute: Elgar was both a 'thinker and dreamer'. Those who listen to his music carefully will perceive the mixture of intelligence and emotion that is so perfectly to be found there.

Another such 'outsider', in terms of the musical establishment, was Frederick Delius – usually known, for the early years of his life, as Fritz. Delius was born in 1862, five years after Elgar, but they died within months of each other in 1934 – the elder man first. Placed close in time, it seems at first sight that little else holds them together. They lived very dissimilar lives, and their music sounds completely different even to the most casual listener. If one compares Elgar's *The Spirit of England* with Delius's *Pagan Requiem* – both works owing their existence to the First World War – one quickly sees that the two composers were worlds apart.

In terms of the social history of music, however, they bear comparison. Both were largely self-taught and owed nothing to the new colleges of music. Both were largely self-made as musicians, only achieving a sure ability in their art after lengthy struggle. Both had also looked to Germany for musical education, and both drew for their initial inspiration from a common fund of German late Romantic music – especially from Wagner. In their domestic lives there were marked similarities also: both relied heavily on devoted wives who had a great influence on their music.

The two men, however, were quite dissimilar, and although in 1907 they both became involved in the founding of the short-lived League of Music (Elgar as president and Delius as vice-president) they did not really know each other. Delius once expressed his boredom with much of Elgar's work, and said that Elgar thought that his (Delius's) music was 'not quite proper'. Yet in the summer of 1933, in the last full year of their lives, Elgar, being in Paris to conduct his violin concerto with the fifteen-year-old Yehudi Menuhin, travelled down to Grez-sur-Loing, Delius's home for the past thirty-six years. Both men have left accounts of the visit, Delius through Eric Fenby. Elgar's great sense of courtesy can be seen to no better effect than on this occasion. He took enormous care to ensure that the infirm, blind and paralysed Delius was up to the visit; he hired a taxi to reach Delius's home at Grez on time when the new Buick belonging to Menuhin père developed engine trouble; he continually sought advice from Delius's wife as to whether the other man was tiring of their conversation, and he bought Delius some records.

Elgar reported that Delius was in much better health than he had feared and that they had had an interesting talk about literature (Dickens and Montaigne) and music. They also talked about Elgar's trip to France by air – the first time that he had flown. Elgar was keen that Delius should consider such a form of transport himself – it would have greatly simplified the long and complicated arrangements that had had to be made for Delius when he visited London in 1929. In a marvellous passage Elgar later recalled a part of the conversation thus: 'What is flying like?' Delius asked. Elgar replied:

Well, to put it poetically, it is not unlike your life and my life. The rising from the ground was a little difficult; you cannot tell exactly how you are going to stand it. When once you have reached the heights it is very different. There is a delightful feeling of elation in sailing through gold and silver clouds. It is, Delius, rather like your music – a little intangible sometimes but always very beautiful. I should have liked to stay there for ever. The descent is like our old age – peaceful, even serene.

Elgar tells us that Delius resolved to fly, as earlier in the conversation he had, also on Elgar's advice, resolved to read Montaigne with his wife. The aged and infirm man had much life left in him.

On his side Delius found Elgar 'very genial and natural and altogether quite unlike what I had expected him to be'. They talked of Delius's current compositions and then of Elgar's, and in an exchange full of reverberations touched on what it meant to be an English composer. Elgar said, 'my music will not interest you, Delius; you are too much of a poet for a workman like me!' Delius replied that he 'thought there was some fine stuff in his Introduction and Allegro for Strings, and that I admired his *Falstaff*, but I always thought it was a great pity that he had wasted so much time and energy in writing those long-winded oratorios'. 'That,' said Elgar, 'is the penalty of my English environment.' 'Well anyhow, Elgar, you're not as bad as Parry,' Delius replied. 'He would have set the whole Bible to music had he lived long enough.'

The two men followed up the meeting in correspondence and Elgar sought Delius's advice on a suitable composition of his for a small orchestra. Elgar later expressed his desire to 'share a few more years with you' and, quoting Michael Drayton, to 'hear your "brave translunary things"'. Delius also had greatly enjoyed the visit: 'Yes, I liked Elgar very much,' he said. Jelka Delius later said that her husband never got over Elgar's death in the following year. Delius himself died shortly afterwards. The meeting in 1933 between the two composers has more than just a sentimental interest, however, for those curious about Frederick Delius. The episode shows how Elgar found Delius in much better spirit than he expected. It was not unusual for people to have to revise their view of the aged Delius. The image of Delius that has come down to us from this period, the image that is still most commonly held in the mind's eye today, is of a gaunt, drawn face with the closed eyes of the blind; a dying man seated upright in an almost aristocratic pose in his chair, the image, in fact of James Gunn's celebrated and well-known portrait of the composer. Photographs of Delius in old age, people's memories of the composer on his visit to London in 1929, Eric Fenby's vivid book, *Delius as I Knew Him*, and striking footage from Ken Russell's BBC television film of his life, have helped to perpetuate this image of a sick, monkish aesthete.

This image of Delius is very far from the mark when one considers his life as a whole. As a young man he was a considerable social success – particularly with women – one of his admirers went to the length of

disguising herself as a man in order to surprise the composer at sea on
a trip to America, a situation from which there was no easy escape. He
lived well, always taking great care over his dress, and enjoyed good
food and wine. There was nothing 'monkish' about Delius. The disease
which struck him down, variously explained as a 'stroke' or 'nervous
rheumatism', was, in fact, syphilis. Even to the end of his life, when he
was continually racked with pain, he went on enjoying himself as best
he could. Eric Fenby wrote of him at this period: 'there was nothing of
the sickly, morbid, blind composer as known by popular fiction here,
but a man with a heart like a lion, and a spirit that was as untameable
as it was stern'. Delius told Fenby, 'I have seen the best of all the earth
and done everything that was worth doing. I am content. I have had a
wonderful life.'

   Frederick Delius's life did, however, have a difficult opening. Delius's
parents held the very formal principles of child-rearing considered proper by the Victorians. Both parents came from Germany and remained
Prussians in their way of thinking. His father, Julius, was a strict disci-
plinarian and little loved by the young Fritz. One of the composer's
sisters, Clare, spoke of her father's ledger mind – always expecting to
see a tangible return for time or effort expended; the Delius family home
was not an auspicious environment for a young composer. Fritz was
born in Bradford where his father had set up a successful wool business.
He was one of fourteen children (two of whom did not survive infancy).
As a child he showed considerable musical talent, as did his brother
Ernest, and music at the salon level was encouraged in the Delius house-
hold. Julius Delius loved music and was a great concert-goer, often
having chamber music in his own house.

   In his sister Clare's published memoir of the period she recalls that:

Fred's musical genius – I write with submission – seems to me in looking
back to have developed from the contacts he made with life. Cheerfully gre-
garious, he made the acquaintance of a young sailor, to whose stories of his
adventures on the Seven Seas he listened hungrily. . . . He would rush back
from one of these intimate talks, his eyes shining, straight to the schoolroom.
There he would seat himself at the Erard and begin to improvise, turning
all those adventures he had just heard of into music. And such wonderful
music – so it seemed to us, at any rate! I can see him seated at the stool, turning
round occasionally to us, and saying breathlessly 'That's a wood, hanging on
the shore of a coral island. . . . That's where the river meets the sea. . . . That's a
bird. . . . That is the sunset in the tropics. . . . This is the dawn.'

The young Fritz was most prominent musically as a violin player and once substituted for an absent player when Joachim and Patti visited his father's house. Fritz impressed the great Joachim with his playing, and Julius Delius as a lover of music would have been a proud man at such a moment. But even after seeing Fritz's talent receive such commendation there was no part of Julius's mind that could ever consider his son making a career in music. Such an idea remained unthinkable for both Julius Delius and his wife all their lives, even after their son had begun to achieve success. Fritz was, rather, introduced to the family wool and noil (wool-combings) business – Delius and Co.; his father made many attempts to get his son started on the right track but the boy was obstinate and spent little effort on the business. After the failure of many stratagems and much exhortation, Julius decided that it would be better for his son to learn business on his own away from home. Fritz was set up as an orange-grower in Florida, sailing from England in 1884. He was, in fact, never to return to live for any appreciable period in England again, although – by his own choice – his body is buried here.

At Solano Grove, away from the direct influence of his father, Fritz worked with extreme devotion – at his music. It was for him a period of withdrawal during which he seems to have come to the conclusion that nothing but the life of a composer would do for him. The orange plantation was not a success. A chance meeting with a New York organist, Thomas Ward, who was in the South for the good of his health, pointed the way forward for Delius. Delius studied with Ward for some months and later recalled his influence:

Ward's counterpoint lessons were the only lessons from which I ever derived any benefit. Towards the end of my course with him – and he made me work like a nigger – he showed wonderful insight in helping me to find out just how much in the way of traditional technique would be useful to me. And it wasn't much. A sense of flow is the main thing, and it doesn't matter how you do it as long as you master it.

Delius had not, however, escaped the long arm of his father. An agent was dispatched from Bradford to report on the prodigal Fritz, who had in fact done a bunk from the orange grove, leaving it in the hands of his even less reliable brother Ernest, who had appeared providentially at just the right moment. Julius now had his son's whereabouts traced by private detectives. Fritz, meanwhile, had been earning his living by teaching and performing, and had ended up in New York, where his father finally caught up with him. Julius Delius was not one to give up easily. Often described as tyrannical he was no worse than most similarly placed Victorian parents and in some respects he was better than many. Clare Delius calculated from his financial accounts, which he kept meticulously in the most proper Prussian style, that he had spent a small fortune - £37,000 - on the education of his children; he was also a generous patron in the public life of his home town. His view on music as a career - an unsteady prospect at the best of times - was the conventional one. After the American episode, however, the father unbent a little towards his son and agreed to allow Fritz eighteen months at Leipzig to study music on condition that he would return to England when the time was over. Julius's hope was clearly that Fritz would reconsider his decision once he had an opportunity seriously to weigh up the bleak future that would confront him as a composer. The bargain was struck and Delius returned to Europe.

As his father had hoped, Leipzig - then a centre of musical activity which attracted the most celebrated composers and performers - proved a disappointment to Fritz, but not for the reasons his father had hoped for. Fritz had long been fascinated by all sorts of music - recently, especially, the music of the Negroes which he had heard in Florida - but he soon learnt that there were few contemporary European composers who interested him. He always acknowledged a great debt to Wagner, but he admired very few others. Of Bach he expressed differing opinions, sometimes flattering, sometimes not, and of Beethoven and Mozart he had nothing good to say. Chopin was the composer he most loved among figures of the past and, among the living, Grieg, whom he first met at Leipzig. (The influence of Grieg, and of Scandinavia in general, remained with Delius all his life.)

His months in Leipzig were not, however, wasted, and he learnt or absorbed much. On returning to England the problem of how to convince his father that a life in music was acceptable still remained. At this point Grieg stepped in and, inviting Julius Delius to dine with him, finally tipped the balance. Julius Delius, while disparaging the life of a composer in general, was a man who obviously loved music, and meeting Grieg would have been a great pleasure for him. It was agreed at this meeting that his son could carry on in his chosen course and a sum of money was fixed for his support. (These all-important financial negotiations were also carried out by Grieg.) Julius had, however, given in in spite of himself - he never showed good grace about it; although he

continued to support his son financially neither of them really had anything more to say to each other.

With his new-won freedom Fritz now went to France, which country
would be his base for the rest of his life. The first years in France were
passed in Paris, where he lived an exciting life in the lively artistic world
of the 1890s. He kept the company of painters rather than musicians.
Osbert Sitwell said of Delius at this time: 'He was the only Englishman
I have ever met who knew personally the giants of the post-Impression-
istic movement, recognized them for what they were and was privileged
to frequent their studios.' His friendship with Edvard Münch is especially
well-documented, but he knew many other interesting figures in Paris
at this time: Alphonse Mucha, Strindberg and Gauguin among them.

Delius was, however, no Bohemian – as he pointed out, he liked
regular meals too much for that – and the financial arrangements forged
with his father took care of his needs. He dressed with accustomed
elegance and if he stayed up at night it was because the noise from the
busy courtyard of the house where he lived distracted his work during
the day. In personal terms he was drawn to Jelka Rosen, who was
painting in Paris at the time. The initial connection between them was
provided by a mutual interest in the works of Nietzsche. At this stage
Delius, however, seems to have postponed a decision on his future for
a while and he arranged to visit his orange grove in Florida once more
to see if he could turn this investment to useful account. With him went
the itinerant vagabond violinist Halfdan Jebe, whose letters Thomas
Beecham, who was privileged to see them, described as 'the most outrageously Rabelaisian I have ever read' – and a young lady. Fritz Delius
was not a man to be easily pinned down.

Jelka Rosen, however, settled in a charming, quiet, picturesque house
in the village of Grez-sur-Loing near Fontainebleau; a well-known resort
of artists, where the writer R.L. Stevenson and the painter Sisley had
lived. On returning from his American jaunt a profound change came
over Delius and he settled with Jelka in Grez: some time later they
married. They lived there until Delius's death and the place and the
composer have become inextricably linked. The colourful incidents and
world-roving that had been such a prominent feature of his early days
now subsided. Delius's prospects as a musician now improved: the period
ahead was to be his most productive as a composer – 'the great noon
tide', as Fenby quotes from Nietzsche.

The fruits of this period were considerable. In 1899 – the year also of the *Enigma Variations* – Delius, who usually made little effort to promote his works, put on a concert entirely of his own music. The critical reaction to the concert was cautious but some clearly felt that here was a force that would have to be reckoned with in the future. As a financial exercise, however, it was a failure: Delius's entrepreneurial skills had never been very well-developed. The composer retired to Grez and from then on the world had to beat a path to his doorway. Early biographers of Delius felt that the following years, between the concert in 1899 and 1907, when Henry Wood reintroduced Delius's music to England with a performance of the revised Piano Concerto at a Promenade Concert, were years in which Delius's music was largely ignored. During this time, however, there is evidence of two developments. First, Delius's music began to enjoy a considerable reputation in Germany, especially under the influence of Hans Haym at Elberfeld, and, second, specialist musicians and writers, alerted by the 1899 concert, continued to take an interest in the composer's progress. And one of those who had attended the Wood concert was, from 1907 onwards, to become his greatest champion.

Thomas Beecham became utterly convinced of the value of Delius's music and promoted it for the rest of his life. Rarely has a conductor become so closely associated with the work of a single composer as Beecham has with Delius, and rarely has such a relationship been so felicitous, for it delighted them both. Delius's reputation began to grow in his native country, although progress, while steady, was slow. The coming of the war in 1914 forced the Deliuses to leave Grez (carefully packing and carrying with them their most treasured possessions, the scores on which Delius was working and Gauguin's *Nevermore*). They lived for a while in England, but in reduced circumstances. Before the war Delius had received both royalties for his music and the proceeds from shares which he held in Germany; the coming of hostilities cut off these funds. His life was not always an easy one from a financial point of view: he was forced in the end to sell the Gauguin and Jelka had to sell the house at Grez. (The Deliuses, however, continued to live there: the house was bought by that ubiquitous patron saint of English composers, Balfour Gardiner, and let to the composer and his wife, rent-free, for life.)

After the war it seemed for a while that things might, broadly speaking, continue where they had left off. Delius had held the opinion that the Germans needed to be 'smashed' but on returning to the house he found it in an appalling condition thanks to its occupation by French soldiers. The all-important wine cellar, which he had buried in the garden, was safe, however, and he began to settle again. But much had changed. By 1922 Delius knew that he was a sick man and many attempts to find a cure for his disease did not halt its course. Within a few years he was a complete invalid, totally blind and almost utterly paralysed. This was the period of his life when with his amanuensis, the young Yorkshireman Eric Fenby, he continued to correct and write music long past the point where most men would have given up. Fenby's book describes the process in detail and is an extraordinarily valuable picture of a composer at work. Delius became considerably more diffi-cult to live with, and the pain of his own life and that of those around him is vividly evoked by Fenby. But the composer never lost his stoic sense of dignity and was dressed as elegantly in his wheelchair as in his hey-day.

In 1929 Beecham arranged a six-day Delius Festival in London to mark the progress of the composer's music in England. All the concerts were packed and Delius attended, seated in an armchair in the Grand Circle of the Queen's Hall. Robin Legge, the influential critic of the *Daily Telegraph*, wrote, 'at the end, the composer bowed his head over and over again and gently waved his arms in acknowledgement of the storms of applause which greeted him'. At the close of the final concert Delius briefly addressed the audience, 'Thank you for the very fine reception you have given me. . . . This Festival has been the time of my life.' The gaunt-faced composer had finally come into his own. On the return voyage to France after the festival he seems also to have become symbolically reconciled with the land of his birth. He asked that his chair should be placed facing the receding shoreline of England so that he could picture it in his imagination. Perhaps this imaginary benediction was going both ways. This image forcibly demands an answer to an important question: how far, and in what way, may we speak of Delius as an English composer?

The composer's own feelings about the land of his birth were am-biguous. He felt that English concert-goers were very conservative. Speak-ing of the then contemporary English passion for the music of Sibelius, he said with considerable prescience, 'The English like that sort of thing just as they like vogues for this and that. Now it's Sibelius, and when they're tired of him they'll boost up Mahler and Bruckner.' But at various times in his life he had turned again to England – in 1907 he had even begun to feel, as many others did at that time, that young composers were achieving something worthwhile there.

Although he rarely visited the land of his birth it was by his own wish that he was buried in the south of England: the violinist May Harrison arranged for his body to be buried at Limpsfield in Surrey. (It seems that Delius had an objection to being buried in the colder north of England, whence he had come.) It was a very controversial move at the time. May Harrison gave the reason for the choice as follows: Delius felt that 'some of the little English churchyards reminded him of Gray's "Elegy", one of his favourite poems, and upon which his last cello work, *Elegy*, was based'. It was a hard decision for those closest to the composer to carry out, for the Deliuses and the house at Grez had become almost inseparably linked. Delius's body was buried temporarily at Grez and then moved to England a year after his death. A few days after he was laid in the Limpsfield churchyard Jelka Delius joined her husband in death, and was buried next to him. Her life had been a continuous and extraordinary sacrifice to Delius and his music.

Beecham's last words at the graveside of the composer included the opinion that Delius's music 'is extraordinarily redolent of the soil of this country and characteristic of the finer elements of the national spirit'. Many people have claimed to hear English qualities in Delius's works but the composer himself did not approve of such sentiments. He once upbraided the young Eric Fenby with the following words: ' "English music? Did you say English music?" There was a pause, and then he added. "Well – I've never heard of any!".'

Delius, born in Yorkshire of two German parents, called himself a 'good European', and in recent years writers have tended to stress his cosmopolitanism. But Delius, like Elgar, had come out of an English environment: the former spending a life reacting against it, the latter working within it, and both of them renewing it for future generations. If not a typical Englishman in his behaviour, Delius was certainly a Yorkshireman: he was deeply moved when the Mayor, Town Clerk and Mace Bearer of Bradford came all the way to Grez to present him with the freedom of the city. After his death Fenby replied to a message from the Mayor, who had expressed his sadness at not being able to lay a wreath on Delius's grave at Grez, that he would perform the office himself; it would be fitting, he explained, for he too was a Yorkshireman.

Although Delius had a deep interest in musical folk culture the 'folk-music' that one finds in his work is not in any way specifically 'English' (*Brigg Fair: an English Rhapsody* excepted of course). He does not belong at all to the Vaughan Williams school. But it is impossible not to treat Delius as part of English musical history: he was thought to be so by his generation, and he enjoyed the friendship of many of his English contemporary and younger composers. In the next generation he had a wide and profound effect on many English composers, especially those who like him had gone to Germany to study. Delius's music has a poetic appeal that has always attracted listeners in England and, to a certain extent, in America (partly due to the work of Percy Grainger there on his behalf). Delius's works are now not heard in Germany and have never really been heard in France, and it is quite appropriate that he should figure large in any history of English music.

We have seen how wrong the 'monkish' image of Delius is. He was, rather, a lively man and his life was full of friendships. He was one of those blunt men – as indeed Yorkshiremen are often characterized – who always said exactly what he thought and many people found his manner rude; his friends, however, knew the man better and remained loyal to him. Delius believed in no half-measures and had a horror of the mediocre. There was about him a great sense of strength and purpose.

There was a lighter side to Delius – he had certainly lived a life of pleasure as a young man and later he enjoyed his life as much as he could, even under the appalling conditions of his illness. His sense of humour extended to teasing the press on the very rare occasions when they were able to interview him. He was also rather changeable – sometimes capricious – in his views. He was fond of lively novels: as a child his favourite was *Sweeney Todd, or the Demon Barber of Fleet Street* and Fenby tells us that as a sick man he enjoyed detective stories 'and any yarn, no matter what it was, that told about the sea'. His roving days behind him, his mind's eye obviously still loved to roam far and wide. But, especially later in his life, his irascibility was also a prominent part of his character. His sister – with fine irony – was reminded by her brother's martinet moods of their father, whom they had both so disapproved of. But his sister pointed to one other characteristic of her brother that is revealing: she thought that even as a child Delius had found it difficult to be moderate in things. It was perhaps the taming of the all-or-nothing struggle in his soul that brought about the strongest mark of Delius's peculiar individuality. Both this individuality brought about by self-mastery, and the isolation it created, can be heard in his music.

In terms of Delius's music the 'monkish' image is all wrong too: his approach is personal, his style unmistakable. Delius knew which music chiefly interested him, and that was his own. His feeling towards Beethoven is revealing – in this respect Delius's iconoclasm knew no bounds. Beethoven's music was, for Delius, intellectual music, and while he was prepared to recognize Beethoven as an 'intellectual giant' he was not interested in his works at all. When a famous string quartet called on Grez they proposed playing one of the last quartets of Beethoven. 'Oh no you won't', was the response they got from Delius. And, listening to the Op. 110 Piano Sonata once, Delius said to Fenby, 'Listen – banal – banal – listen – listen, my boy – fillings – fillings!' Schoenberg and the 'wrong note' school, as Delius called that composer and his followers, also came in for his scorn. Of Schoenberg himself Delius said, 'when a man has to write about his methods of composition you may be sure he has nothing to say'. To the Cambridge musicologist E.J. Dent, who had come to visit Delius in connection with their mutual friend Busoni, Delius said, 'Dent! You're not musical any more! Too much learning!' To which the Cambridge professor goodnaturedly agreed.

It was not to learning or the intellect that Delius felt music should speak. 'Real emotion' was what he was after. We are fortunate in having a clear statement of what Delius did believe the role of the composer to be. In his correspondence with the young Philip Heseltine (published in Cecil Gray's biography of Heseltine, who is perhaps better known today under the name he used as a composer, Peter Warlock) Delius gave his intense young friend clear advice about becoming a composer. Heseltine began the correspondence by asking, odd as it may seem, whether he should go in for the Civil Service or music. Delius replied, 'I think that the most stupid thing one can do is to spend one's life doing something one hates, or in which one has no interest; in other words it is a wasted life.... I think that you are sufficiently gifted to become a composer. Everything depends on your perseverance. One never knows how far one can go.' Three years later Heseltine sent a song to Delius. The older man replied, this time, 'Your song ... is lovely and gave me the greatest pleasure. Turn to music, dear boy, that is where you will find the only real satisfaction. Work hard at composition; there is real emotion in your song – the most essential quality for a composer.' And later Delius wrote to Heseltine, 'For me music is simple: it is the expression of a poetic and emotional nature.' Writing to another composer, C.W. Orr, Delius also made the following characteristic remark, 'But do not let anything I say influence you in any way. Always stick to your likings – *there are profound reasons for them.*'

Delius disliked the sensational in music as much as he did the intellectual. In a rare article of 1920 on 'The Present Cult' he attacked the contemporary lust after the 'latest' – especially in ballet. He noted that even Bach fugues and Beethoven sonatas were being 'interpreted ... by every hysterical nymphomaniacal old woman who can gull the public into seeing "a revival of the Greek Spirit" '. (He shared with Elgar this irritation with the balletomanes of their day.) Delius felt that the time had come for serious composers to declare their views on 'the Russian impressionists, the Parisian Decadents and their Press agents', musical art having been degraded by these people to the 'level of a side-show at a fair'. He attacked Dixie, Dalcroze, Duncan and Diaghilev and mockingly said, 'In an age of neurasthenics, music, like everything else, must be a stimulant, must be alcoholic, aphrodisiac, or it is no good.' This was not Delius's way: his music makes an immediate appeal to many people but never for these reasons. Delius detested vulgarity in any form. (Of Hindemith's works, for example, he claimed that the listener could hear the composer's 'vulgar soul' in the music.)

Delius believed that music should not become a vehicle of melodrama on the stage or even in a song. In his best-known opera *A Village Romeo and Juliet* the development of the plot is presented to the audience in a series of musical 'pictures' rather than conventional acts and scenes: opera to him was as much a musical form as any other. Writing of Beecham's conducting of *A Village Romeo and Juliet* he said, 'Every gesture of the actors in my work must be controlled and ordered by the conductor, for my music is conceived in that spirit. Only thus can the whole be made comprehensive to the public. An old actor stage-manager will be no good whatever for he will make the singers act from the stage and not from the music.' The voices were only one part of his operatic works, which should be taken as a whole. When listening to Wagner he would say, 'Never mind so much about the singers, or even what they are singing about; the narrative is in the *Orchester*.' (He always used the German word for orchestra.)

We learn little about the kind of music that Delius wrote by examining the texts that he chose to set, although we can see much about the man from them. Delius was particularly fond of the works of the Danish writer Jens Peter Jacobsen and of various other Scandinavian authors. His greatest choral works, however, are settings of Nietzsche (whose philosophy he was devoted to) and Whitman – both great believers in the affirmation of life. Delius's choice certainly reflects his own positive approach to life, and his belief in the strength of the individual. It should be added that Delius wrote no conventional religious works – for he disliked what he called the 'Jesus element' in music. His music is rather that of the high hills and the sea, of nature and of man inasmuch as he is part of the great beauty of nature.

It is necessary to turn to the music itself to hear this. Neville Cardus pointed out that Delius's is the most difficult of all music to talk about without playing or hearing illustrations of it. And one also has to hear it played well – Beecham was able to bring Delius's music to life, but he devoted much study and rehearsal time to it. Indifferent performances of Delius's music are their own worst enemy – for it is music that becomes quite unravelled if not played properly.

To the technical musician, the interest of Delius's music lies in his vast harmonic language, and in the particular sense of form that lies behind his works. To the ordinary listener, Delius's music suggests a deep love of nature, a beauty of expression, a fine sense of musical colour, and a poetry of its own that is clear and sincere. It is music 'full of a great kindliness', as Heseltine put it: but also sometimes full of a sadness that is part of a sense of infinite space and beauty stretching out for ever. There is, however, nothing of the woolly 'pastoral' in this: Percy Grainger's description of Delius as the 'Marcus Aurelius of music' is a good one and shows that a sensitive nature may still be vigorous and disciplined. Delius certainly shares this with the philosopher emperor.

The death of Delius in 1934 – lion-hearted to the end – contributed to a terrible year for English music, in which Elgar, Norman O'Neill and Gustav Holst were also carried away. Delius's death was an event marked by sadness in England. Beecham worked for the rest of his life to record and perpetuate his music, and the Delius Trust continues that work today. Delius – showing the sense he had of being part of a community – had hoped that the money raised by his royalties would help other young musicians to get public performances of their works, but Beecham overrode this wish. He was keen to sustain Delius's own works, for, as Delius himself said, 'My works have been the most important event in my life.'

CHAPTER THREE

# Traditions – Old and New

## HURLSTONE, COLERIDGE-TAYLOR, BOUGHTON, HOLBROOKE

The 1890s, as well as being an important, formative period for Elgar and Delius, were exciting years in the history of the musical schools in London: at the Royal College of Music in particular great promise was beginning to be shown by a number of pupils, two of whom, William Yeates Hurlstone and Samuel Coleridge-Taylor, have now slipped into an obscurity that neither deserves. Both were considered at the time to be among the brightest hopes for English music, but both died very young and neither became properly established: Hurlstone, who died at thirty in 1906, received even less recognition than his friend Coleridge-Taylor, who died in his thirty-seventh year in 1912. They flashed over the sky like a pair of comets but both deserve observation, and, in looking at them, we get, if only briefly, an excellent general view of the musical life of England at the turn of the century. Of these two young men, Hurlstone was the better, and more interesting, musician, while Coleridge-Taylor was by far the more popular. In considering them we get a chance to see what it was that contemporary audiences wanted from their composers, and the problems facing composers who were developing within the basic framework of national musical life.

The early loss of William Yeates Hurlstone was held by his contemporaries to be a serious one and the tributes paid to him were fulsome and sincere: Adrian Boult wrote of Hurlstone that 'his loss was a very great loss to English music, comparable perhaps to that of George Butterworth': Thomas Dunhill noted that he 'was regarded by those in whose company he studied as unquestionably the most significant musical figure of his generation'; Stanford, who said of him that 'he goes deeper down than Taylor', believed that he was his best pupil, and Walford Davies also referred to Hurlstone as 'his most beloved pupil'. Sadly Hurlstone's output is small and although there is nothing of the prentice in his early works – indeed they are marked by a real sense of confidence and maturity – none of them achieved sufficient popular fame to be put on today, although his *Variations on a Swedish Air*, highly thought of by Elgar, were still to be heard publicly performed in the 1940s.

Hurlstone came from a family that had produced distinguished artistic figures in the past but had been reduced to poverty. His father had been a gifted amateur musician and the son showed marked precocity. When he was only eight George Grove and Hubert Parry travelled down to Salisbury to hear him play the piano and were very struck by him. Parry said that he was impressed not just by Hurlstone's advanced executive ability but also by his 'grasp' of music. Bronchial asthma was already in evidence, however, and a career as a piano-player was clearly not going to be possible. From a very young age Hurlstone determined to be a composer and had his first piece published when he was nine. At eighteen he won a scholarship for composition at the Royal College and his career there was most distinguished.

During his college days Hurlstone lived at South Norwood and he would often travel to and fro on the train with two fellow-pupils at the RCM – Samuel Coleridge-Taylor and Fritz Hart. These three young men learnt much from each other's company on their journeys: Hurlstone holding that the composer on which he modelled himself was Brahms, Coleridge-Taylor taking Dvorak and Hart – representing the new order – following Wagner. (Hurlstone, in his short life, never really 'understood' Wagner's music, as he put it.) Of these three young men, the relationship enjoyed by Hurlstone and Coleridge-Taylor was particularly close. Coleridge-Taylor left an interesting account of his and Hurlstone's conversations in the obituary notice he wrote of his friend.

I recall that in our student days we each had a musical god. His was Brahms, mine was the lesser-known Dvorak. We agreed that, when either of these composers was really inspired, there was not much to choose between them; but he (Mr Hurlstone) insisted that when Brahms lost inspiration he became merely dull, whereas Dvorak became commonplace. How we used to argue over that vexed question, as to which was the greater crime, to be dull or commonplace.

When the train reached South Norwood or Croydon they would re-enter the suburban world of 'music making' which was the fertile seed-bed of so much talent. This was Hurlstone's musical world for most of his life. Hurlstone, like Coleridge-Taylor, was a poor man: he had begun teaching music at sixteen, an activity he hated; he also undertook to make arrangements of music for popular performance. He took part, in Fritz Hart's words, in 'those polite and painfully innocuous "Musical Evenings" which were still given in London suburbs in that fast-dying Victorian Era'. Like his friend Coleridge-Taylor, Hurlstone enjoyed the patronage of a local worthy - a Captain A.S. Beaumont of South Norwood Park - and the music making at the Captain's home was of a high calibre. Here a few chosen friends would meet to perform chamber music in the music-room; and here also Hurlstone met W.W. Cobbett, who was so instrumental in the revival of chamber music in England.

Hurlstone's contemporaries agreed that it was in chamber music that he excelled as a composer, an opinion that was underlined by his winning the first Cobbett competition. The Fantasy Quartet which he wrote for the prize set something of a precedent and was seen as a model for all future 'phantasies' - a form which Cobbett was particularly keen on. But Hurlstone did not restrict himself to chamber music works: his *Variations on a Swedish Air* were produced at the first concert of the Patrons Fund at the RCM in 1904. He wrote a stirring Piano Concerto, a choral ballad, *Alfred the Great*, and various songs. He was also known at one time for his 'Fairy Suite for Orchestra', *The Magic Mirror* - a piece based on Snow White and the seven dwarfs.

Hurlstone, although poor and in ill-health all his life, was a cheerful and popular man widely known among his contemporaries. The *Daily Mail* of 5 August 1904, while asking the question 'Are we on the eve of a Great Musical Triumph?', printed pictures of various 'promising composers who may help to bring back the golden age of English music', and Hurlstone was one of them. In the years after leaving the Royal College he followed the career of a local musician in the Croydon area, having been appointed Professor of Music at the Croydon Conservatoire. As a teacher and conductor he kept very busy, and in his work he was a keen supporter of British music. As a composer he was attracting ever-increasing interest and in 1905 he got the break he needed when he was appointed Professor of Harmony and Counterpoint at the Royal College of Music. He moved to Battersea Park to be closer to this work, and for a moment it might have seemed that he had escaped one of his life's two great enemies - poverty. The other, however, ill-health, then extracted its full toll, and in the very next year, on the threshold of a real career as a musician, he died of his illness.

Following Hurlstone's death the leading musicians of the day paid handsome tributes to him both as a man and as a musician. Stanford and others pressed successfully to have his manuscripts published. Hurlstone's friends Fritz Hart (later conductor of the Melbourne Symphony Orchestra and the Honolulu Symphony Orchestra), and Thomas Dunhill (for a time assistant music-master at Eton College and well-known later as a composer of light operas, songs and piano works) helped to keep Hurlstone's name alive, as did certain English conductors - notably Guy Warrack. But little could be done to promote a talent that had been snuffed out almost before it had begun to develop. It is futile but intriguing to speculate which direction Hurlstone might have taken had he lived. He did not belong to the Vaughan Williams/Holst group at the Royal College or to the 'coterie' of the folk-music people. His was an independent way and his music shows that he had learnt an enormous amount from his teachers, who, in return, were united in their admiration for him. But while Hurlstone was, at the time of his death, still clearly a musician of the conventional school, his own interests - especially in English music of an earlier period - prefigure many of those of later composers of the musical renaissance. He showed every sign of meaning to retain his individuality: it is almost too sad to wonder where Hurlstone's talents for writing beautiful music might have led him.

Hurlstone was obviously an attractive man. Fritz Hart remembered his affectionate ribbing of Holst's perhaps rather over-serious views; in artistic matters also Hurlstone was not a man who could take himself too seriously. He did not look like a contemporary musician of the period - keeping his hair short and carrying his music in an ordinary bag in which he would declare were 'writs and debentures'. But he knew exactly what he wanted. Fritz Hart observed that 'Art was never a problem to him that demanded discussion and argument.' Hart went on, 'Will, without, however, making a song about it, was as consciously a nationalistic "English" composer as were several of his contemporaries. But it was the instrumental music of the Tudor composers and of Henry Purcell that influenced him, rather than the choral music of the great English masters.' Hurlstone's early death was a real blow to English music, all the more so as his areas of interest were exactly those which were to prove so remarkably fruitful for many later composers.

Samuel Coleridge-Taylor was another man whose musical development was cut short by an untimely death. As a young musician he rose higher in public esteem than Hurlstone ever did but he later lost the support of the musical establishment. Coleridge-Taylor flared bright in his day but his talent was much more uneven than that of his friend. His moment of fame was, however, remarkable. He rose to the position of 'musical man of the hour', just before Elgar reached fame, and long before Vaughan Williams, although he was younger than both of them. His life was remarkable in other ways also. Born in 1875, he died tragically young in 1912. He began his musical career by being hailed as the rising hope of music by Sullivan, Stanford, Parry, Elgar and Elgar's friend August Jaeger; but he soon disappointed these early champions. His music, with the exception of the great choral work *Song of Hiawatha*, did not long survive his death. In more recent times, however, Coleridge-Taylor has become an object of interest again not specifically because of his music but because of the colour of his skin: for Samuel Coleridge-Taylor was a black man and, it need hardly be said, this was unusual in London at the turn of the century. (A clergyman who once travelled with Coleridge-Taylor in a train compartment apparently assumed him to be Japanese.)

The composer's father, Daniel Taylor, was a West African who came to England to study medicine at King's College Hospital Medical School, London. He graduated as MRCS in 1874. Samuel Coleridge-Taylor's mother was a white Englishwoman. (The name Coleridge-Taylor was adopted by the composer later in life: his friends and teachers referred to him as 'Taylor', his wife as 'Coleridge'; he was, however, always known in the musical world by the full hyphenated form.) Daniel Taylor seems not to have been able to build up a successful practice in England and returned to West Africa where he remained for the rest of his life. It seems in any case that he deserted his wife and child at an early date, for the young boy was brought up entirely by his mother, who went to live in Croydon.

This suburb of London was to be Coleridge-Taylor's main home for life, and it is interesting to see how he emerged through the particular musical culture of that town. His early musical training came through the patronage of two local men interested in music: a Mr Beckwith (who is said to have spotted the young child from a window playing the violin) and a Colonel Walters – both men being aware that Coleridge-Taylor was an exceptionally talented child. How far colour initially drew attention to him it is impossible to speculate, but to both these men and to George Grove at the Royal College of Music the important thing was 'his musical gift, and not his colour', as Grove put it.

Coleridge-Taylor's patrons did well for him: Beckwith gave him violin lessons and Walters arranged for him to have a much sought-after position in a good local choir of which he was honorary choirmaster. Walters also took the trouble to compare all the London musical training colleges and decided in favour of the Royal College. George Grove was impressed with Coleridge-Taylor, who began at the College in 1890. He was a shy, timid person at that time, and remained very sensitive throughout his life although his confidence grew to a marked degree in his last years. In 1891 his setting of *In thee, O Lord* was published by Novello and in 1892 Grove arranged for Coleridge-Taylor to take composition as his first study with Stanford.

Of Stanford's many famous pupils Coleridge-Taylor was the first really to shine. Many of Stanford's pupils were, in one way or another, to achieve a firm position in music in later life but none were ever so devoted to their master as was Coleridge-Taylor, who kept a photo of Stanford framed by his mother in a velvet horseshoe on one of the candle sconces of his piano. It is too easy to picture Stanford as an ogre; to his early pupils he was something of a hero. On one occasion Stanford overheard one of the students calling Coleridge-Taylor a 'nigger'; Stanford sent for Coleridge-Taylor and begged him to ignore such vulgarisms, pointing out that his talents were far greater than those of the other boys. On another occasion Coleridge-Taylor consigned one of his manuscripts to the fire because it had not met with Stanford's approval. Coleridge-Taylor's studies at the Royal College were successful, and although he did not mix closely with many of the other pupils except Hurlstone, he seems to have derived great benefit from the years he spent there. In 1896 both Coleridge-Taylor and Hurlstone made important contributions to a college concert at St James's Hall – Coleridge-Taylor with his Symphony in A minor and Hurlstone with his Piano Concerto in G major (the orchestra included Gustav Holst playing the trombone and Ralph Vaughan Williams the triangle). Coleridge-Taylor left the College in 1897.

In 1898 the full measure of Coleridge-Taylor's progress was visible.

The first performance of *Hiawatha's Wedding Feast* took place in that year in the Royal College of Music and according to Parry it was:

one of the most remarkable events in modern musical history. It had got abroad in some unaccountable and mysterious manner that something of unusual interest was going to happen, and when the time came for the concert the 'tin tabernacle' [the makeshift concert room of the College] was besieged by eager crowds, a large proportion of whom were shut out – but accommodation was found for Sir Arthur Sullivan and other musicians of eminence. Expectation was not disappointed.

Coleridge-Taylor quickly went on to expand the original cantata to three parts by adding *The Death of Minnehaha* and *Hiawatha's Departure*, and in 1900 the Birmingham Festival decided to perform all three parts. (Coleridge-Taylor finished off his work by adding an overture.) The concert took place on 3 October: the date is important for in the morning Hans Richter gave the first performance of Elgar's *Gerontius*, one that has become famous for being the most disastrous in modern English music. The *Song of Hiawatha* was given by Richter later in the same day and, unlike the Elgar, it went down very well with the audience; although Coleridge-Taylor shared Elgar's reservations about Richter as a choral conductor. It is said that Jaeger had originally suggested to Novello that they should invite the celebrated conductor Julius Buths over from Düsseldorf for the Birmingham Festival to hear *Hiawatha*. This is a fine irony, because it was Buths's presence at Birmingham that led to the German performances of *Gerontius* which, in turn, established the work properly in England. *Hiawatha* did not, in the event, appeal to Buths: it was not felt to be 'sufficiently philosophical'. To the Birmingham audiences and to many others, however, Coleridge-Taylor was the man of the moment; but that moment was passing almost as soon as it had arrived. Elgar recovered from the set-back of the first performance of *Gerontius* and in the following years rose from success to greater success, while Coleridge-Taylor was never able to regain the position that he had held between 1898 and 1900.

The change in Coleridge-Taylor's fortunes seems to have come with the last section of the *Hiawatha* trilogy. Both Elgar and Jaeger had initially been very impressed with the young Coleridge-Taylor. In 1898 Elgar, being too busy himself to write a work for the Gloucester Festival, had suggested to Dr Herbert Brewer of the Three Choirs committee that they should approach Coleridge-Taylor instead: 'I wish, wish, wish you would ask Coleridge-Taylor to do it. He still wants recognition, and he is far and away the cleverest fellow going among the young men.' Elgar knew of Coleridge-Taylor from Jaeger, who had written of him to his friend, 'I have long been looking for a new English composer of real genius, and I believe that I have found him.' Coleridge-Taylor was duly asked to write for the Gloucester Festival and Elgar was delighted:

> I hope he won't write anything *too* startling – that is founded on a too remote subject – of course he will want to show the critics what's in him but the easygoing agriculturists who support these things also want a tiny bit of consideration and, if he can please *them, without the slightest sacrifice of his own bent of course*, it would be well in view of future commissions.

The resulting piece, the *Ballade* in A minor, was as great a success at Gloucester as the composer's colour was a surprise.

Coleridge-Taylor's support from other leading musicians quickly diminished, however. Jaeger had greeted the early parts of *Hiawatha* with enthusiasm, but of the third part, *Hiawatha's Departure*, he wrote to the composer, 'This will never do. The public expects you to progress, to do better work than before; this is your worst.' Coleridge-Taylor took Jaeger's advice and recast the whole work; but the doubts that had formed in the minds of Jaeger and Elgar grew. Elgar wrote to Jaeger in early 1900: 'I think you are right about C. Taylor – I was cruelly disillusioned by the overture to *Hiawatha* which I think really only "rot" & the Worcester prelude did not show *any* signs of cumulative invention or effect: the scoring is altogether uninteresting & *harsh* of both these works ... His later work is insincere & cannot do any real good.' The problem seemed to be that Coleridge-Taylor was getting rather too fluent in his music without becoming sufficiently self-critical at the same time. Stanford in particular thought Coleridge-Taylor deficient in this respect; and this problem was to remain with the composer for the whole of his life. He 'spoke from the heart' perhaps a little too easily.

With the choral singers of England, however, Coleridge-Taylor remained a firm favourite, and it was for the festival singers and audiences that he wrote in the next few years: in 1901 *The Blind Girl of Castel-Cuillé* for Leeds, in 1902 *Meg Blane* for Sheffield, and in 1903 *The Atonement* for Hereford. None of his later works caught on quite as *Hiawatha* had done, but they were great successes, performed with the very best box-office draws – well-known singers like Madame Albani, the so–called 'Queen of Song'. (The effect that such singing stars could have on the success of a piece of music was remarkable. Novello were originally concerned, for example, that Elgar's *Gerontius* did not have a big enough role for Madame Albani, without whom, it was believed, no work could be a major success.) Coleridge-Taylor was now, in a real sense, a popular composer, but he was not in any position to earn a living solely by composition. The first and most famous part of *Hiawatha, Hiawatha's Wedding Feast*, was sold to Novello for only 15 guineas, although they later gave him a further £25 once it had achieved its great popularity. The second and third parts the composer sold entirely for £250. On top of this, the musical activities with which he was concerned could actually cost money rather than bring it in – running a local orchestra was a case in point. Also, in order to secure the copyright of his Violin Concerto he had to stage a ludicrous copyright performance of it: he wrote to W.H. Reed, a close friend of both his and Elgar's, that it was 'only a farce; only a half-dozen people need to be present, and you need only play a few bars from each movement, *but it must be advertised* on the bill'. Jessie Coleridge-Taylor, the composer's wife, was particularly bitter that her husband was only ever given one full score by his publishers – a copy of *Hiawatha's Wedding Feast*: the rest, along with seats at concerts where his works were played, he had to buy for himself.

Coleridge-Taylor earned his living by teaching and conducting, a familiar enough way for composers to survive at the time: Elgar, after all, had only just emerged from many years of like toil. Like Elgar, Coleridge-Taylor hated teaching: 'Never teach, it will kill you physically and artistically. Everything you give to a pupil is something taken from yourself', he told a friend. He taught at the Croydon Conservatoire, at the Crystal Palace and later at the Trinity College of Music and the Guildhall School of Music. He conducted local choral and instrumental bodies as well as travelling widely, particularly to Wales as an adjudicator at eisteddfods. His stories of the Welsh musical festivals give entertaining sidelights on the period. A notable feature of these gatherings was their great desire for complete impartiality in the judges. This led to extremes of caution: at one eisteddfod the adjudicators were restricted in curtained-off 'Punch-and-Judy like erections, set on poles. . . . As each choir finished a man mounted the ladder, poked his arm through the curtains, and took our folded lists of marks, which were added together on the platform.' Coleridge-Taylor also adjudicated from a hotel window while the bands passed, playing, along the street below him, and once from a deep hole in the ground covered over with boards. Of his many musical activities it was, however, conducting which seemed to suit his talents best: in his last years he was making a good name for himself in this field and his wife seems to have thought that her husband's future would have lain in that direction.

It was an exhausting life but one which he seems to have hugely enjoyed. In 1912, however, he caught pneumonia and died within three days. Those close to him put his contraction of the illness (in those days often fatal) down to the strains and pressures of overwork. His death came as a great surprise to all who knew him. Music dominated his life until his very last moments; he died, propped up on pillows, conducting the air by beating time with both his arms, smiling approval at this, his last performance. He had said at an earlier moment: 'I wanted to be nothing in the world except what I am – a musician.'

Coleridge-Taylor's life had been affected at many points by his colour. Over the years he had suffered from colour prejudice in England and had seen it much more vividly at work on his visits to the United States of America. A very shy child, Coleridge-Taylor grew in confidence over the years, and learned to respond effectively to racial prejudice. He was liked and admired by those who were close to him. He married a fellow-pupil at the Royal College, although her family was bitterly opposed to a mixed marriage. At the College he was remembered for his industry and sense of purpose but he never belonged to any of the 'groups' that existed at that time. He was a meticulous and neat man, as his scores show. He was given to long solitary walks in the open air, and his appearance was always very proper. A friend remembers that, 'He was invariably dressed in black, and wore a black broad-brimmed felt hat, after the style of those worn by clergymen, with a hat-guard. He walked with a quick, nervous, swinging step, always carried a walking-stick, and was always in a hurry.'

It is quite impossible to gauge now, and doubtless it would have been as difficult then, how far Coleridge-Taylor's colour affected the reception of his works in England. The festival audiences and others were keen, it seems, to be seen and heard to be impartial in their dealings with a 'coloured' man. Lionel Bingham, the music critic of the *Standard*, once wrote in a letter to a correspondent who had protested at the apparent omission of articles on Coleridge-Taylor's music, 'on one point you may rest perfectly assured, namely, that the young composer's race and blood, far from detracting from his progress in this country, give him a dis-tinction as a "representative" composer that he would perhaps not otherwise enjoy'. Some writers, however, openly, if discreetly, wrote about the effect of the composer's colour and race on his music or else made reference, probably unconsciously, to it in their choice of words. To the critic of the *Daily Graphic* in 1898 his *Ballade* had passages of 'barbaric gaiety'. *The Times* wrote of the *Ballade*'s 'strong instinct and almost savage character'. Sometimes writers reached ridiculous levels of speculation. They questioned where Coleridge-Taylor's inspiration for music had come from; one writer looked for 'atavism' in Coleridge-Taylor's music and told his readers that: 'The primordial instinct was strong in Coleridge-Taylor.' Others pointed to supposed characteristics of the music of the 'coloured races' coming through in Coleridge-Taylor's works – though this was a matter almost impossible to speculate on at that time as virtually nothing at all was known about African music. Even the composer himself was not immune from such speculation. Coleridge-Taylor apparently held the view that Beethoven had coloured blood in his veins: according to his biographer, W.C. Berwick Sayers, he held that this supposition was 'supported by the great composer's type of features and many little points in his character, as well as by his friendship for Bridgewater, the mulatto violinist'.

For all such speculation Coleridge-Taylor's musical output followed a very conventional pattern especially in the large-scale choral works; he also wrote chamber music, songs, incidental dramatic music for stage performances, keyboard music and orchestral music. The composer he most admired, as we have seen, was Dvorak. A more conventional beginning in the musical world of his time could hardly be imagined. To try to measure the influence of race in his music is, in any case, as unrewarding as it is impossible. When giving speeches in public (a thing he hated to do) Coleridge-Taylor would stress the traditional 'European' virtues and values of music: he would urge his listeners to strive after excellence with enthusiasm, to aim for a higher artistic ambition than mere technical ability, to try to understand, rather than just perform, music. There is nothing here out of the ordinary. As an example of a poor struggling composer/conductor/teacher living and working in a suburb of London it would be difficult to imagine a more typical case than that of Samuel Coleridge-Taylor.

Although almost nothing was known about the music of the black races at the time, Coleridge-Taylor once said that he wanted to do for Negro music 'what Brahms had done for Hungarian folk-music, Dvorak for the Bohemian, and Grieg for the Norwegian'. After the publication of *Hiawatha* he found that interest in the work grew quickly among black singing groups in the United States, and in Washington a Coleridge-Taylor Choral Society was set up with the specific purpose of performing *Hiawatha* with an all-black choir. (Other such choirs were later to be founded elsewhere in the United States.) *Hiawatha* had the makings of a black *Messiah*. Andrew Hilyer once wrote from Washington:

> In composing *Hiawatha* you have done the coloured people of the US a service which, I am sure, you never dreamed of when composing it. It acts as a source of inspiration for us, not only musically but in other lines of endeavour. When we are going to have a *Hiawatha* concert here for at least one month we seem, as it were, to be lifted above the clouds of American colour prejudice, and to live there wholly oblivious of its disadvantages, and indeed of most of our other troubles.

The Coleridge-Taylor Choral Society pressed the composer to visit the United States and to conduct his famous work. This he did in 1904, the first of three visits to America.

In the United States Coleridge-Taylor was seen by many coloured people as 'the living realization of their highest ideal', as his biographer Berwick Sayers put it. The press were no less restrained in their language and by the time of the third visit in 1910 he was called by Carl Stoeckel 'the African "Mahler", as it is generally conceded by orchestral musicians that the greatest conductor who ever visited this country was the late Gustav Mahler of Vienna'. Enormous audiences turned out to hear his *Hiawatha* and he was forced to shake hands with literally hundreds of people who wanted the privilege of seeing and touching him. (On one occasion, missing his physical presence, a life-sized photograph of the composer was displayed on stage.) Thousands attended his concerts and many more were turned back at the doors. (A certain alliance of feeling between the 'Red Men' of North America and the 'Black', commented on by Booker T. Washington, goes some way towards explaining the great popularity of *Hiawatha* among Negroes in the United States.) Interest in his music was not restricted to black people: at his first concert in Washington in 1904 the audience was about two-thirds black and one-third white. (In this respect Coleridge-Taylor felt that it helped with white Americans that he was a black Englishman and not a black American.) He achieved celebrity status in the United States: he was even received by President Roosevelt at the White House, where the two men had a long talk.

Coleridge-Taylor wrote only a few works based on African or Negro tunes and these were not a great success. In England such music was greeted with polite interest. He sent a copy of his *Twenty-four Negro Melodies* to Stanford, who replied, 'It is very good of you to send me the *Melodies*. They look most characteristic and interesting. I wish you would send a copy to Percy Grainger ... who is greatly interested in folk-songs.' In musical effect these melodies were indeed, as Stanford was implying, folk-songs, and folk-song material, whatever its derivation, shares the same limitations the world over. Coleridge-Taylor's Violin Concerto, for example, was originally written around African melodies but he scrapped the whole work and rewrote it entirely, remarking that 'those native melodies rather tied me down', a problem familiar to his composer contemporaries who were using English folk-tunes.

In the last few years of his life Coleridge-Taylor seems to have come to an impasse with his African/Negro music: the rewriting of the Violin Concerto was a case in point. After a period of no really big public success in England his setting of Alfred Noyes's *A Tale of Old Japan* was put on at the Queen's Hall with the London Choral Society in 1911. This work shares much in common with *Hiawatha*. In both cases it was the exotic names that initially appealed to the composer: 'I think the names attracted me first. Think of "Yoichi Tenko the painter" – the opening line – then of "Little O Kimi San" and "Sawara, lissom as a cherry spray". Then, as I read on, the beauty of the poetry and imagery held me, and I *had* to express it musically.' It was, like his earlier works, an enormous success. Coleridge-Taylor's love of exotic names and places mirrored contemporary fashion. The most encouraging aspect of the new work was that the composer had again found a poem which could stand extensive musical treatment.

Coleridge-Taylor's music has many 'definite characteristics', as Parry put it in an obituary notice. He went on to explain: 'He was fond of strong, clear-cut rhythms, which are often much repeated. Warmth of melody and abundant colour are nearly always features.' What Coleridge-Taylor loved in Dvorak's music, Parry thought, was its open-air sound and the 'genuine simplicity which our modern music so often lacks'. His music was popular without becoming trite. He was able to write tunes of great immediate appeal and his daughter could remember the second piece of the once very popular *Petite Suite de Concert* being 'pumped out over the public address system of Victoria station', in a 'vulgarized version, à la Blues'. It was, maybe, all a little too easy. As Coleridge-Taylor's first biographer W.C. Berwick Sayers wisely noted.

'*Hiawatha* was at once his glory and his bane: it had genius and novelty combined; and thereafter the critics demanded novelty of him rather than music.'

That Coleridge-Taylor was an immensely talented man none would deny, but his development was stifled. Why was this, and what does it tell us about the state of music in England at the time? A clue is to be found in an opera that Coleridge-Taylor worked on during 1907 and 1908. He chose Marie Corelli's novel *The Amulet* as his text, intending to call the opera *Thelma*. He was a composer who could work very fast when he wanted to (his wife would read to him while he was scoring, apparently without distracting his concentration), but in this case he took his time and spent much effort on the work. He took the finished opera to the director of the Carl Rosa Opera Company in Nottingham, and while the music was considered to be fine, the work itself as a whole was deemed utterly unsuitable for presentation. Referring to Coleridge-Taylor in his book on Vaughan Williams, Hubert Foss said that he was 'another man who was stifled by English lack of operatic opportunity'. Here is the real clue.

Coleridge-Taylor loved the theatre and was never so happy as when he was writing incidental music for the stage – he would frequently attend rehearsals of plays that he was writing music for and try to capture the spirit and atmosphere for his scores. He also loved the exotic and the wonderful and, recalling the two-year effort on his opera, we can perhaps venture a guess as to the extent of the problem caused him by the 'English lack of operatic opportunity'. Coleridge-Taylor had surpassed many of his contemporaries in popular choral composition: some choral societies regarded *Hiawatha* and *Gerontius* with equal veneration for years. But at this period in English musical history most people, Parry included, knew that the traditional narrative type of cantata was becoming discredited. Parry, indeed, even thought that Coleridge-Taylor's works were the exception to this tendency; but it was clear to all composers that the form was getting stale. (With audiences, however, such works remained highly popular for some time to come: *Hiawatha* reached its greatest fame when it was presented at the Albert Hall in 1924 and the following years as a full-dress 'Red Indian Drama'; and Sir Thomas Armstrong observed that when Malcolm Sargent was asked what he would like to conduct for his seventieth birthday celebrations he 'surprised some of his friends by saying that he would like to conduct a full-scale performance of *Hiawatha*'.)

Coleridge-Taylor was, like other composers – Vaughan Williams, Holst, Delius and even Elgar – investigating new forms of English choral music and opera, but he had scarcely begun this search for a suitable vehicle for his talent when he died. Like his contemporaries he found himself in something of a vacuum, and looked to opera for a possible solution, and it is a great pity that this man, who had such a flair for dramatic and poetic music, was not able to develop in this direction. As it turned out there was no real, lasting success in this respect until the years after the Second World War, while in the inter-war years large-scale choral works (Walton's *Belshazzar's Feast*, for example), greatly in the teeth of the prevailing conventional wisdom, enjoyed something of a come-back. But the search for an English operatic form was utterly necessary for men like Coleridge-Taylor and we can learn much from the zeal and purpose with which this challenge was undertaken.

Of all the tireless prophets of English music in the early part of the twentieth century none was more remarkable in his day than Rutland Boughton; and none has been so quickly forgotten. He was a man whom it was hard to ignore: George Bernard Shaw initially replied to the composer's letters, 'Why do you want to come and play your King Arthur to me? I do not insist on reading my plays to you'; and, a little later, 'I loathe your music.' Yet Shaw, like many others, was won over by Boughton's energy and his determination to do something new and different. His *The Immortal Hour* was one of the most outstandingly successful English operas to be staged this century, and yet it is hardly ever heard today. Boughton's appeal stretched widely, from the devoted band of men and women who worked for him at Glastonbury to the grand men of music and prominent public figures who signed a Civil List pension petition for him: Granville Bantock, H.C. Colles, Walford Davies, Edward Dent, Ralph Vaughan Williams, Herbert Morrison, Bernard Shaw, Lady Londonderry and Dame Elizabeth Cadbury included. But it came to nothing in the end; his life-long belief in communism and free love, in the national destiny of music-drama and in the central position of the theatre in the community died with him, with only half his work in print and his prophetic mission in ruins.

Rutland Boughton's sense of mission was visible even in his youth. He was born in 1878 in Aylesbury, where his father had a small grocery business. Boughton's background was conventional enough: his mother played the harmonium and he became involved in music early as a choirboy and as a member of the local Sacred Harmonic Society. As a child Boughton formed an 'orchestra' of his friends and wrote out music for them. But then a curious element entered his life, for without ever having been to a theatre or opera, he began to conceive a cycle of music-dramas on the life of Christ. This basic idea – although the cycle of music-dramas he actually wrote has as its hero King Arthur rather than Christ – was to be with him for the rest of his life, and the writing of music-dramas was to be his main concern as a composer.

At the age of fourteen, further education being out of the question, Boughton found a job in the offices of a London concert agency. His musical compositions began to receive some attention. In 1893 a song of his was published and in 1898 a piano concerto was put on at St James's Hall; it was very badly received. Just as Elgar had a few years before, Boughton now left London and went home to attempt to earn his living by building a local reputation. Boughton was, however, always a tryer and it was not long before some of his music came to the attention of Stanford. At the age of twenty he began again – now as a student at the Royal College of Music, his fees being paid by the Member of Parliament for Aylesbury at the instigation of Stanford, who liked to refer to Boughton as 'a fellow who's been playing Beethoven in a barn'. Boughton still had a strong Buckinghamshire accent and had a very different background from many of the other students. Like Coleridge-Taylor he was not closely associated with any of the groups at the College that were such a feature of the time, his only close friend there being Edgar Bainton. He left the College in 1901 when the money ran out and Stanford had obviously lost interest. Of one of his works – *An Imperial Elegy for the Death of Queen Victoria* – Boughton recalled that 'Dr Stanford told me that it was the ugliest thing he had heard, apart from the music of Richard Strauss', to which Vaughan Williams, who was not on the best terms with Stanford at the time, added, 'some of Strauss's uglinesses are better than Stanford's beauties'. The *Imperial Elegy* was a setting of Whitman's lines:

> Darest thou now O soul,
> Walk out with me toward the unknown region,
> Where neither ground is for the feet nor any path to follow?

It was a passage also set by Holst and Vaughan Williams at about this time. Boughton said that *The Times*'s critic, in a 'a jolly slashing notice', had written of his setting that 'Mr Boughton had made ground solid enough for the feet even of a Fafner'.

Boughton began to earn his living again by hack work; he occasionally tried his hand as a music critic but these jobs seldom lasted long as he was unable to keep his opinions in line with those of his employers. Northcliffe himself got rid of him from the *Daily Mail* after an article in which he wrote 'Melba won't do'. Boughton worked for two years playing a harmonium in an orchestra pit, but in 1905 finally got off the treadmill when he was offered a job at Birmingham by Granville Bantock as a teacher of piano and rudiments; he later added singing to his duties. He was also involved at this period of his life with the Birmingham City Choral Society and the Cadbury pageants, and he was still composing: from 1907 until 1910 he wrote sets of choral variations of English folk-songs. Things were looking up for Boughton, but now his life underwent a major change in direction: in 1910 he left his wife for Christina Walshe (who designed many of the sets and costumes for his productions), and the couple were obliged to leave Birmingham, where the scandal created by their behaviour became a serious problem. They went to Berlin and while in Germany visited Bayreuth, which one might assume would be Valhalla for the young composer. Boughton, however, was no slave of Wagner's. He had for some years been working out in his own mind the specific problems that faced him as a composer in England, and in 1911 he was ready to share his results with a larger world. In that year a book appeared, *Music Drama of the Future*, by Boughton and the poet Reginald Buckley; this was both an advertisement and a justification for the Arthurian Cycle that the two men had begun to produce. The pamphlet combatively began: 'the following pages contain a half-taste of a work which achieves what Wagner failed thoroughly to achieve'.

Boughton was never a man to lack confidence in his own theories. In 1907 he was contacted by Buckley, who also worked on a joint project with Coleridge-Taylor for an exotic 'West African drama, with strong imperial interest'. Boughton replied, 'Your letter made me feel that the dream of my life was within grasp.' Buckley's four poems of 'the coming of the Hero, his Manhood, the Quest of the Grail and the ultimate fading of those glorious days' had first been sent to Elgar – who had rejected them – and then to Bantock. Bantock had suggested Boughton and here the poems ended their journey, although Boughton and Buckley's was not a smooth partnership. The two men fought over the texts until Buckley's death in 1919, and in the end there were in fact five music-dramas in Boughton's completed Arthurian Cycle.

Boughton explained his theories of music and drama in some detail in the publication of 1911. He ranged over Euripides and Ibsen, Aristophanes, Molière and Shaw, not overlooking Aeschylus and Sophocles, Shakespeare and Tolstoy. Like all of Boughton's writings this is a *tour de force* and the reader is more bowled over by the energy of his prose than convinced by its arguments. He drew a clear distinction between 'opera' and 'music-drama'. Opera, he said, was designed for the amusement of theatre audiences with music thrown in, while 'music-drama is a story of the symbolic type which can only be adequately expressed in the continuous emotional mood of music'. 'An opera can be written at any time. A music-drama must be waited upon, because the composer must first of all undergo a living religious experience.' Wagner was taken to task for failing to divest himself of the 'analytical, argumentative methods of the prose-drama' and in *Pelléas et Mélisande* Debussy is accused of having 'merely crawled after the words' with his music. Boughton felt that in the process of underlining the drama Maeterlinck's play had been ruined by the music.

Boughton developed a theory that 'the Wagnerian drama lacks just that channel of musical expression which is absolutely necessary to the English people – the channel of the chorus'. His work on 'Music and Democracy' had convinced him of 'the truly popular nature of all the greatest art and of the fact that the greatest artists acquire their superhuman powers by acting as the expression of the oversoul of a people'. The choral element was vital to Boughton and he held that 'drama was choral in its origin. The mass-atmosphere is one of the great and precious splendours of the Greek drama; and the same atmosphere is preserved in the most important dramatic celebration in the churches – the Mass!' Like an increasing number of composers of the period Boughton was not a conventional Christian and he was looking for new channels for his spiritual impulses. He believed in the Hero – the Hero of Beethoven's great symphony – and he felt that 'the production of a hero can only come about in the unity of the people'. Arthur, Prometheus and Christ were 'all of them the direct production of mass-feeling'.

The British people, he believed, were the ideal vehicle for his views. 'The outstanding value of the orchestral chorus to the public is that by its means they themselves enter into the art-work. The choral singing which is the chief glory of British music, and the love of pageantry which is now so happily reviving finding their inevitable union and climax in such a work as ours.' This was a heady philosophy, but Boughton's enthusiasm was infectious. Most of his followers did not want to go the whole way with Boughton and live in a communal farm of craftsmen and artists, from which he hoped a new order would arise, but there were many who were prepared to give their money and time to help realize his visions of the union of Carlyle's 'toil-worn Craftsman', the provider of the daily bread, with the 'Artist' who strives after the 'Bread of Life'.

Boughton's first practical step was taken in 1912 with a plan to start up 'a new sort of Summer School for grown-ups' as the composer told the *Daily Mirror*. His scheme, which was in fact unrealized, was to take a school for the month of August, rehearse an opera, and then play it in the woods.

There will be two acts (two scenes in Act I) and we have specially chosen the night of August 27th for playing the first act because of the full moon then. A night literally elapses between the acts, Act II being played after breakfast on August 28th.

Another novel point about the opera will be that each scene will take place in a different part of the woods. Mr Frederick Jackson of 'Tarn Moor' is giving us the run of his extensive grounds for our 'stages', and there will be a mile walk for the players and the audience between scenes one and two in the first act.

Performers will be expected to provide their own costumes, which will be of the simplest kind, mostly green in colour.

Sadly, it didn't work; and Boughton now began to try to realize his vision in a much more realistic way. He and Buckley fixed on Glastonbury as an appropriate place to accomplish their plans and in 1913 they set about drumming up support. While there were those who always regarded Boughton as a crank and others who considered his views 'dangerous', from this point onwards he began to command the respect of some of the greatest of his fellow-musicians. Bantock and Elgar were enthusiastic about his plans for Glastonbury, the latter writing, 'I am very glad indeed to make acquaintance with your fine work *The Birth of Arthur* and am delighted to learn that there seems to be an opportunity to produce it next August in the district most eminently suited by association and tradition for its production.' In 1913 the conductor, Dan Godfrey, put on an experimental performance of a section of the work at Bournemouth for the seaside holiday-makers – hardly the audience

Boughton originally had in mind for the work. At Glastonbury plans were being made for 1914 and an appeal for money for a 'National Festival Theatre for Music and Drama' was launched, signed, among others, by Thomas Beecham, Henry Wood, George Moore, John Galsworthy, Edward Carpenter, Bernard Shaw and Percy Grainger.

The coming of the First World War, however, took much of the steam out of the project. Boughton was reluctant to join the armed forces, and when he was called up in 1916 Shaw argued in print that he should be exempted. Boughton's appeal against military service was rejected, and between the end of 1916 and the beginning of 1919 he served in various regiments, ending up in the Royal Flying Corps under the Director of Music, Walford Davies. The festivals at Glastonbury did get under way but much was lost when the original momentum was broken, and Boughton's *magnum opus*, the Arthurian Cycle, was seriously checked (the first part to be put on was *The Round Table* in 1916). In the first two festivals in 1914 and 1915 works which were to achieve a considerable fame were, however, performed: *The Immortal Hour* and *Bethlehem*. The latter, based on the Coventry Nativity Play, was, in Boughton's own words, 'deliberately composed as a folk opera, the lyrical quality of the play being increased by the insertion at suitable moments of Early English Carols, either as choral interludes after the manner of Greek tragedy, or as part of the play itself'. The work enjoyed very considerable popularity with choral societies for many years, and it fulfilled its purpose of being a work that could be performed entirely by local players.

But an even greater success was enjoyed by *The Immortal Hour*, a setting of the Celtic play by that strange figure known as Fiona Macleod – really the pseudonym of William Sharp – who died in 1905. Sharp concealed the fact that he was Fiona Macleod throughout 'her' life: he even submitted a separate and fictitious entry for her to *Who's Who* where her favourite recreations are described as 'boating, hill climbing, and listening'. Both writers were extremely prolific, but the 'continual play of the two forces in him, or of the two sides of his nature' produced 'a tremendous strain on his physical and mental resources, and at one time, 1897–8, threatened him with a complete nervous collapse', according to Sharp's wife, Elizabeth. Sharp encouraged the view that Fiona Macleod was a 'dreamy Celtic genius' and *The Immortal Hour* is certainly shot through with the kind of feeling that might have come from the pen of such a figure.

The main characters of the music-drama - Dahua, Lord of Shadow, Etain, a princess of the Land of Youth, Eochaid, the king, and Midir, Etain's rightful lord who has come to claim her back to the Land of Youth - are figures from the land of dreams. It appealed to people on many different levels, but, above all, it was a work containing a number of memorable tunes and this was the major reason for its quite unprecedented popularity. Boughton's biographer, Michael Hurd, has calculated that by the time of its third revival in London, there had been over 500 performances of the opera in London alone and a similar number elsewhere. Its first run, in 1922 in London, totalled 216 performances, breaking the record for any serious English opera. A certain Miss Parker held the record number of attendances - 133 performances - and Princess Marie Louise saw it fifty-two times. It also won the first Carnegie Trust Award. Composers as different as Bax, Holst and Ethel Smyth expressed their admiration for the work and on the rare occasions when it is revived nowadays it invariably charms its audiences.

*The Immortal Hour* may have been Boughton's most popular work in the public mind but it did not hold that position in the composer's. He understood, and indeed could make his plans on, the commercial strength of the work; but at the same time this success worried him, for he had no intention of becoming the London season's operatic lion. He felt much more at home in small communities: 'the London prestige is largely bluff', he said. Instead he concentrated on his Glastonbury Festivals and the touring company which developed from there. In 1922 his *Alkestis* (from the Gilbert Murray translation) was first performed, and in 1924 a work based on Thomas Hardy's *The Queen of Cornwall*, which Hardy spoke of as a 'glorification of the play', was staged. In Boughton's account of his visit to Hardy he says that they went for a long drive together during which the author

pointed out some of the places and houses mentioned in the books, and referred to his characters as if speaking of real people, making it clear that the world he had created, beginning in realism, had to some extent passed over into the world of vision. In the evening he brought out some old music in the hope that we might find a song suitable for the drunken choruses in *The Queen*.

(Hardy attended a performance of the complete work in the company of T.E. Lawrence.)

As is often the way with such artistic endeavours, the Glastonbury Festival began to lose steam after a time. For various personal, practical and political reasons – nothing in Boughton's life was simple – his associations with the festival that he had brought into being began to be less productive, and by 1927 it had collapsed. Boughton was, however, to complete four more music-dramas: *The Ever Young* (performed at a festival in Bath in 1935), and the last three parts of the Arthurian Cycle – *The Lily Maid* (performed at a festival in Stroud in 1934), *Galahad* and *Avalon* (both still unperformed). The writing of the Arthurian Cycle had been the work of his life but the great series of five music-dramas never appealed to the musical public as much as *The Immortal Hour*, *Bethlehem* or even *Alkestis* and *The Queen of Cornwall*. Boughton had faced the problem of writing opera or music-drama in English for English audiences head-on and his works met with considerable enthusiasm and success. He always knew that they would not go down well in the Covent Gardens of this world but, produced locally, with local people involved, he felt that justice could be done to the spirit of his works. Shaw, Edward Dent and Vaughan Williams were among those who wrote to him of the fond memories that they had of the exciting times at Glastonbury. Edward Dent, who as Professor of Music at Cambridge held one of the most prestigious musical posts in the country, wrote to Boughton in 1946 that he had heard *The Immortal Hour* recently at Walthamstow,

and I still find it as beautiful and moving as ever – indeed I think I find it more beautiful and original than I did before. People in the old days used to say it was Wagnerian, but all that has faded away now and it really is very much all of a piece; a complete musical unity and completely and uniquely your own. I really begin to think it is one of the best operas ever written, and when I say that you must bear in mind that I judge all opera as complete wholes on the stage, not by details of music or libretto.

Writing on another occasion Dent further explained his views: he said that while *The Immortal Hour* may not always be good music, judged by purely musical standards, 'there is no getting over the fact that it is an opera of marvellous compelling power. That is because the voices dominate it ... the point is that the voices have the music which expresses the composer's most essential thoughts.'

Boughton had achieved much of what he had set out to do: he had composed ten music-dramas; he had finished his five-part work of the Arthurian Cycle; he had established a practice of organizing local music, drama and dance schools and festivals; and he had lived a life in accordance with his beliefs. It is one thing for a young man to write about living as part of a self-supporting artistic community but quite another much later in life to get up early in the morning to feed the animals before starting to compose, as Boughton did. He worked throughout his life to advance the ideas he held dear. As a young man he had published a pamphlet called 'The Self Advertisement of Rutland Boughton'. In this work he had outlined the main problem he saw facing a musical artist – how to compose and survive. 'If you like to give me a nice little farm near a town on such terms as will allow me to do my musical work when I feel moved to it, I will *give* you my music.' Boughton had no desire to '*sell* himself' but he realized that he would have to 'sell my soul to you – to advertise my music and ask what price I can get', for he was always a practical man, however unlikely some of his schemes may have seemed at their inception. No idle dreamer could have had the great successes – or the great failures – that Boughton had year after year. 'All art should be a free gift', was the centre of his position, but he knew that, in practical terms, composers needed a fair return for their works, and he suggested that many composers had fallen victim to the 'humbug' which had placed them in a class apart, to their own undoing. His proposition was that composers should join together, as the instrumental musicians had in the Musicians' Union, to obtain better conditions.

A publisher with whom I was discussing the point (a knowing old bird) met this argument with the complacent remark that 'composers are not expected to live by their composition, but in other ways – teaching and so on'. That is largely true as a statement of the position of British composers; and that is why we have had so few of the best kind during the past two hundred years.

Boughton never saw much for the labours of his lifetime in terms of financial reward. In theory he did not approve of patronage but in practice he accepted some modest financial assistance. There was always somebody ready to help Boughton on his way, from an early landlord who supported him, to Lady Londonderry – his 'Circe' of later years. He was responsible for one 'dismal pot boiler', as Michael Hurd calls his *Burglar Bill*, but, for the rest, his musical output was prodigious and the rewards slight. As well as the full-dress music-dramas there were four shorter dramatic works, two ballets, three symphonies, four symphonic poems, four overtures, five concertos and a wide variety of other pieces.

Boughton had been influenced by the English folk-song movement and, especially in the composition of *The Immortal Hour*, by the work on Hebridean folk-song carried out by Marjory Kennedy-Fraser. Vaughan Williams very much admired his three songs to words by Hardy and wrote to him, 'I rather believe that that kind of music growing out of those kinds of words is what will go down to future generations as the best type of our generation and country. Probably a Frenchman or a German would hate them, and I rather hope he would.' Boughton himself had been influenced by a wide variety of people in his life: by Ruskin, Whitman, William Morris and George Bernard Shaw. An important early influence was also that advocate of the brotherhood of mankind and the simple life, Edward Carpenter. Boughton became a frequent visitor at Carpenter's cottage but was scared away after Carpenter admitted to him that he was a homosexual.

Boughton was also an active writer: as well as his pamphlets he wrote a book on Bach and a general work, *The Reality of Music*. Bach was clearly his ideal as a musician: he wrote, 'All expressions of modern musical art have their fount in Bach.' Both books reveal an eclecticism that is characteristic of writers who have had little formal education but whose love of learning is sincere. Boughton's politics coloured much of his journalism. Hamilton Fyfe, Editor of the *Daily Herald*, had to call him to order in 1924: 'My dear Boughton, Will you *please* write about music? That is what the readers want. We get quite enough of Trade Unionism in other parts of the paper!' Boughton was a life-long communist, although he broke with the Communist Party on two occasions – the second time in 1956 after the invasion of Hungary. He felt, especially in later life, that his political views were responsible for his lack of success. Boughton would argue with anybody and everybody. He accused the BBC of victimizing him; he berated the government in 1931 for Philip Snowden's attempts as Chancellor of the Exchequer to subsidize the Covent Garden Opera Syndicate, when no provision had been made for English Opera; he 'broke' with Herbert Morrison, one of the leading Labour politicians of the 1920s, over what he considered to be the ineffective policies of the Labour Party in 1929. Even in Moscow in the 1920s he was disappointed at 'the lack of political insight shown in the presentation of Wagner', as Michael Hurd has observed. Boughton *contra mundum* was a familiar sight to his friends and contemporaries, and in his later years many of them noticed that he had developed a persecution complex, convinced that there was a conspiracy against him and his works.

Boughton had worked hard to organize and promote his festivals, pageants and summer schools at Glastonbury; he had conducted numerous choirs – as prepared to use a barn as a theatre for his purposes. Most of his productions there were accompanied only by piano not orchestra, and he saw virtue in this also. The scenery and costumes were always kept to a minimum, partly no doubt for economic reasons but also because it was felt that the suggestive and symbolic value of undistracting sets and costumes was a plus in terms of the whole music-drama. He promoted English music of all periods at his festivals – Dowland and Byrd, Purcell, Parry and Ireland, Elgar and Vaughan Williams – but he was not narrowly 'English'. He had once considered an Irish festival and, at another time, a Welsh one – this latter in collaboration with Vaughan Williams and Holst, although nothing came of either of these ideas.

Boughton's political views sometimes obviously influenced his musical works. In 1926, the year of the General Strike, he wrote a 'workers' ballet' called *May Day*: it is one of the many ironies of his life that *May Day* was only performed once and then by Dan Godfrey in Bournemouth, where it was unlikely to have the revolutionary effect planned for it by the composer. Boughton never gave up trying, however. He once presented his *Bethlehem* in modern dress – Herod a cigar-smoking capitalist, Christ born in a miner's cottage, etc. – which caused some scandal at the time.

Boughton's private life provided much fuel for gossips and ill-wishers. Having walked out of his first marriage, he repeated the process some years later, this time falling in love with one of his pupils, Kathleen Davies. Shaw once wrote to Boughton urging him to send in an entry on himself to *Who's Who* and humorously suggesting that for 'recreation' Boughton should put 'being seduced by his pupils'. But the people who surrounded Boughton in his working life – 'my crowd' as he called them – were devoted to him and his vision of music-drama, and although he clearly was not an easy man to get on with most people gave him the benefit of the doubt in the end.

Boughton was one of the most colourful characters in English musical history. But how important was he as a composer? In the pre-First World War period he wrote on the subject of the 'Death and Resurrection of the Musical Festival', showing that he had a good understanding of what had happened to English music in the previous twenty years or so. Boughton thought that the great traditional musical festivals – Birmingham, Leeds, Norwich, Sheffield, the Three Choirs, and so on – had been, at best, 'gatherings of such wealthy folk as are too kind, or too lazy, to pot grouse'. He was much more in favour of the newer competition festivals and felt that they provided a basis for the 'festivals of the future'. These, he believed, should be non-competitive festivals held as the central moment of a civic public holiday in specific communities. In such views and in his belief that 'musical art is an important factor in building up human character' Boughton was in line with many of his contemporaries. While recognizing the success of Elgar and Bantock, Boughton envisaged for himself a more radical course than theirs. The central position he gave to the choral music-drama was a particularly English solution to one of the main problems that he and his fellow English composers faced, and his attempts to create an opera for English people, based in some part on music that would be characteristic of the nation, was a considerable achievement. In 1934 Shaw wrote, 'Now that Elgar has gone you have the only original personal English style on the market, free at last of all survivals of the Wagnerism and Debussy-Ravelism that give an exotic flavour to your rivals', and there is a considerable truth here.

But the next year Shaw wrote something equally true: 'You are still only half awakened to your art.' Boughton did in fact fail to realize his idea of a permanent Temple Theatre, as he once referred to his vision of an ideal location for his work, and even though he did have some considerable success in getting his work staged he did not manage to establish a new form of choral drama for his fellow-countrymen. Like Ethel Smyth, but in a different way, he was able to keep up interest in his work as long as he was alive but this interest quickly faded after his death. Boughton was not, however, searching for glory but rather for the well-springs of a viable national musical art in a world where he saw materialism and ugliness encroaching on his higher ideals.

In his time Boughton was often referred to as the 'English Wagner' and this was a title that he shared with another English composer, Joseph Holbrooke, who was, in addition, also known as the 'English Strauss', the 'English Berlioz', the 'English Mussorgsky' and, in a phrase of the journalist Hannen Swaffer's which perhaps comes closest to the truth, the 'Cockney Wagner'. (On many of his published works Holbrooke's forename appears as Josef, a form that he seems to have favoured for a while.) Like Boughton and Bantock and others of that generation, Holbrooke thought on a colossal scale. He, too, engaged in many activities:

he championed the right of composers to a fee for performances of their work; he was a zealous propagandist of his country's music and did much to get young British composers a hearing; and he was a tireless advocate of his own works. In his journalism and his speech Holbrooke was known to be a man with a caustic turn of phrase. Such a forthright man is always going to attract enemies and Holbrooke had his critics, but, at the same time, there was an eccentric 'character' about both Holbrooke's life and his work that drew people to him. Indeed, as a young man he attracted considerable notice: Ernest Newman once thought that he was the composer most likely to leave his mark on English music, and Beecham put on his works.

Holbrooke was born in 1878 in Croydon, where his father was a 'professor of music', in fact a teacher and performer. As a boy Joseph Holbrooke was a chorister at St Anne's, Soho. His father wanted him to be a conductor but the boy had other ideas. Joseph was entered for the Royal Academy of Music in 1893 and studied composition under Frederick Corder, the prominent teacher, composer and conductor; his time there, however, was not long and he did not make a real mark. Domestic circumstances forced him to leave the Academy and for a while he earned his living touring Scotland with a production called 'Two Hours' Fun', conducting the Woodhall Spa orchestra, and other minor jobs. By 1900, however, Holbrooke was beginning to attract more senior attention. In that year August Manns did his *The Raven* at the Crystal Palace (throughout his life he was fascinated by the work of Edgar Allan Poe) and Ernest Newman wrote asking how any 'competent observer' could fail to see how significant Joseph Holbrooke's works were both in themselves and 'as a landmark in our English Renaissance'. In the following year another of his pieces was performed by Granville Bantock at New Brighton. When Bantock took up an academic position at Birmingham Holbrooke got a job with him there; things began to look up and he became firmly established as a festival favourite. In 1904 his *Queen Mab* was given at the Leeds Festival. These were the years when the great names of the hour at the festivals were Elgar and Bantock, and in 1906, at Birmingham, Holbrooke's *The Bells* joined Elgar's *The Apostles* and the first part of Bantock's *Omar Khayyám* for their first performance under Hans Richter.

Holbrooke was the *enfant terrible* of English music of his time. His work was regarded by many as experimental, even outrageous, and he made much of how technically difficult some of his scores were. Hol-

brooke's manners and way of life matched his music and he was grouped
in the public mind with his 'Bohemian' friends – among which were
Augustus John and George Moore. Granville Bantock's daughter Myrrha
recalls how Holbrooke, when living in the Bantock ménage, once remained immured in his study for a whole week, appearing only for
meals. 'One day when Joseph suddenly failed to present himself at table
my mother became anxious. Entering the study she discovered him in
a dead faint on the floor. He had completely worn himself out, but he
had composed *Queen Mab*, one of his most attractive works.' Holbrooke
would even try to get away without wearing a collar and tie, but
Bantock's wife insisted when he stayed with them that he put on such
apparel, objecting strongly to his informal manners.

Holbrooke's production of music was ceaseless: piano works and
songs, operas, ballets, symphonies, concertos, a great variety of other
orchestral pieces, music for brass bands and a substantial number of
chamber works. He was strongly influenced by Wagner's *Der Ring des
Nibelungen*, by the works of Liszt and, especially, by Strauss's music. His
orchestral works often call for extremely large numbers of performers.
He liked to score parts for unusual instruments (Richter was particularly
averse to the concertinas used in *The Bells*). In his time his work was
widely heard – although probably never as widely as he would have
liked.

As an experimentalist Holbrooke was as daring for his time as Bliss
and Walton were to be in the years after the war. A marvellous example
of this is recorded in the pages of Thomas Beecham's volume of autobiography, *A Mingled Chime*. Holbrooke approached Beecham with the
idea of putting on his work *Apollo and the Seaman* (to the poem by
Herbert Trench). Beecham was intrigued and even helped Holbrooke
search Paris for a sarrusophone and player, an instrument that the composer – but evidently, from his account, not the conductor – considered
was vital to the artistic scheme of the work. They finally succeeded in
their quest, unearthing a certain Monsieur Doloville, and leaving Beecham free to proceed to Grez to visit Delius, his initial purpose in
crossing the Channel. For the performance of *Apollo and the Seaman* the
orchestra and conductor sat behind a screen on which magic-lantern
slides of the poem were projected. Beecham's account of the first performance of the work in 1908 is well worth repeating and may, to a
certain extent, remind readers of the celebrated reports of the first public
performance of Walton's *Façade*:

In order that the performance should begin in an atmosphere of impressive mystery, a time-table had been drawn under which at eight o'clock the doors of the hall were to be closed to further admittance. At one minute past the lights were to be lowered, at three minutes past further lowered, and a minute later the lowest pedal note on the organ was to begin sounding as softly as possible. On the fifth minute the hall would be plunged into complete darkness, the organ would cease, and a soft blow on the cymbals would give a signal for the appearance on the screen of the first lantern slide, Apollo himself.

On the night, due to the non-appearance of a cab, Beecham arrived fully six minutes late; attentive readers of the above account will realize that by this stage the audience at the Queen's Hall were beginning to feel that something had gone wrong, and a 'slight apprehension of danger was brewing', as Beecham delicately put it.

The central work of Holbrooke's career, like Boughton's, was operatic. Compared with Boughton, Holbrooke had slightly more modest ambitions; his greatest work is a mere trilogy of operas – *The Cauldron of Annwyn* – and was the labour of only twelve years. In this project Holbrooke collaborated with Lord Howard de Walden (T.E. Ellis), a wealthy property owner and lover of the arts, known in his time as a proficient swordsman, motor-boat racer and explorer as well as an antiquarian and collector of armour; who also helped support many other artists including Gustav Holst and Dylan Thomas. Ellis wrote the librettos for the trilogy, *The Children of Don* (first put on in 1912), *Dylan* (1914), and *Bronwen* (not staged until 1929).

Holbrooke and his librettist shared a common interest in 'British Music' and it seems that the composer even accompanied the peer on his honeymoon cruise in order to play the piano for him. The first opera to be staged. *The Children of Don*, was put on at Oscar Hammerstein's Kingsway Theatre (as an opera house this project cost the promoter dearly; it was later to be turned into a picture palace). Howard de Walden sank money into the production, even getting Nikisch over from Berlin to conduct. Hannen Swaffer's account of the occasion reveals that all did not go smoothly:

There was wicked trouble on the stage. In one scene, men were supposed to change into wolves, and, after Howard de Walden had tried in vain to use dogs to play the part of wolves, trick mechanisms was used. But, by a devilish scheme on the part of someone on the stage, the mechanism went wrong, the wolves fell down in front of everybody, the audience shrieked with laughter, and Lord Howard de Walden rushed out of the theatre, livid with rage.

Holbrooke's ambitions were considerable and he was prepared to take great risks. Such accidents apart – and the novel staging techniques that Holbrooke favoured always entailed certain practical dangers in performance – *The Children of Don* went on to be heard in both Venice and Salzburg in 1923, not an inconsiderable achievement.

Holbrooke's journalism and his book *Contemporary British Composers* (of 1925) did much to promote the works of his fellow-musicians, and for many years he put on a series of chamber concerts where new British works could be heard. Holbrooke believed that 'England's music craves a *character*', and he worked hard in his life to try to discover, both in his own works and in those of other composers, what character that might be. His book on contemporary British composers was the work of a self-confessed 'nationalist in art as in politics'. In it he voiced his complaints about the finances of composers, the lack of proper opportunities to hear native music, the role of music critics, the need for patronage, and so on. He called also for greater organization of music. The main part of his book, however, was a survey of the leading native composers of the day: Edward Elgar, Granville Bantock, John Ireland, Cyril Scott, Ralph Vaughan Williams, Arnold Bax, Havergal Brian, Frederick Delius, Gustav Holst, Eugene Goossens, and a group of young men which included Arthur Bliss, Herbert Howells and Lord Berners. Holbrooke's book and his work for his fellow-composers show that he could be a generous and inspiring man; but he was in some ways his own worst enemy also.

In the post-war world Holbrooke lost his position as *enfant terrible* and innovator. In referring to the earlier years Beecham had called him 'a musician of natural ability handicapped by a poor aesthetic endowment and a total want of critical faculty', and other writers of the time commented on his rather slapdash way of writing and his inability to be sufficiently critical of his own work. Myrrha Bantock thought that Howard de Walden's generosity had possibly been his undoing. She said that Holbrooke 'led a very easy life, with a flat in the South of France, a London house and a cottage in Wales, and as a composer he never really developed beyond a certain point, which was reached early in his musical career'. Cyril Scott believed that the death of Holbrooke's patron in 1946 changed the whole position of his life. Holbrooke lived until 1958 and in his later years the music writer Peter Pirie says he 'settled into deeper and deeper eccentricity and solitude; even his habit of engaging in controversy, which in his youth was heated and violent, seemed to have left him', although, according to Scott again, he censored the 'excruciationists', as he called the new musical school.

It is hard to separate the wheat from the chaff in Holbrooke's work and while some of his symphonic poems may be played on occasion the reluctance of promoters and conductors to put on his larger works is readily understandable. Like many others, Holbrooke never fitted into the post-war world and nobody was prepared to take a risk with his work any more. As was the case with Rutland Boughton, Holbrooke spent much energy and effort trying to develop a national form of opera that he believed would appeal to his fellow-countrymen. In this brave attempt, however, it became more and more obvious that they were both going down the same cul-de-sac, and the new young men of the post-war world were to do better by travelling in different directions. We should not, however, underrate the sincerity and deep sense of purpose that impelled Boughton and Holbrooke on their quest for an 'English operatic opportunity'.

# CHAPTER FOUR

# Shifting Horizons

## BANTOCK, BRIAN, DAVIES, SMYTH

The growing English musical traditions of the first years of the century were fundamentally and irrevocably changed by the First World War. In the lives and works of Granville Bantock, Havergal Brian, Walford Davies and Ethel Smyth we can see the great material and psychological changes brought about by the war reflected in a vivid way. Before the war they had each been considered, although in different ways, to be in the vanguard of English music – figures from whom a new lead could be expected – but none of them were able to live up to this expectation. They were among the many composers who found that their voices were no longer listened to with much interest in the post-war period. The link between them and their audiences was broken beyond repair.

Before moving on to consider their separate careers, however, something may be said about them in more general terms, for they illustrate well one particular point. In their different ways – Ethel Smyth especially so – the story of each of these composers shows that the capital city was not the only major musical influence in England at the time. While London was unquestionably the centre of national musical life the physical impact of the provincial centres of England and Wales and the psychological influence of the Celtic worlds of the North of Scotland and West of Ireland were of considerable importance. Havergal Brian, who came from a very poor background, was able to take his first steps in a musical career in the Potteries, for example; Bantock worked both at Liverpool, and, as did Elgar, Holbrooke and Boughton, at Birmingham; Walford Davies adjudicated at festivals all over the country and did especially valuable work in Wales; and, in a very different way, Ethel Smyth made her mark outside the metropolis, her *Fantasio* first being put on at Weimar and *Der Wald* in Berlin. Her best known work, *The Wreckers*, was heard in both Leipzig and Prague before being performed in London.

Provincial towns and cities often boasted considerable musical resources, in many cases certainly greater than exist today. The Hallé Orchestra in Manchester under Richter was thought by many to be the best in the country and Elgar's musical journeys frequently took him to North Staffordshire, Birmingham or Liverpool. The great choirs of the regions were often excellent, and metropolitan conductors were glad of the opportunity to conduct them. This widespread musical life meant that at this period many composers had a reasonable chance to hear their own work, although the quality of performance was uneven. Some composers found it difficult to live in the metropolitan musical world – even Elgar was never really at ease in London and his close friend Granville Bantock preferred to stay in Birmingham, where he enjoyed a considerable musical career.

Before the First World War there was a time when the front line of English music seemed to be held by two men – Elgar and Granville Bantock. The two knew each other well and shared friends in common. Bantock played Elgar's music whenever he had the chance, earning from Elgar the highest praise – 'Bantock *is* a real brick and *really* understands things.' Elgar recommended Bantock for an important job in Birmingham and the younger composer succeeded Elgar as Professor of Music there. Their friendship lasted well: when he was dying Elgar asked his old friend to come and pay him a last visit to bid him goodbye. There were those who were even prepared to put their money on Bantock rather than Elgar. Gerald Cumberland (the pseudonym of C.F. Kenyon), for example, in a mischievous book of 1918, *Set Down in Malice*, compared the two men to Elgar's disadvantage: the 'only two names that are of vital importance in British creative music – Sir Edward Elgar and Granville Bantock. No two men could be in more violent contrast: Elgar, conservative, soured with the aristocratic point of view, super-refined, deeply religious; Bantock, democratic, Rabelaisian, free-thinking, gorgeously human.' Cumberland concluded 'of the two, Bantock is the more original, the deeper thinker, the more broadly sympathetic'.

Granville Bantock was born in 1868, eleven years Elgar's junior. His father was a distinguished surgeon and gynaecologist and objected strongly to his son's desire to devote his life to music. Granville Bantock's passion for music may have been all the stronger for having started rather later than most – at the age of sixteen. But by 1889 he was safely in the Royal Academy of Music where he studied under Frederick Corder. There was, in the 1890s, an energetic group of young men at the Royal Academy who, like the parallel groups at the Royal College, were to do well later in life. Bantock kept in touch with many of his contemporaries there and often played their music in public. He had been a leading social figure of the Academy and a prolific composer, showing for the first time his interest in Oriental subjects and writing pieces of a 'colossal' nature. Bantock thought in the biggest terms: he planned, at this time, a series of twenty-four symphonic poems on Southey's *Kahama* (he finished only two) and also six Egyptian dramas (of these only one saw the light of day – *Rameses II*). Another important feature of Bantock's life that developed early was his adherence to programme music. We are told that one of his pieces at the Academy was an overture about Satan and after a passage in which the players had got badly tangled up, the Principal, Mackenzie, asked the young composer 'Where are we now?' Bantock replied, 'In hell, sir.' As a young man he hero-worshipped Wagner and Liszt – the father of the tone poem.

Having left the Academy, Bantock tried his hand at a variety of musical activities: he was the conductor with George Edwardes's party taking the musical show *The Gaiety Girl* on a world tour, and he then settled down to the job of Musical Director of the New Brighton Tower Pleasure Gardens near Liverpool. One might be forgiven for the thought that Bantock now seemed set on a career at the 'lighter' end of the musical spectrum, but he was not that sort of man. At New Brighton between 1897 and 1900 he began to introduce his audiences to more serious music than they were used to. His ambition was to transform an open-air military band into a small orchestra capable of playing complicated modern works, following the example of Dan Godfrey at Bournemouth. Bantock was especially keen to introduce contemporary English music to his audiences and arranged concerts of the music of Cowan, Parry, Elgar, Corder and Wallace, conducted by the composers themselves. He also championed the music of Sibelius, who came to England for the first time to conduct his First Symphony at Liverpool for Bantock. (Sibelius's Third Symphony is in fact dedicated to Granville Bantock.) He gathered to himself men of talent at New Brighton. His programme notes, for example, were written by the young Ernest Newman, who later followed the composer to Birmingham and lectured for him there. At New Brighton, however, his relations with the owners of the Tower deteriorated and he was fortunate that, through Elgar's influence, he was offered the job of first Principal of the School of Music at the Birmingham and Midland Institute. He also at this time (1900-1901) conducted two concerts of British music at Antwerp.

Birmingham was to remain Bantock's base for many years, although, as his daughter has recalled in her sympathetic account of her father's life, the family made frequent moves around that city. During this period he wrote the three parts of his *Omar Khayyám* for chorus, soloists and orchestra, a massive work performed in its various parts in 1906, 1907 and 1909 and then all together. (It was also put on in Vienna in 1912.) In 1908, when Elgar could no longer face being Peyton Professor of Music at the University, Bantock was successfully put forward for the job and during the period between then and the onset of the war he set up many new musical activities in the area. Choral societies looked to Bantock as a leading member of the competition festival movement (an enthusiasm of his; he even went to Canada once to try to encourage the setting up there of a similar movement) and his new works were keenly awaited. The texts he chose show a characteristic eclecticism: between 1911 and 1914 he published, among other things, *Atalanta in Calydon, Vanity of Vanities* (from Ecclesiastes), *The Great God Pan, Lucifer in Starlight, Kubla Khan, A Pageant of Human Life* (with words by Thomas Moore). All of these works reflect in some part the spirit of the time – perhaps none as much, however, as his *Omar Khayyám*, which was particularly popular.

Bantock was, like Elgar, firmly planted in the Edwardian world. He was a man given to crazes for things Indian, Chinese, Persian, Arabic or Japanese. (His house was decorated with numerous Japanese prints and oriental curios.) His interest in the music of the British Isles was especially concentrated on the romantic 'Celtic fringe'. In this respect he was similar to a fellow-pupil of the Royal Academy, Arnold Bax, but whereas Bax was devoted to the land and the people of Ireland, Bantock was inspired by the Hebrides. He was specially interested in the work of Marjory Kennedy-Fraser, who had journeyed all over the Hebridean islands collecting the local folk-songs. She and her harp-playing daughter

Patuffa later travelled widely performing them. Bantock's *The Seal Woman* was based on such Celtic songs, the libretto being written by Marjory Kennedy-Fraser, who played the part of an old crone in its production.

Bantock was well-known for his idiosyncratic behaviour and for his love of excess – he would never have one thing if a dozen would do. He was devoted to the cult of Napoleon; as a child his daughter was rather overawed by him. Many of his fads were only short-lived: once, for example, having visited a Trappist monastery, he made his whole family eat for a while out of wooden bowls with spoons. It is not really surprising that he and his family acquired the reputation of being Bohemian. He was extraordinarily fond of animals and had many un-usual pets in his various homes. He also kept open-house for a wide variety of humans: as we have seen Joseph Holbrooke lived in his house for a time, as did the curious H. Orsmond Anderton, Bantock's first biographer, who, in his own phrase, 'hermitized' on the composer's estate. Anderton, a man of spartan habits, known to Bantock as 'the Colonel' because he had once been a lance-corporal (a typical example of Bantock's sense of humour), was the composer's private secretary for some years, even though it would be hard to imagine two less similar men.

Bantock's was a large personality. Like Elgar he did not fit easily into the post-war world. His music too came to be regarded by younger musicians as belonging to a past age. He continued to write very suc-cessfully for large choral societies and it was in the forms associated with this type of music that contemporaries thought that he did his best work. But the gradual decline in popularity of choral singing and the increasing lack of interest in his sort of programme music meant that Bantock slid into obscurity. Very little of his music has survived, a fact which com-mentators before the First World War would never have predicted. Beecham was keen on his *Fifine at the Fair* and that work has been performed in recent times perhaps more than any of Bantock's others. It is a straightforward piece of programme music with some excellent moments; but there is about it and about Bantock in general such a strong feeling of belonging to a past age that it is hard to feel any close sympathy with it. It is the music of a very different world, and it catches its moment so well that it is of only restricted interest to us.

In his day, however, Bantock was thought to be a very modern figure. He was a member of an all-male 'revolutionary movement against conventionality' known as 'Step off the Pavement', together with Havergal Brian, Gerald Cumberland and Hans Richter: eating, drinking and sending each other postcards were the main concerns of the members of this confraternity. They struck a 'modern' attitude in their opinions. Writing just as the war was coming to its close, Cumberland looked forward to getting back to the 'real' world after his war service. Cumberland was, as we have seen, a great supporter of Bantock's, whom he took to be the new man of the hour. His attack on Elgar, or on what Elgar was supposed to stand for, was foolish. But in looking to the future Cumberland expected something new and different in English music and he expected it from Bantock, Holbrooke and others. He was sadly wrong; but it is revealing that one of the other composers of the time who came in for his scorn – Walford Davies, to whom we shall shortly return – had a much wider mission than Cumberland's favourite composers ever had. Cumberland characterized Davies as representing 'asceticism, fine-fingeredism, religiosity, "mutual improvement", narrowness of intellect, physical coldness'. The believers in Granville Bantock saw themselves in quite a different light. Their zest for life came out in works of great and obvious passion, often characterized by prodigious overflowing of emotion. Some people felt that such baring of the soul was altogether un-English; but to Beecham Bantock was a 'true lyrical and dramatic' writer and Eugene Goossens admired his use of the 'full resources of orchestral colour'. Bantock found, however, as did Elgar also in later life, that his works became progressively unpopular with promoters faced with the great and ever-increasing expense of putting them on. The days of Wagnerian or Straussian orchestras were over, and Bantock, who had once been in the front line of British music, was overtaken all too soon. He died in 1946 and his ashes were scattered to the winds from the top of a Welsh mountain by his sons, a last romantic gesture for this non-church-going but deeply religious man.

A fellow-member of 'Step off the Pavement' and in his way quite as extraordinary a character as Bantock, was Havergal Brian. Brian first rose to notice before the First World War and was thought by many to be a composer of considerable interest. A variety of circumstances, however, brought about a reversal in his fortunes and between 1922 and 1954 three excerpts from an opera and a short overture were the only works of his to receive first performance. A second phase of interest in Brian began in the 1950s, increasing in intensity in the 1960s and 1970s:

the 'unknown warrior' of British music (as some called him) was, supposedly, being honoured at last in his own land. The story of Havergal
Brian's life and the extraordinary second chance given to his music is
unique in the annals of music history. It is a curious tale made more
curious by the composer himself. Kenneth Eastaugh's biography of 1976
revealed a complex and contradictory man, and the evidence presented
there is important if we are to escape the over-simplified views of those
who would have us see Brian as a working-class, anti-war hero who
defied the musical establishment and went on composing in the face of
great odds ... and so on. Brian is a much more interesting man, and the
story of his life more instructive, than that view allows.

Havergal Brian was born in Longton in the Potteries in 1876. His
father and his mother had both worked in pottery factories. Both parents
sang in choirs and Brian - although he had no formal musical training
- learnt to play the organ as a child. He became an apprentice-joiner
with a jobbing master and all family and local conventional wisdom
would have suggested that should he continue to 'play it safe' with his
job he would - in material terms - be all right. But Brian was never a
man to play it safe for long. The musical life of the Potteries was, at the
time, thriving, and Brian left regular employment and lived for a number of years off a variety of jobs, for he was determined above all else
that he was going to compose music. Some of the jobs he did enabled
him to sneak away and engage in musical activities on the quiet. He
frequently attended concerts at Manchester of the Hallé Orchestra under
Richter. He also came to the attention of Elgar, whose *King Olaf* Brian
greatly admired. It seemed possible that he might be able to break out
of the constraints of his background and earn a living in music. It was,
however, a great gamble.

As a composer Brian's first real breakthrough came in 1907: in that
year his *English Suite (No 1)*, a setting of Psalm 137, and a concert
overture, *For Valour*, were heard. Brian had achieved a considerable
status in local musical circles and now interest in him began to spread
further afield. In the following years both Bantock and Wood put on
his works and the performance of the *English Suite* at the Queen's Hall
was very well received by the audience. All seemed set now for a
favourable career in music and in 1909 Brian attracted the attention of
a wealthy man, Herbert Minton Robinson, whose middle name displays
his connections with the wealth of the pottery world. Robinson offered
to be Brian's patron on the grounds that he was 'very certain that you

are the only composer of any account who is not financially well off – and, it is a crime to be poor!' Until his death in 1923 Robinson paid out to the composer's family considerable sums of money, and this, ironically, seems to have been Brian's downfall. That Brian wished to escape the poverty of his working-class background is understandable enough, and Reginald Nettel, whose book on Brian, *Ordeal by Music*, of 1945, first brought the composer back to the public's attention, rightly says that Brian belonged to a people who were trying to make the world more acceptable to themselves – not trying to put it to rights. Brian had no sense of mission for his class – far from it. He longed to live in the world in which his great friend Granville Bantock moved, with a large house, domestic servants, fine food, books and cigars in front of the fire; and, while Brian had the money, that was how he lived.

This vastly different style of life brought with it problems for Brian. He took to drinking heavily, he was often extremely bad-tempered and violent and eventually his behaviour led to a break with his wife: he went off with another woman in a scandal which almost ruined him. At this stormy time he lost the sympathy of Elgar, his friendship with Bantock cooled (although Bantock continued to support Brian's music), his relations with Henry Wood and Arnold Bennett also ended, and he nearly lost the financial support of his patron. He had risen high and fallen far. Brian moved to London and later said that the next few years were a period of the greatest depression for him. Here he experienced some of the problems of a provincial musician in London that Elgar too had come across: Brian complained bitterly of what he thought of as the London 'gang' with, as he saw it, their 'Oxford' manners. (Again, we should be careful not to read too much into such remarks. Brian was no straightforward 'class warrior' at all: only a little while later, for example, he was inveighing against the 'addlepated labourers' in a munitions factory where he worked for being paid more than he was.) He did little composing during these troubled times and with the onset of the war he joined up with the Honourable Artillery Company (having first, in a typical gesture, considered joining the French Foreign Legion). The more settled life in the army meant that he was again able to direct his attentions to his music, and he soon got leave to attend performances of his pieces; Dan Godfrey at Bournemouth was now showing interest in him. In May of 1915, however, he was discharged for flat feet and worked in a number of minor civilian jobs for the duration of the hostilities.

In the years following the end of the war Brian made his most determined attempt to assault the musical world, trying to enlist anyone
that could conceivably be of any help to him. He was busily writing
music again and it is to this period that his opera *The Tigers* and the
Gothic Symphony belonged – the two works of his which have created
most interest in recent years. Havergal Brian found the post-war musical
world quite different from that existing before 1914, and although he
had been his own worst enemy in the years immediately before the war,
the effect of the Great War on his progress as a composer should not be
underestimated. Another serious reverse was the death of his patron in
1923. In the following years Brian ceased to be a composer of even
passing interest. He became almost a different man – supporting himself
and his new family (the children of which never knew of their father's
earlier marriage and family until he had died) with a variety of jobs. As
an individual he became calmer and more settled. He continued to write
music but his output was not substantial, especially so when one comes
to consider what he would achieve in the 1950s and 1960s after he had
been 'rediscovered'.

Brian's rediscovery was above all due to the work of two people:
partly to Reginald Nettel for his book *Ordeal by Music*, and, more
importantly, Robert Simpson, who as a music producer at the BBC was
well placed to promote a revival of his music. For a second time Brian
became the object of public interest and this time he responded well to
the attention. All his earlier anger and desperation had gone and interest
in his work now spurred him on to the most extraordinary efforts of
composition. Between 1951 and 1968 Brian wrote four operas, twenty-
five symphonies and a number of other pieces. He still had a deep
romantic streak, however: Nettel has shrewdly pointed out that three of
these four operas are about the period of the French Revolution and its
aftermath – from Schiller, Goethe and Shelley – the fourth was an
Agamemnon. It was almost as if Brian was drawn to periods of history
and to individual characters who were responsible for bringing order
out of the chaos of the world. Like Bantock, Brian had a great admiration for Napoleon; and he was also an admirer of the German state and
people, especially the Kaiser, with whom he once corresponded. During
this period of his life Brian also enjoyed performances of his works that
had lain unplayed for years. In 1961 his massive Gothic Symphony was
put on (his only really important first performance since 1907), a second
staging in 1966 involved some 700 performers at the Albert Hall. Brian

responded to those who were interested in him by giving them exactly what they wanted - more music. In return they gave him, at last, a chance to hear his work in performance; something without which few composers can really develop.

In 1969 Brian was asked in an interview the following revealing question: 'Half a century ago you were regarded as a rising star among composers; then you went into almost complete obscurity. Why was this? What went wrong?' The composer replied, 'It was the First World War - of 1914 - it obliterated other men besides me - Bantock's and Holbrooke's stock went down. Others. And more particularly, the great choirs of the Lancashire Coast and the Midlands all went out. They never came back again.' There is a lot of truth in what Brian said, as we have seen; but, in his case it was not the whole truth, as we now know. Brian's personal problems, as revealed in his letters, betray a deeply worried, sometimes almost paranoid character; at times he even imagined that someone was getting into his house at night and tampering with his manuscripts. Moreover Brian threw away his best early chances to work at his music. Struggling against the odds was, ironically, what seems to have brought out the best in him although there were times in his life when the odds were stacked - mainly by himself - too high.

When Brian finally and quite unexpectedly received attention and performances he wrote for all he was worth - but one suspects that the real tragedy in his life was that he had not done so at a much earlier phase. His new music displayed many of the characteristics of the earlier period. He had Bantock's tendency towards the massive. The cost of putting on a work such as the Gothic Symphony is enormous and the forms in which he chose to write as an older man - operas and symphonies - were still in the tradition of Wagner/Bruckner and way outside all but the most ambitious budgets. Many musical influences can be heard in his works, including those of Elgar and Delius.

In the 1960s music critics and a part of the musical public warmed to Brian as a phenomenon. It must be said, however, that his music has not struck a deep note of sympathy with a significant public - there are still many people unconvinced that Brian is an 'unknown warrior' and merely suspicious of what they see as special pleading. A case in point is afforded by Brian's opera *The Tigers*. This work, written against the background of the Great War, is held by some of Brian's supporters to be an important 'anti-war' work - but it is no more 'anti-war' than, say, in their very different ways, Delius's *Pagan Requiem* or even Elgar's *For the Fallen*. Brian's work is, rather, a satire on the world of the time and especially the army: there is a 'Bishop', a 'Colonel' and the splendid Mrs Freebody – 'I want you to know her,' says the Bishop, 'for she is keenly interested in all moral and social work. Anything which will tend to uplift the sorrows of the great poor. The decline of the national birthrate. She is especially devoted to the mission of the heathen.' But sharply amusing as it is – as it is meant to be – we must remember that the composer had shown no qualms in joining up at the outbreak of the war. His supposed 'anti-war' phase was really only a part of his anti-almost-everything phase. He was, indeed, always a most contrary man, refusing to the end to do what was expected of him. Even in his last years when the popular press had got on to the idea that he was a neglected composer-genius he would not play up to them. If Brian was an outsider it was largely because that is what he wanted to be; and although we must be grateful to the BBC for bringing Brian back to our attention it is easy to sympathize with the view that it is high time that they put Brian back into the pack again, shuffled the cards, and dealt us a new hand.

A much more conventional figure of the period, also once considered to be a potential leader of English composition, was Walford Davies. Born in 1869, his life reflects some aspects of the period more clearly than the lives and works of other composers that we have looked at, showing particularly how one man – albeit at a high cost to his own creative art – did fruitfully adapt to changing circumstances: Davies became very well known in the later part of his life as an educator, especially on the radio. Like many of his contemporaries his main energies were put to the service of expanding and extending musical life in England in general rather than working solely for his own art as a composer. In Davies's case this was in part due to his character – for he possessed a naturally didactic disposition. He once said of himself 'I notice more than ever now my fatal tendency to lay down the law. I believe I do it in everything. I notice in the primers that I have read marginal notes of mine intended for the work I was to write on the subject. I think if I am told the ingredients of a pudding my instinct would be to start a treatise on cookery.' Some people found, on occasion, that this didactic streak meant that Davies was not the easiest of men to deal with, but he showed over and over again that he possessed an original and rare talent

for communicating his knowledge and, equally important, his enthusiasm, to a wide audience.

Davies came from a family devoted to music and as a boy had been
a chorister at St George's Chapel, Windsor. When his voice broke he
became a pupil-assistant to Sir Walter Parratt, then Windsor's distinguished organist. In 1890 he was awarded an open scholarship in composition at the Royal College of Music, and in 1895 he was appointed
a teacher of counterpoint at the College. Works of his now began to be
performed – his Symphony in D was put on by Manns at the Crystal
Palace – and in 1896 he visited Brahms at Ischl. The great composer's
comments on Davies's music were critical but encouraging.

In 1898, however, Davies began the first of many appointments – as
organist to the Temple Church in London – that were to determine his
life's main activity, and effectively prevented him from concentrating
his major attentions on composing. Some of his friends felt that Davies
was in danger of achieving too little because he kept trying too much.
For example, in 1918 Parry wrote to H.C. Colles (who later wrote
Walford Davies's biography), 'Walford is going to stir up great enthusiasm for music in the Air Force. And then?' As a composer Davies
suffered from the multiplicity of his interests and activities, but he had
consciously chosen this life and his achievements were considerable even
if he never fully developed as a composer.

Throughout his life Davies was devoted to English church music: he
was one of the first members of the Church Music Society (founded in
1906) and proposed the motion in 1927 for the setting up of the School
of English Church Music and its college of St Nicholas. His knowledge
of English church music was extensive. (Parratt declared that compositions from every decade of the past 400 years of English church music
were represented at Windsor: Davies himself had a particular interest in
the work of Merbecke.) The choir at the Temple, under his training,
became extremely well-known and there even evolved a Templer's
Union for half-yearly concerts given by past and present choristers.
Among Davies's choristers were many who went on to distinguish
themselves later – perhaps none rose to greater heights in the public eye
than Leopold Stokowski who, after singing in the choir, went on to
take up an appointment at St James's Church, Piccadilly, before making
his fortune elsewhere. Indeed, much of Davies's effect as a popular
educator can be seen in his pupil Stokowski.

The personal effect that Davies had on a choir was evidently considerable and his high standards were infectious; Granville Bantock entrusted his son to Davies's training. Walford Davies was also an able organist and the application of modern technology to the king of instruments was one of his passions. He championed the work of Frederick Rothwell, whose patented console with tabs between the keys to ensure a quicker change of registration made more rapid variations in sound possible. (The last organ that the two worked on together – that of St George's, Windsor – was redesigned completely with two consoles; Walford Davies was prepared to pay for the extra one himself if the dean and canons were not.)

During the First World War Davies showed another side of his character. He greatly wished to 'mobilize' music, as he put it. He was keen to be sent over to France for this purpose and in 1916 he began working there through the YMCA, who provided many services for the fighting troops. (It was in connection with this that Parry gave Walford Davies his celebrated tune for Blake's poem 'Jerusalem' with the words 'Here's a song for you. Do whatever you like with it.' With the troops he sang 'John Peel', 'Land of My Fathers', 'Will You No Come Back Again?' and other favourite songs of the time; but he also moved them on to harmonized hymns and more serious works, such as 'When Israel Came out of Egypt'. Throughout his life Davies was motivated by a desire to spread good music as widely as possible to all groups of people. In London, for example, he conducted the West London Bach Choir and also worked at the People's Palace in the Mile End Road. In the Second World War he was instrumental in getting CEMA (the Council for the Encouragement of Music and the Arts – it is interesting to note the emphasis in this title on music) set up, in order to 'mobilize' music once again.

Another great expenditure of energy came with what he saw as his 'mission' to Wales. Davies was appointed Professor of Music at Aberystwyth University College, Musical Director to the University of Wales and Chairman of the National Council of Music. His duties were demanding but he was quite tireless in his enthusiasm for taking music to the Welsh. Bearing in mind the reputation for musicality that the Welsh enjoy some might think that such a mission would be like taking coals to Newcastle; but musical education was badly lacking there at that time, particularly instrumental teaching. A later review of the activities of the Welsh Council of Music between 1917 and 1941 wrote of this time, 'In rural districts queues often formed up before the opening of the doors, the people curious to see and hear the instruments. In some cases they had never seen a violoncello and the question was once asked, "Is it played with the fingers?".' There were in Wales many choirs but competitive singing had become a habit and there was an overemphasis on singing for prizes. (This was also visible in many English choirs, especially in the Midlands: the initial enthusiasm for and encouragement of competition singing had been fired by a desire to help improve the quality of performance, but the end result all too often was that the technical aspects of performance were concentrated on at the expense of the musical.) Davies was opposed to such a practice. And when the firm opinions of Davies met the equally tough-minded people of the Principality there were problems: on one occasion Davies tried to get a Welsh crowd to sing a chorus from Bach's *St Matthew Passion* only to meet with revolt in the ranks, for 'Land of my Fathers' broke out from the back of the marquee where he was conducting.

But it was in yet another field that Davies was to become best known and that was the radio. Davies impressed John Reith with his strong sense of purpose and his belief in bringing good music to the attention of a wide public, and he was involved in many series of broadcasts between 1924 and his death in 1941. Davies aimed his broadcasts either at children or at the 'ordinary listener' and would illustrate them with examples which he played on the piano. He also used compositions sent in over the course of the previous week by listeners to his programmes to illustrate his points as he went along. He was remembered for the informal style which he adopted on the air, and his popularity was considerable. He also worked to uphold the standards of music in the religious broadcasts on the BBC. On Walford Davies's death the Director-General of the day, F. W. Ogilvie, said of him, 'people often say that broadcasting has "made" so-and-so; but Walford Davies, with his seventeen years at the microphone, is one of those by whom broadcasting itself has been made.'

Davies was also involved with educational work through his many books, lectures and essays. But there was in this seemingly practical man a streak of the dreamer. In his early days in Wales he had considered founding a 'monastery' of music, where a colony or brotherhood of musicians and music-lovers could live a life devoted to their art. His sense of the importance of the more spiritual side of life can also be seen in his last book, *The Pursuit of Music*, a strange mixture of instruction and intuition.

What had happened in all this activity to Walford Davies the composer, the man who had set off to Germany with his youthful works to consult the mighty Brahms? As an English composer Davies had taken the conventional route and became celebrated for major choral works commissioned by the great festivals. His first major commission, *The Temple*, he owed to Elgar, who recommended him personally to Ivor Atkins, the conductor of the Worcester Festival for 1902. He was asked for another work by Leeds for 1904 – for which he set the text of *Everyman*. His other major work – the *Song of St Francis* – was also for a festival, this time for Birmingham in 1912. His output of choral music, church services, songs, chamber music and orchestral pieces (including his once very well-known *Solemn Melody*) was prodigious and continued throughout his extremely active life; it is ironic, however, that he is now chiefly remembered for the still frequently heard march-past that he wrote for the RAF in 1921.

It was a considerable achievement of Walford Davies's to have composed so much and lived such an active life. There was, however, no time for Davies, and, perhaps after a while, no great desire, to develop a clearly marked personal musical style. Davies wanted the maximum number of people to be involved in music and the music he wrote had this purpose very much in mind: it is interesting that he wrote almost no music for the keyboard. His music was practical and developed little.

Walford Davies was knighted in 1922 in recognition of his services at the Temple Church, and in 1934, on the death of Elgar, he was appointed Master of the King's Music. In the following year he conducted a programme of music for the Silver Jubilee of George v, who insisted on having 'Jerusalem' in the concert. The King is said to have remarked 'We must have "Jerusalem", and if there is no room for it, I shall go down myself to the platform and *whistle* it.' (The King got his way, and later said that it was the 'best show I've ever seen'.) In 1937, for the coronation of George vi, Davies wrote a children's suite called *Big Ben Looks On* for the two royal princesses. From the People's Palace to that of the royal family Walford Davies had exercised his considerable powers to great effect, and if much of his music has not survived him it is in part due to the enormous successes that he had in other fields.

Quite different in character from Walford Davies was the last of the four composers in this chapter. Ethel Smyth was an indomitable woman: her main energies – and they were considerable – were spent on her own behalf rather than on the musical public. She is now best remembered for her autobiographical writings and for her association with the Bloomsbury group; in her seventies she fell in love with Virginia Woolf. It is as a character and a celebrated sapphist that she is likely to continue to be best known in the future, for her music – the chief interest of her life – has gone into almost total eclipse, and there are no grounds for believing that this position will or should be reversed. While she was alive and promoting her own works Smyth's music received performance and attention. After her death, in 1944, however, the musical works slipped from sight; some would say deservedly so. But her career as a musician has much of interest in it, especially from the point of view of the writing and reception of English opera before the First World War.

Ethel Smyth shared one initial disadvantage with many other English composers of her time. Her father was a general and his opposition to her following a serious path in music was formidable. In his daughter, however, he met a match for his determination and obstinacy and she eventually managed to bludgeon him into allowing her to go to Leipzig to study in 1877. Her connections with the German musical world were similar to those which other English composers of the period enjoyed and she had about her an easygoing cosmopolitanism that later generations would envy. We have already seen that early works of hers were staged on the Continent – Berlin, Weimar, Karlsruhe, Leipzig and Prague – but she also had performances in New York as well as London, and her best-known work, *The Wreckers*, was originally intended (as *Les Naufrageurs*) for the Paris Opéra-Comique, but it was in fact first performed (as *Strandrecht*) at Leipzig.

The celebrated German conductor, Bruno Walter, once characterized *The Wreckers* as 'typically English': what did this mean in Ethel Smyth's case? Smyth, as a musician, really belongs to the world of nineteenth-century English opera that produced such highly successful figures as Wallace and Balfe, a world that also included the popular works of Arthur Sullivan. Her operas were certainly very different from those of the last-named composer – they were more dramatic, some would say more melodramatic – but many of the same ingredients went into both. They shared an English tunefulness and a significant use of choral singing, and one suspects that in the opera house they appealed to similar audiences. One of the reasons for Ethel Smyth's success on the Continent may well be that, at the time, there was a large market there for what has come to be called 'operetta'. And in England Beecham, for one,

knew that her works could spell relative success in box-office terms. But
Ethel Smyth wrote works that, compared to those of other contemporary composers, were unadventurous and uninspired.

Her works include six operas and a Mass in D major that was once
highly thought of. She suffered in her later years from deafness and this
is, perhaps, one reason why she never really developed as a composer.
She was yet another example of an English opera composer who was
zealously working away in a cul-de-sac of musical history, mainly
because her work was highly imitative and she made no attempt to
develop a distinctive musical style. As a woman, however, she will
doubtless never cease to be of interest; her work for the suffragette
movement was important and she proudly went to prison for her beliefs.
While in prison Thomas Beecham visited her and saw her conduct a
group of prisoners in her famous 'March of the Women' – she leaning
out of a window beating time with a toothbrush. One suspects that both
Beecham and Smyth hugely enjoyed themselves on this occasion.

Like Coleridge-Taylor, in whose work music writers tried to trace
'savage' qualities, Ethel Smyth's was subjected to nonsensical examination for supposed 'femininity'. Nothing, really, could be further from
the mark. But in terms of the social history of music in England Ethel
Smyth was important, for she opened doors for women in the musical
world that had hitherto been firmly closed. A highly distinguished group
of women composers in Great Britain have much to be grateful for in
Dame Ethel Smyth, whose services to music were recognized in her
title. She stands at the head of a new departure for women, and in her
day she stood there alone. Her artistic talents may not have been properly
developed but they were nevertheless considerable. She too suffered from
a 'lack of operatic opportunity', she too was unable to find an appropriate form in which to write good English opera; but she had such
confidence in her own abilities that she perhaps never really noticed it.

# CHAPTER FIVE

# Heirs and Rebels

## VAUGHAN WILLIAMS, HOLST, BUTTERWORTH

In 1934, when Beecham observed (at Delius's graveside) that Ralph Vaughan Williams was now the undisputed leading figure in English music, that composer was already sixty-two years old. No other figure so spans this entire era of English musical history as does Vaughan Williams. He was born fifteen years after Elgar and died eighteen years before Britten. He first entered the Royal College of Music in only the seventh year of its existence, in 1890, and finished his last symphony in 1957, having composed music for no fewer than eighty of his almost eighty-six years. His really was a career in music.

The composer's family background was a strong asset. He was brought up, after the early death of his father, in his grandparents' home, at Leith Hill Place in Surrey. His father's side of the family was distinguished in law, and on his mother's were the Darwin and Wedgwood families – Ralph's mother had once collected earthworms with Charles Darwin. Leith Hill Place was a Wedgwood family house and ran on the traditions of that hard-working, independent and somewhat radical family. It was a cultivated world: the house contained pictures by Reynolds, Romney and Stubbs. Interested in the arts in general, music had always been an important part of the life of those who lived at Leith Hill Place. Unlike many other English composers Vaughan Williams was given every encouragement in his youth: when he showed early signs of interest in music the family installed an organ in the house for him. His schooling was conventional. He was sent to Charterhouse, where he organized a concert which included a piano trio of his own composition; this elicited encouragement of a sort from the mathematics master: 'very good, Williams, you must go on'. After leaving school he spent two years at the Royal College of Music studying with Parry before going up to Trinity College, Cambridge to read for a degree in history. At the same time he undertook a Mus.B., studied composition with Charles Wood and organ with Alan Gray at Cambridge, and continued his weekly lessons with Parry in London. At Cambridge he fell into one of the 'magic circles' that were so characteristic of that period and formed friendships with other remarkable men which lasted throughout his life. During one vacation he was one of a party of friends at Seatoller in Borrowdale. With Vaughan Williams was his relation Ralph Wedgwood, George Macaulay Trevelyan, George E. Moore and Maurice Amos – three of the five in later life were to be awarded the Order of Merit.

Vaughan Williams had, by any standards, made a good start in life. He was clearly very musical but he had taken care to acquire an excellent all-round education. He was now determined to be a composer and so, after Cambridge, he returned to London and the Royal College where he studied with Stanford. Following this, he briefly held a job as organist of St Barnabas in South Lambeth – the organ-loft being considered at that time one of the very few respectable, 'proper' positions in the musical world. In 1897 he married Adeline Fisher (whose elder brother was the historian H.A.L. Fisher, later President of the Board of Education), and they spent their honeymoon in Berlin so that Ralph could hear Wagner's *Ring* in the full version and study with Max Bruch. When they returned to England their life fell into a settled pattern and Vaughan Williams passed the examination for his Doctorate of Music at Cambridge in 1899. At this time he was also giving university extension lectures, writing articles for musical journals and composing.

Vaughan Williams began with many advantages, but he made good use of them. He opted for a life of music – chiefly composition – and he did not have to worry too much about financial considerations. It seemed that he was going to combine his composing with a multitude of other musical activities: in the years ahead he would write articles for Grove's *Dictionary*, edit a volume of *Welcome Songs* for the Purcell Society and undertake the editing of the music for *The English Hymnal*. But in 1903 Vaughan Williams as a composer met his fate in the person of Mr Pottipher, an elderly labourer of Brentwood in Essex from whom he 'collected' the song 'Bushes and Briars', thus beginning the period of his life when he first found confidence as a composer. He was already thirty-one years old; fifty-five years were, however, left to him to develop, and he put those years to the fullest use.

At the Royal College his closest friend was Gustav Holst and their relationship was a close and fruitful one. Vaughan Williams and Holst helped each other with their compositions and, perhaps just as important, helped each other think about what they were doing in larger terms. Many people would have despaired of becoming a composer if they hadn't managed to establish themselves by the age of thirty-one. Musical history is full of musicians who did their best work before reaching that age. But Vaughan Williams and Holst both knew what they needed to do; they knew that it would take time to achieve anything really worthwhile and they paced each other over the years like long-distance runners in a race. Vaughan Williams may be thought a late developer but that was because he learnt by doing. He once said, 'I have always found it difficult to study. I have learnt almost entirely what I have learnt by trying it on the dog.' Vaughan Williams and Holst knew – if they truly were to be 'heirs and rebels' – that their path would be long and hard. As we have already seen they shared a favourite quotation from the writings of Gilbert Murray: 'Every man who possesses real vitality can be seen as the resultant of two forces. He is first the child of a particular age, society, convention; of what we may call in one word a tradition. He is secondly, in one degree or another, a rebel against that tradition. And the best traditions make the best rebels.' It would be a life's work – in the circumstances in which they found themselves – to be both a rebel and an heir.

Vaughan Williams went to Parry because he was impressed with his devotion to the art of music. Parry inspired in Vaughan Williams the idea that an artist must be loyal to his art, and the younger man picked up from his teacher the search for a 'characteristic' music. Vaughan Williams was impressed with Parry's integrity: they had much in common as men and musicians. His debt to Parry was great: if anyone could be said to be Parry's heir it would be Vaughan Williams. He subscribed to his teacher's view that style was 'ultimately national' and appreciated the 'peculiarly English' quality of Parry's music. From Stanford, Vaughan Williams learnt much less – which he later regretted.

Vaughan Williams claimed that he went on learning throughout his career: even in the later days he said that he was still learning – this time from his own pupils. As a young man he had also studied in both Berlin and Paris. He went to Ravel in Paris in 1908 because he had come to the conclusion that he had become 'lumpy and stodgy; had come to a dead-end and that a little French polish would be of use to me'. Vaughan Williams and Ravel may seem today a curious mixture but, after an initial misunderstanding, the two men got on well, and in 1912 we even find Ravel making plans for a concert of English music in Paris.

In 1941, in a letter to Lord Kennet, giving advice on a possible musical career for his son Wayland Young, Vaughan Williams stated his views on the training of British composers abroad.

Almost all the British composers who have achieved anything have studied at home and only gone abroad when they were mature - Elgar, Holst, Parry, Bax, Walton. Stanford is an exception, but he was by no means a beginner when he went to study abroad and as a matter of fact he never quite recovered from Leipzig. On the other hand I have known many young composers with a genuine native invention who have gone to Germany or France in their most impressionable years and have come back speaking a musical language which can only be described as broken French or German. They have had their native qualities swamped and never recovered their personality.

Vaughan Williams also believed in learning by going to the best man in the field. As a young man he had approached Elgar to be told by Alice Elgar that her husband was too busy to give lessons. He also went to Delius, to whom he insisted on playing through the whole of *A Sea Symphony*. 'Poor fellow!' Vaughan Williams later related, 'How he must have hated it. But he was very courteous and contented himself with saying, "*vraiment il n'est pas mesquin*"' - indeed Vaughan Williams always composed on a generous scale.

But it was with Gustav Holst that Vaughan Williams was really able to discuss the problems that he faced as a composer and they developed the habit of occasionally having full-day sessions on each other's music - 'field days' as they called them. (Roy Douglas, who worked with Vaughan Williams in his later years clearing up his very confusing and untidy manuscript scores and preparing them for performance and publication, said of the period after Holst's death in 1934, 'I was often aware of how profoundly he missed being able to submit his new works to the unsparingly critical eye of his beloved friend Holst.') Holst and Vaughan Williams knew that the training they had received at the Royal College was only a beginning. 'We must not get old for the next forty years because we have such a stiff job,' wrote Holst in 1903. They exchanged hints and criticisms and on their walks in the countryside, and on other meetings, they kept alive a friendship that they had both valued from their student days. Although the heat of youth went out of their correspondence and a certain drifting apart in artistic matters is noticeable in later days, they remained close friends. It was clear to both of them that if they were to achieve anything it would be by dint of hard work, and Vaughan Williams was a zealous worker all his life. A true child of his background, he felt, for instance, that Delius 'would perhaps have more backbone in his music if he had gone down into the arena and fought with beasts at Ephesus instead of living the life beautiful in a villa in France'. Vaughan Williams believed that it was essential for a composer to be in touch with 'practical music' and, throughout his career, he constantly acted on his own advice.

Vaughan Williams constantly revised his music, sometimes many years after its first composition. In his later days Holst's role as critic was undertaken, in a rather more formal setting, by a 'jury' of Vaughan Williams's friends who would be invited to hear a play-through of his latest composition on the piano. These people would offer advice and, while firmly keeping his independence to the end, the composer would make changes if the advice offered to him seemed good. He would also make further changes to the score even after the work had gone into orchestral rehearsal. He was not, in this way, like Elgar who knew exactly what effect he wanted and exactly how to obtain it.

Roy Douglas has given a full account of the composer at work. Vaughan Williams could always hear in his mind what he wanted. His problem as a composer lay in finding the way to create the effect he desired with an orchestra. His struggles and his patience were, in time, well rewarded. We left Vaughan Williams's career in 1903 where he met Mr Pottipher at Brentwood and we must return there to pick up the most important single thread in his musical life – his work with English folk-song. Vaughan Williams worked independently of the most celebrated figure in this field, Cecil Sharp, but they were friends and both held modern views, by contemporary standards, of how best to record and 'use' folk-song. The subtle variations of specific folk-songs, far from being an irrelevance to them as many musicians had hitherto thought, were rather a source of great interest and pleasure.

Many stupid and poorly thought-out opinions have been voiced about the popularity of English folk-music earlier this century and there is good reason to look closely at Vaughan Williams's own views. There was nothing folksy about Vaughan Williams either as a man or as a composer. His lectures of 1932 on 'National Music' clearly state his position. He asserted that, contrary to a widely held belief, music was not an 'international language'. Following Parry, Vaughan Williams looked at the beginnings of national music with the eyes of a Darwinian. Folk-music was the music that had 'for generations voiced the spiritual longings of our race'; it was an unpremeditated form of music 'and therefore of necessity sincere'. He held that 'any school of national music must be fashioned on the basis of the raw material of its own national song'. There was nothing antiquarian in Vaughan Williams's interest in folk-song – he knew the art of the folk-singer was dead – but he felt that there was everything to be gained from drawing on the 'living waters' of national music. He quoted Emerson, 'The most original genius is the most indebted man', and he and a whole generation following him drew on folk-song for their inspiration. Vaughan Williams believed that English composers had to learn how to use their own national idiom as had other nationalities – the Bohemians and Russians, for example – but they must also rebel against it. He said in his 1932 lectures:

> I know in my mind that if it had not been for the folk-song movement of twenty-five years ago this young and vital school represented by such names as Walton, Bliss, Lambert and Patrick Hadley would not have come into being. They may deny their birthright; but having once drunk deep of the living waters no amount of Negroid emetics or 'Baroque' purgatives will enable them to expel it from their system.

Vaughan Williams also quoted Sir Henry Hadow, the distinguished music writer, with approval: 'the composer bears the mark of his race not less surely than the poet or the painter and there is no music with true blood in its veins and true passion in its heart that has not drawn inspiration from the breast of the mother country'.

It is all too easy to misunderstand Vaughan Williams's point of view nowadays and if he had left his argument there, one would be tempted to wonder if this was not a form of musical chauvinism. But Vaughan Williams was a man of far greater vision than this. He knew that to an extent his turning to folk-music was part of a larger national impulse to shake off the dead hand of the German or Italian idiom. But there was much more to it than that. Vaughan Williams was a visionary in many ways: he believed in a 'universal popular art' for all the people – for the 'divine average', as Walt Whitman had put it. He said, 'I hope you do not think that I am preaching artistic chauvinism. That purely negative attitude of mind is, I trust, a thing of the past.' Music must, he considered, be 'for the people', and should know no national boundaries. In order to achieve this objective he felt that English composers should first find out what they had to offer from themselves to the 'universal popular art'. He summarized his thought thus: 'Until our music becomes a really spontaneous expression, first of ourselves, next of our community, then and then only of the world, in fact until it is as unpremeditated as that of the folk-singer, it will not be vital.'

Vaughan Williams' aims and ambitions were, therefore, all-embracing: there was no narrowness in his thinking. He stressed, above all, a sincerity of purpose, 'which it is so difficult to follow and so perilous to leave'. Folk-music, although the greatest, was only one of Vaughan Williams's many interests. He also worked on Purcell, made a study of the music of Tudor times, and edited the music of *The English Hymnal*. (He had been approached by Percy Dearmer whose name Vaughan Williams vaguely knew 'as a parson who invited tramps to sleep in his drawing-room'. Dearmer belonged to a group who were dissatisfied with the new *Hymns Ancient and Modern* and who hoped to be able to do better. Vaughan Williams was never a conventional professing Christian but his love and knowledge of the Christian tradition were extensive and he fully knew how to write music that would embellish that tradition.) As a writer of pieces for choral festivals he had no peer in his day (interestingly his own favourite English choral piece was Parry's *Blest Pair of Sirens*). He also inherited Elgar's mantle as England's leading 'official' musical figure although he did not become Master of the King's Music. At the end of the Second World War it was, for example, to Vaughan Williams that the BBC turned for a special commission, *A Thanksgiving for Victory* (later renamed *A Song for Thanksgiving*).

Unlike Elgar or Delius, though, Vaughan Williams was interested in the rising vogue for dancing, his *Job*, of 1930, 'A Masque for Dancing', is ample evidence of that, although it is a quite different work from those of the 'modern' ballet composers of that time – Bliss, Berners and Lambert. Opera engaged more of his attention; it is easy to forget that six operas came from his pen. But here, like so many others, he was not successful with the critics or the public, something that seems to have disappointed him greatly. He held that opera should be performed in English, and would make no concessions to the smart opera set; but his attempt to create an appropriate form for English opera failed to find any real support. He wrote concertos for violin, piano, oboe and bass tuba as well as the romance for violin, *The Lark Ascending*, a suite for viola, *Flos Campi*, and a romance for harmonica for Larry Adler in 1952. He also wrote music for the cinema – a form of entertainment of which he was very fond.

His outstanding achievement was, however, his symphonic work. He started his first symphony in 1903 and finished his ninth in 1957. The symphonies, spanning over fifty years of his life, show better than anything else the independence of Vaughan Williams both as a man and as an artist. It was Elgar who had shown the way in terms of the English symphony, but Vaughan Williams did not take up where Elgar had left off. He developed a symphonic style and practice of his own.

The fact that the first three and the seventh of Vaughan Williams's symphonies are known by names rather than by numbers – *A Sea Symphony*, *A London Symphony*, *A Pastoral Symphony*, and *Sinfonia Antartica* – begs the question as to how far they may be regarded as conventional symphonies. From our present-day viewpoint there is little heat left in the controversy about the nature and merits of 'programme' and 'absolute' music. The case of the *Pastoral Symphony*, completed in 1922, affords a good example of the controversy and its sterility. There were many people ready to read into this work the rolling landscape of the Cotswold hills and pictures of a green and pleasant land – Philip Heseltine's amusing remark that it was 'like a cow looking over a gate' became notorious in its day. But this was all wrong: the work was in fact a war-time piece, set abroad, as the composer later explained. Recalling 1916 when he had been in France with the Royal Army Medical Corps Vaughan Williams said, 'It's really war-time music – a great deal of it incubated when I used to go up night after night with the ambulance waggon at Ecoives and we went up a steep hill and there was a wonderful Corot-like landscape in the sunset – it's not really lambkins frisking at all as most people take for granted.'

In the case of the *Sea Symphony* and *Sinfonia Antartica* it is possible to be rather more precise with associations because the former is a setting of a text of Walt Whitman's and the latter has literary superscriptions to each of its movements, ending with a passage from Scott's journal for the sixth movement. *A London Symphony*, described by the composer as 'a symphony by a Londoner', suggests to the listener many of the sights and sounds of the capital city but Vaughan Williams said that such associations were 'accidentals, not essentials'. Of the other symphonies no programme is suggested, but both the named and the numbered symphonies clearly belong to the same main line of musical development. This procession of symphonies continued to his last days. Ursula Vaughan Williams, the composer's second wife, has a story about the Eighth Symphony that reveals her husband's tenacity as a composer. 'Frank Howes's book on Ralph's music had recently been published and when I invited him [to a play-through of the new work] by telephone he said in a voice of horror – "He's not written *another* one?".' Indeed there was yet another still to come.

Vaughan Williams was a tuneful composer: throughout his life he referred to his major compositions as his 'tunes'. A student at Cornell University who played Vaughan Williams a movement from his own dissonant quartet on the piano provoked the observation: 'If a tune *should* occur to you, my boy, don't hesitate to write it down.' In his later days, when deafness troubled him and he could not be sure of the balance of sound when listening to rehearsals of his works, Vaughan Williams would ask Roy Douglas, 'Does the tune come through?' Although as a young man Vaughan Williams had urged his fellow-composers to do away with 'good taste' and said 'what we want in England is *real* music', that did not mean that he intended to write in a language incomprehensible to his listeners. He was convinced that music should be 'for the people', but he would 'write up' to them rather than write down. It is inconceivable that a narrow and dry academic style would have appealed to him. And he was able to combine his beliefs with a confidence that he had been true to himself as a man and as a musician. In a speech he made when he was eighty-five Vaughan Williams summed up his point of view when he said: 'Bach was behind the times, Beethoven was ahead of them, and yet both were the greatest of composers. Modernism and conservation are irrelevant. What matters is to be true to oneself.'

In his music one can hear both Vaughan Williams's sincerity and the struggle, both technical and spiritual, in which he was engaged. Right at the end of his life he addressed the following words to schoolchildren: 'Music will enable you to see past facts to the very essence of things in a way which science cannot do. The arts are the means by which we can look through the magic casements and see what lies behind.' The visionary element in Vaughan Williams is never far below the surface and it is precisely a lack of vision and a lack of personal strength that distinguishes many of his imitators. Remaining true to himself, he still played the part of the senior figure in his field with a sense of responsibility; to many he was an avuncular figure – 'Uncle Ralph' – and he was much loved.

The story of his life between the First World War and his death was outwardly an uneventful one. He became a professor of composition at the RCM in 1919, and conductor of the Bach Choir in 1921. He moved from London to near where he was brought up as a child, and lived there as long as his first wife was alive (she died in 1951 at the age of eighty). He was a popular man and had a wide variety of friends, many whom he had known since his Cambridge days. He knew many of the younger composers – Gerald Finzi was perhaps the closest to him. He was also a friend of Bruce Richmond, the founder editor of *The Times Literary Supplement*, both men being interested in each other's work. Vaughan Williams was responsible for founding the Leith Hill Musical Festival and was in charge of the musical side of it for many years. His energy and hard work were evident throughout his life (he was to have attended a recording of his last symphony on the day he died). Once, when he was confined to bed for some time, it was typical of him that rather than waste valuable time he set about learning the clarinet. His stamina frequently amazed those who met him for the first time. Vaughan Williams's physical appearance was once very well described by Clare Mackail. She recalled the composer sitting in the nave of Worcester Cathedral in 1914 next to his strikingly beautiful wife Adeline, 'with the sun shining through the windows on her hair which looked like pure gold. It was an unforgettable sight, the two of them. He had a thick thatch of dark hair, a tall, rather heavy figure, even then slightly bowed; and his face was profoundly moving, deep humanity and yet with the quality of a medieval sculpture.'

Following Adeline's death he married, in his eighty-first year, his second wife, Ursula, whose biography of her husband, coupled with Michael Kennedy's study of his music, is such a rich source for those interested in the composer. The last years of his life with his new wife were an Indian summer. He moved back to London, travelled abroad: to Rome, America (he particularly wanted to see the Grand Canyon), Greece and Ischia, to stay with the Waltons. Vaughan Williams's curiosity about the world remained fresh until the end. In America in 1954 he was awarded the Howland Prize at Yale University, a prize that his close friend Gustav Holst had won some thirty years before. This gave Vaughan Williams the greatest pleasure, and must have struck a deep note in him, bringing together again as it did these two men over the divide of so many years.

The great span of his life and the wide range of his music and ideas makes Vaughan Williams a central figure of the English musical renaissance. In his life we can see all the difficulties that had bedevilled English music for so long and we can also see many of them finding their solution. Vaughan Williams was aware of the need for a well-developed national musical life if England were to be a musical nation. He knew, as he wrote to his friend Hubert Foss, that without the foundation of 'the humblest of music makings, the choral competitions, school music etc.... the Elgars and Waltons can't exist'. On this basis he advocated a sound training in basic craft for young composers. Following Parry's search for what was 'characteristic' in his pupils, Vaughan Williams encouraged his own students to turn to themselves and to the 'English idiom' that he felt was part of their background. And in 1948 he wrote of 'this renaissance from Parry to Britten' and how he felt it was due to the realization that 'vital art must grow in its own soil and be nurtured by its own rain and sunshine'.

Gustav Holst was another musician who responded to this impulse. Like Vaughan Williams he too had had a musical education at the Royal College quite unlike anything that a previous generation of composers had enjoyed, but the problem, as they both saw it, was how to make this education count for them as individuals. The two men were close in many ways and the great friendship that existed between them was quite unique in the history of English music. Gustav Holst, however, had come from a different background from Vaughan Williams, and he was to develop into a very different sort of composer.

Holst was born in Cheltenham in 1874. His family had originally been Swedish and his great-grandfather fled Riga with his Russian wife in the early years of the nineteenth century. Both Gustav Holst's father and grandfather had, however, married English wives. (The composer was named in full Gustavus Theodore von Holst – he dropped the 'von' during the First World War.) The von Holsts were an intensely musical family and the idea that Gustav might grow up to earn his living by music was not a strange one to them. His father was training him to be a concert pianist but by the age of seventeen it was already clear that Gustav suffered from neuritis in his right arm and would never earn his living on the concert platform. Gustav was never a healthy child – he suffered from asthma and was short-sighted – but he enjoyed music greatly, especially the lyric pieces of Grieg, and he had determined at an early age to be a musician.

Holst's mother died when he was eight and his father later remarried; his stepmother was a theosophist, and from an early age Holst was introduced to unconventional ways of seeing the world around him. He arrived at the Royal College of Music in 1893 – having already been an organist and a choirmaster, and having worked in many parts of the music business at a local level. Like Parry and Elgar he had been born in Three Choirs territory (Vaughan Williams had also been born in this fertile area but his family had moved when he was too young for the fact to be significant). The Royal College was an exciting place to be in the 1890s. Vaughan Williams wrote of his time there:

> What one really learns from an academy or college is not so much from one's official teachers as from one's fellow-students. I was lucky in my companions in those days; other students at the college were Dunhill, Ireland, Howard-Jones, Fritz Hart and Gustav Holst. We used to meet at a little teashop in Kensington and discuss every subject under the sun from the lowest note of the double bassoon to the philosophy of *Jude the Obscure*. I learnt more from these conversations than from any amount of formal teaching.

Unlike Vaughan Williams, however, Holst's greatest concern in the early days was how to make a living and during the holidays from the Royal College he had to play in bands to pay his way. His engagement with Stanislas Wurm's White Viennese Band, where he had to wear a white uniform with brass buttons and was required to speak in a 'foreign' accent when within earshot of the customers, was an indication of the pull that foreign names had over English music at the time. Holst characteristically benefited from his time with Wurm, and Vaughan Williams later said that his friend's years of trombone playing had enabled him to 'get at' music from the inside. In the year after he left the Royal College he earned his living as a trombonist with the Carl Rosa Opera Company and the Scottish Orchestra.

In the early days money was always short and it was not until Holst settled down to a career of teaching music that he solved the problem of how to find a financial basis for his life as a composer. Holst was essentially a teacher for most of his professional career. He taught at schools, notably St Paul's Girls' School, and at universities and colleges, notably the Morley College in South London. Like Vaughan Williams he lived a very active musical life. During the First World War he went to Salonica and Istanbul with the YMCA, which had charge of the cultural activities for the troops. Holst, with immense vigour, spent his time organizing choirs and concerts wherever he found himself. He set out to show the soldiers that music could be taken seriously by anybody and that there was such a thing as British music. Holst was a peaceable man, but it was inevitable that during this time with the army he should see and be affected by the great violence surrounding him. In 1919 he wrote a moving account of a visit to the Struma battlefield, an account that is highly revealing of the man: 'On Saturday we went straight over the battlefield, and the driver showed me the trenches, machine-gun pits, sniping posts and all the other horrors. And then we came to where the ground had been cleared, and there we found peasants with their oxen ploughing the battlefield, and I realized I was witnessing the greatest sight on earth.'

On his return from Turkey he resumed his teaching and practical musical activities and in 1920, all of a sudden, he became a success. *The Planets* and *The Hymn of Jesus* made Holst's public reputation, as the *Enigma Variations* and *Gerontius* had made Elgar's, and for three years he was a very popular composer. The Queen's Hall was twice sold out in one week for a concert of Holst conducting his own music, and it seemed that a new star had risen on the horizon. In 1924, however, he suffered a complete physical and nervous breakdown and on his doctor's advice retired to his house in Thaxted, Essex, where he lived a solitary life. He was never to regain the earlier public acclaim; many who value his later music more highly than his early works think that in the end that was as well thus.

Holst re-emerged from his period of isolation a noticeably older man. He had also changed as a composer: he now developed many of the highly personal traits implicit in his earlier works and in the process lost touch with the broad musical public. His later works never achieved the popularity of his brief heyday, and at the end of his life publishers were sending back his compositions as unsuitable for publication. Holst was not thrown by the fickle nature of fame, indeed he seems to have found much to be grateful for in the loss of the accolade of popular composer. He spent the rest of his life teaching; he made a practice of working on his own compositions during school summer holidays.

Holst was both a very private individual and a man of wide interests, as may be seen from a list of the books that he kept. (He was not a man

of many possessions.) They included texts that he set to music – Humbert
Wolfe, Helen Waddell, novels by Hardy and Greek plays in Gilbert
Murray's translation; also A.N. Whitehead's *Adventures of Ideas*, *The
Upanishads*, books of James Jeans's on space and time, and Robert
Bridges's *The Testament of Beauty*. Holst, characteristically, left no auto-
biography. He was devoted throughout his life to the countryside of the
Cotswolds, which he had known as a boy. He was fond of walking and
cycling, and although often not in the best of health, he led a busy life.
In his early days in London he was keen on the socialist vision of William
Morris and he joined the Hammersmith Socialist Club and became the
conductor of the Hammersmith Socialist Choir, which met in Kelmscott
House. Here he met the woman he was to marry, Isobel Harrison. His
work at Morley College also reflected his desire that the practice of his
art should be spread as widely as possible and his belief that, given the
real thing, most people – of all backgrounds – would respond to music.
When teaching in schools he insisted that the music studied and performed there should be real music of the highest possible standard, and
he believed in active participation rather than passive 'appreciation'.

Holst, like Vaughan Williams, learnt by doing and encouraged other
people to follow suit. He was once one of a party on a visit to Spain in
the company of Arnold Bax, his brother Clifford, and Balfour Gardiner.
The party arrived at Gerona and promptly lost Holst. He reappeared a
little later and when asked what he had been doing replied, 'Losing
myself. . . . If you want to know a city, you must manage to lose yourself.' This was typical of the man: he was always losing himself – in his
interests and his work – whether it was Sanskrit, Greek, astrology or
music, where he would, as he himself said, 'spoil as much music paper
as possible' in order to get results.

Holst believed that the 'modern renaissance' of English music, as he
called it, had begun with Elgar's *Enigma Variations*. 'I felt that here was
music the like of which had not appeared in this country since Purcell's
death.' In notes for lectures he gave in the 1920s he developed his own
view of English music:

Something is happening in England in the 20th century that has never happened before. For the first time in the history of English music we are trying
to learn to honour and appreciate our forefathers.

We know our national folk-songs and dances (I knew none till I was over 25).

Less than 12 years ago we were able for the first time to know all the Tudor
madrigals.

Less than 12 years ago we *began* to learn the complete Tudor sacred music. . . .

We are laying a sure foundation of our national art.

In this passage we can see two of the main interests in Holst's life: folk-music and the music, both sacred and secular, of Tudor England. These interests, as well as an interest in Purcell (whose *The Fairy Queen* was given its first performance in modern times by Holst and his pupils at Morley) he shared with Vaughan Williams and others of their generation. But it was folk-music, above all, that proved the real starting-point for Holst as for Vaughan Williams. Writing about 1905, the same year as Elgar gave his celebrated series of lectures on 'A Future for English Music', Imogen Holst noted that a great event took place in the life of her father, for in that year his interest in the revival of folk-song began: Holst 'had already begun to dream of a renaissance in English music; there to his delight he found English music at its very best'.

Holst, like Vaughan Williams, was a late developer as a composer. In a series of letters written from Germany to Vaughan Williams in 1903 Holst gives us an opportunity to watch him think over his development as a composer. He wrote, 'When under a master I instinctively try to please him whereas our business is to learn to please ourselves which is far more difficult as it is so hard to find out what we want.' For Holst as for Vaughan Williams there was much to unlearn before he could really believe that he had started; and, again like Vaughan Williams, as well as Elgar and Delius, Holst was past his first prime before he began to write music for which he would care to be remembered. (Around forty-four for Holst, forty for Vaughan Williams, thirty-five for Delius and forty-four for Elgar.) Success in the eyes of the world never appealed to Holst. (In this context Vaughan Williams once wrote to him of the 'awful stigma to have gone through life with a prize opera on your back – almost as damning as a Mus. Doc.') Holst's solution, rather, was to work hard at composition and to go on working hard until he could tell that he had done something worthwhile. He did not subscribe to the idea that the composer should be an exclusive slave to the art of composition and recommended periods of complete change from music, which included 'absolute laziness', as he put it. Learning to please himself was in part a matter of trial, error, rewriting, trying and erring again. He wrote of 'going into training' for his music and, like Vaughan Williams, he was planning his life's work, knowing that it would take many years to achieve what he had set out to do.

Holst's intention was to make a definite break with the immediate past. Along with Elgar and Delius, Holst and Vaughan Williams had grown up under the influence of Wagner, an influence both liberating and restricting: Holst described his three-act opera *Sita*, which was finished in 1906 when he was thirty-two, as 'good old Wagnerian bawling'. But there are also clear traces in this work of his own developing style.

Of all the composers who were influenced by English folk-song, Holst was the most rigorous. He had, as he said, been brought up to believe that folk-songs were 'either bad or Irish' but like Vaughan Williams, he had discovered that in them lay a liberating power hitherto unsuspected. In the words of his daughter and biographer Imogen Holst, 'the tunes had the simplicity and economy that he felt to be essential in any great art. They combined an emotional beauty with an impersonal restraint. The words and the music had grown up together, and there was a spontaneous freedom in the rhythm that made each other phrase sound inevitable.' His folk-song works are, however, not central to his work as they were to Vaughan Williams. Holst later wrote of folk-song-inspired composition that it was a limited form of art and he accurately pointed out the main artistic problem involved – 'when one works for long in a small form, mannerisms are almost inevitable.'

Holst's greater concern was to find a way of setting English to music. In 1917 he wrote to his friend W.G. Whittaker, 'I find that *unconsciously* I have been drawn for years towards discovering the (or *a*) musical idiom of the English language. Never having managed to learn a foreign language, songs always meant to me a peg of words on which to hang a tune', a view which is a curious half-echo of the old folk-singer Mr Pottipher who had first interested Vaughan Williams and who said, 'If you can get the words, the Almighty sends you a tune.' To the music critic Wilfrid Mellers it seemed that in Holst's 'preoccupation with the relation between English music and the English language is the real significance of his interest in the folk-song movement'. And, as Mellers went on to point out, in Holst's music there is a 'sustained *prose* rhythm' rather than the 'contour of lyricism'. Holst wanted to write music that would be at one with the words.

Holst had set himself a difficult task in trying to discover a musical idiom for the English language and his early achievements in this field came from an unusual direction. His breakthrough derived, curiously, from his interest in Sanskrit literature, although one should not imagine that there was anything 'Sanskrit' in his scores like the Orientalism that pervades some of the work of Granville Bantock, for example. But his study of the *Bhagavad Gita* had a lasting influence on him personally. In 1908 the more mature Holst style was clearly heard in his chamber opera *Sāvitri*. The music of this piece had stripped off most of the Wagnerian clothing of *Sita* and the sparse economic style which is so characteristic of Holst's later music was coming to the fore.

Holst's rise to great popularity after the war came with a work that is still a mixture of his old and new styles of music – *The Planets*. Wilfrid Mellers cleverly observed of *The Planets* that 'their enormous popularity can perhaps be traced to the fact that they were to contemporary audiences superficially startling without being fundamentally disturbing to emotional complacency'. The success of *The Planets* led many to feel that Holst might be the new popular composer. The post-war years at the Royal College were years of the greatest excitement. In 1918 Hugh Allen had become the director following Parry's death and a new generation, full of vitality and enthusiasm, were coming into the college. Allen took in many new staff, among them Vaughan Williams and Holst. At this period Holst was thought to be one of the exciting new voices in music, to be spoken of in the same breath as Arthur Bliss and Constant Lambert. Holst's pupil Edmund Rubbra later recalled the RCM of those

electrically-exciting after-war years when the god Stravinsky reigned in his heaven and all was right with the musical world. R. O. Morris had to escape to the only room in the College (No. 21 in the basement) where he could teach counterpoint without the deafening distractions of *Le Sacre du Printemps* [*The Rite of Spring*] played on two pianos. (I admit I was the principal culprit in this matter.) Arthur Bliss had written his joyous but immature *Rout*, *The Planets* was becoming known, and the Russian Ballet's 1921 season so stirred us to further enthusiasms that Prokofiev's *Chout* was added to our two-piano repertoire. Constant Lambert, still in his teens, came armed with the score of *Green Fire*, and Gordon Jacob appeared with a ballet whose forgotten title I am sure will not be recalled to me by the composer. If most of the output was derivative, yet its fresh vitality and directness of speech augured well for the future of English music.

To Rubbra Holst and Vaughan Williams were the 'big figures of the cultural renaissance of music in England'. But the two men were, in truth, already being eclipsed in many respects by the public attention given to the surface brilliance of the new young composers and their friends. There were writers whose enthusiasm for the music of the new composers of the 1920s meant that they regarded Vaughan Williams and Holst as being yesterday's men, figures of the musical establishment from whom no good could be expected. It was almost as if Holst and Vaughan Williams had reached their destination only to find that they were already too late, such was the difference between their slow development and the much quicker arrival of their own heirs.

In fact Holst took many years to reach a point where he could begin to relax his attention to the practical considerations of earning a living. (Vaughan Williams said of himself that if he had not possessed other means he would not have been able to rely on the proceeds of his composition until he was forty, and Holst was less well-placed in this respect than his friend.) Before and during the war he was the recipient of Balfour Gardiner's great generosity, and in 1918 a private performance of *The Planets* was given at Gardiner's expense as a present to the composer. Gardiner hired the Queen's Hall and laid on the Queen's Hall Orchestra with Adrian Boult conducting so that Holst and his friends could hear the new piece. After the war Holst was fortunate in being given a large sum of money by a secret patron (Claude Johnson, a director of Rolls Royce) who had been impressed by his *The Perfect Fool*, and Holst was able to cut down his teaching by half.

Holst never pursued popular fame with his music; he wanted to be left alone to develop his own way. Vaughan Williams wrote that in Holst's music 'there is no attempt to tickle jaded nerves with "new effects".' His compositions became more and more austere in musical terms. The quintessential example of this last period of Holst's music is his *Egdon Heath*, inspired partly by Hardy's *The Return of the Native*. In 1927 Holst wrote to the American musician Austin Lidbury from Dorchester where he had walked from Bristol via the Mendips, Wells and Sherborne, 'I got here on Monday, and on Tuesday I had an unforgettable lunch and motor trip with Thomas Hardy himself, who showed me Melstock, Rainbarrow and Egdon in general. I've promised him to go up Rainbarrow by night. He is sorry I'm seeing it in summer weather, and wants me to come again in November.' *Egdon Heath* shows Holst's musical style at its most austere, and the piece – slow, quiet and ethereal – left many who heard it feeling uncomfortable. His music was full of a new and brave quality of thought and there were not many who understood at the time what he was trying to do.

In the setting of Humbert Wolfe's poem 'Betelgeuse' we can again see the remoteness that Holst had achieved – the solitariness of his position.

Gerald Abraham, the English musical scholar, wrote, quoting Humbert Wolfe's poem, that at this last period of his life the planets were

too near ... too closely linked with human destinies – bringing war and peace, and jollity and old age. His mind was set on that distant star where 'there is nothing that joys or grieves ... nor ghost of evil or good', nor birth, nor death,
and the God, of whom we are
infinite dust, is there
a single leaf of those
gold leaves on Betelgeuse.

In his later life Holst was often unwell and in pain. In 1932 he was in America when he was taken ill. He was convinced that he was going to die. He could later recall thinking of many things at that time, things that were at the very centre of his being: his family and friends, walks, the Parthenon, his Morleyites singing the Byrd *Mass* in a cellar during an air-raid, and the Struma battlefield which he had seen in January 1919. He had 'one clear intense and calm feeling – that of overwhelming gratitude. And the three chief reasons for gratitude were music, and the Cotswolds, and Ralph Vaughan Williams.' Holst recovered this time. Two years later, however, the messenger of death appeared to him again, as in his opera *Sāvitri*, and this time he took Holst with him. The composer had had to make a decision whether to opt for a minor operation which would have meant him leading a restricted life for the rest of his days or a major operation which, if he survived, would have allowed him to lead a normal life. Holst knew the risk involved in the latter choice but, quite in character, he opted for it. He did not survive.

Holst was a curious man. On the one hand he was a convivial fellow who would 'take an enormous delight in food and good wine and good company', according to Imogen Holst. He had a fine sense of humour – an account of him eating at the George in Hammersmith with Clifford Bax (Arnold Bax's brother) and Helen Waddell shows him full of liveliness, grace and charm. But he was also a very private man, reminding one of E. M. Forster's description of the Greek poet Constantine Cavafy, 'standing at a slight angle to the universe'. Holst could withdraw far into himself. After a concert at the Wigmore Hall of his Humbert Wolfe songs, his daughter tells us that 'Holst felt numb':

His mind was closed in a grey region. He had sunk, once more, into that cold region of utter despair. After the songs the programme ended with the Schubert Quintet in C.... As he listened to it, he realized what he had lost, not

only in his music but in his life. He could cling to his austerity. He could fill
his days with kindliness and good humour. He could write music that was
neither commonplace, unmeaning or tame. And he could grope after ideas that
were colossal and mysterious. But he had missed the warmth of the Schubert
Quintet. At the moment, it seemed as if this warmth might be the only thing
worth having.

Gustav Holst's was an entirely original mind, and his isolation was
partly a result of this originality, for he cut a path for himself that few
could follow. His pupils – like Edmund Rubbra – were very attached to
him. Rubbra appreciated the way that in his dealings with his pupils
Holst would get straight to the point and would detect insincerity in
any statement 'either verbal or musical'. Rubbra also approved of how
Holst would not push his pupils if they were having a barren period.
The enthusiasm and independence of many of Holst's other pupils testify
to his great abilities as a teacher. He was not, however, at all interested
in encouraging them to follow his own style: he never taught from his
own scores, for example, as many composers do. Holst was keen to
draw out from his pupils what was in them, although he did encourage
them to follow his excellent practice of stripping away all that was
unnecessary in their work. 'With what enthusiasm did we pare down
our music to the very bone!', wrote Rubbra.

As a composer Holst had many distinguishing traits: his use of 5/4 and
7/4 time signatures, and his writing for different voices in different keys
at the same time would immediately strike a musician as characteristic.
To the general listener, however, it is probably the mysterious dying-
away voices that are the most memorable aspect of his music – Holst's
signature in another world – or the pulsing rhythms of 'Mars' from *The
Planets*, again not quite of this world. Holst's works are full of a mysterious contemplation, but he is never sentimental; even his mysticism
is stark and economical.

Holst's works, relatively speaking, are not many in number; he only
spent a small proportion of his life composing. Much of his work is
choral, including *The Hymn of Jesus, The Choral Symphony* (from Keats's
poems), a work for which Vaughan Williams had only a 'cold admiration', and the *Ode to Death* of 1919 (dedicated to Cecil Coles 'and the
others' who had been killed in the war). Holst was keen on the idea of
chamber opera and many of his later operatic works were examples of
*opéra intime: Sāvitri, At the Boar's Head* (an interlude based on the Falstaff
scenes in Shakespeare's *Henry V*), and *The Wandering Scholar* (later edited

by Benjamin Britten and Imogen Holst). Holst also wrote for wind bands and his *A Moorside Suite* of 1928 is generally considered in brass-band circles to be one of the finest and most expressive pieces of music written for that medium. He is probably best remembered today by the general music public for his orchestral pieces, notably the *St Paul's Suite, The Planets, Hammersmith* and the *Brook Green Suite* (of 1933). For all the sparseness of much of his later work Holst was always a master of tuneful music: Vaughan Williams wrote of him that he 'never shirks a definite tune when the occasion demands', and this is certainly the aspect of his music that has remained most popular with the wider public.

At the time of his death Holst had travelled far down the road that he and Vaughan Williams had mapped out many years before – but their routes had grown widely apart. Both heirs to the same traditions and rebels against them, they had chosen different ways in which to develop. On Holst's death Vaughan Williams wrote of his ability as a teacher and the high standards he demanded of himself and others: he said that there were works of his own that he was too ashamed to show Holst. Vaughan Williams, better than anybody else, understood the problems that Holst had had to face up to in his career, both within himself and also with his prospective public. As an example of the latter problem Vaughan Williams wrote of 'that brilliant tour-de-force *Beni Mora*, a work which if it had been played in Paris instead of London would have given its composer a European reputation, and played in Italy would probably have caused a riot'. But Holst never compromised in his music and this conveyed itself unmistakably to the audiences of the day. The general musical public would not follow Holst on his solitary adventure into music, and his music has never really enjoyed the attention that it so clearly deserves.

Professional musicians, however, realized that Holst's reputation was undervalued and there has been real progress in establishing Holst in his proper place with a wider musical public in recent years. We are also increasingly seeing that important memorials of Holst's work live on at the places where he taught: the active musical life that goes on in the sound-proof room specially built for him at St Paul's and the room that bears his name at Morley College. Vaughan Williams once observed that Holst's influence would long outlast him because of the pupils he had sent into the musical world, pupils who all shared his sense of the purpose of music; and time has shown how right this view was.

Holst had come a long way in his life from the early days when he had
first felt the liberating influence of folk-song, but one composer who,
due to his early death, never developed past a similar initial enthusiasm
with folk-song was George Butterworth. It is worth looking at his life
and work in some detail for two reasons: first, because he was a composer who was able to create excellent and original music from folk-
song material – and there were not many who could – and second,
because the story of his life is not well-known, and we can see here, in
the most striking way, the disastrous effect of the First World War on
the national musical life of the time.

Killed in action on 5 August 1916, George Butterworth was the most
lamented of the English musicians who died in the Great War. His
life story is told in a now extremely rare book of letters, diaries and
memoirs, printed privately in 1918. One is only too well aware of the
end of the story before one has read a word of it. The reader can follow
Butterworth through his education, into his restless twenties, and then
into the army and over to the Front in France. Butterworth's diary
entries and letters have an innocent simplicity about them that makes the
horror of his death painful to read about even today. Behind the
apparent simplicity, however, there was both a very attractive and a
very complicated man.

George Sainton Kaye Butterworth, born in 1885, was the only son of
Sir Alexander Kaye Butterworth, successively Solicitor and General
Manager of the North Eastern Railway Company; his mother had once
been a professional singer. He grew up in York and went to Eton as a
King's Scholar in 1899, where he studied music with Thomas Dunhill,
now chiefly remembered for delicate piano pieces that generations of
young English piano students have hammered their way through. At
Eton, Butterworth's interest and ability in music was encouraged: among
other distinctions he held the position of Keeper of College Harmonium
between 1902 and 1904. He went on to Trinity College, Oxford, where
he continued his musical activities (he was President of the University
Musical Club), but his studies suffered and he had an undistinguished
academic career. On leaving university he was undecided what to do
and, having turned down the idea of reading for the bar, he spent the
years of his twenties in a variety of pursuits: he wrote criticism for *The
Times*, he taught at Radley College, he studied, for a brief period only,
at the Royal College of Music, and he collected folk-songs and dances
from around the country. This last activity was the one in which he

seemed, at last, to have found his own musical way and he began to feel sure·enough of his own compositions to publish a few of them. Like Vaughan Williams and Holst, Butterworth had taken his time reaching this stage in musical composition but once his music had begun to appeal he was pointed to as a man of great promise. Those who knew his work well at this time were convinced that had he survived the war he would have become a considerable composer.

It was entirely characteristic of Butterworth that he should have enlisted at the earliest moment following the declaration of hostilities in 1914. He joined up with friends in a 'group' - a social form that seemed to them to fit the occasion. Their sense of loyalty to each other and decency to people in general was striking. Butterworth wrote to his father - about a possible commission, it would seem - that, 'It was very kind of Captain H to take the trouble, and if you get a chance I hope you will thank him for me. All the same I expect you agree that it would be the wrong thing to take advantage of private influence at the present time.' The 'group' - which included musicians Geoffrey Toye, R.O. Morris and Bevis Ellis - was the thing that really mattered, and at first the members of it turned down the possibility of commissions in order to stick together. (Vaughan Williams later referred to them when writing to Holst from France: 'I sometimes dread coming back to normal life with so many gaps - especially of course George Butterworth - he left most of his MS to me - and now I hear that Ellis is killed - out of those 7 who joined up together in August 1914 only 3 are left.')

Butterworth's diary reveals an all too familiar picture of the early days of the war. The young men were keen to see action: 'If only we could get going', Butterworth complained. It was already late in the year of 1914 and he wanted to 'get out and finish off the war'. In fact he did not get to France until a year after the war had begun and by then the 'group' had been replaced in his life by the platoon of Durham miners which he commanded; 'they all seem astonished at finding they can't understand the language', Butterworth wrote home. He was in the firing trenches by September 1915 and was shot dead by a German sniper in August the following year. From his own account of the period you would be forgiven for doubting that he saw any fighting, let alone that in his calm closing pages the author was in the middle of the second battle of the Somme. Butterworth's account, like many others of the period, is deliberately understated. His military career was a highly distinguished one: he won the Military Cross for bravery in action, and was recommended for it again for his part in the events of the day on which he died. General Page Croft, who had visited Butterworth's trench just before he was shot, described his last action thus:

I went up to the farthest point reached with Lieut. Kaye-Butterworth. The trench was very low and broken, and he kept on urging me to keep low down. I had only reached the Battalion headquarters on my return when I heard poor Butterworth, a brilliant musician in times of peace and an equally brilliant soldier in times of stress, was shot dead by a bullet through the head. So he who had been so thoughtful for my safety had suffered the fate he had warned me against only a minute before.

There were many tributes to the dead man but perhaps none so sadly revealing of the times as the comment of Lieutenant-Colonel G.H. Ovens. In a letter to Butterworth's family Ovens praised Butterworth as a soldier and went on, 'I did not know he was so very distinguished in music. . . .'

At Oxford Butterworth had been a close friend of Vaughan Williams, who later said that he owed the idea of the *London Symphony* to him (it is dedicated to Butterworth). Vaughan Williams wrote:

I showed the sketches to George, bit by bit as they were finished, and it was then that I realized that he possessed, in common with very few composers, a wonderful power of criticism of other men's works and insight into their ideas and motives. I can never feel too grateful to him for all he did for me over this work and his help did not stop short at criticism. When Ellis suggested that my symphony should be produced at one of his concerts I was away from home and unable to revise the score myself, and George, together with Ellis and Francis Toye [Geoffrey Toye's brother], undertook to revise it and make a 'short score' from the original – George himself undertook the last movement.

It was the folk-song and folk-dance movement that gave Butterworth his direction in music. Vaughan Williams's opinion that it was folk-song that 'freed' Butterworth's music puts it very exactly. Vaughan Williams also said of Butterworth that he 'could no more help composing in his own national idiom than he could help speaking his own mother tongue'. Butterworth was a fine morris dancer. He devoted much time and energy to collecting folk-songs and dances in England, and he co-edited a number of important publications with Cecil Sharp, whom he had also met at Oxford. Even in the trenches Butterworth is reported to have been collecting songs from the men under his command. From peace-time an attractive picture of him collecting a dance is given by his colleague R. Lloyd:

> I well remember the first time I met him at Bucknell, near Bicester, which was an important 'hunting ground'. I found him already at work in a picturesque and ancient cottage with a stone floor and white-washed walls and wheel-backed chairs. An incredibly old man was dancing about the floor, and though sometimes he hobbled and stumbled or paused for sheer lack of breath, he seemed on the whole to have vanquished his years for a space and one felt a ghostly presence of revels that had had their being half-a-century before. George Butterworth sat by the wall, smoking his pipe, mostly in silence, and busily noting down the dancer's steps in a book. Now and then he would put a question or suddenly demand a repetition of a particular figure. But the dancer paid little attention to us and passed from one dance to another as the fragrance of youthful memories inspired him.

One knows that all that is now left of these dances are Sharp and Butterworth's notes and diagrams. It is not much, but it is at least something.

Butterworth's compositions are few but distinctive. All are pervaded by the 'national idiom', as Vaughan Williams put it. Sometimes his works quote directly from folk-songs but more often they only allude to them or to their spirit in a general way. Vaughan Williams also wrote of Butterworth that 'in harmonizing folk tunes, or using them in his compositions, he was simply carrying out a process of evolution of which these primitive melodies and his own are different stages'. Butterworth is best remembered for his rhapsody *A Shropshire Lad* of 1912, and *The Banks of Green Willow* of 1913, an idyll for small orchestra, both superbly well-orchestrated works. The rhapsody was first given by Arthur Nikisch at the Leeds Festival in 1913, where it was very well received. Both works have deservedly retained their popularity. His songs are also sometimes still heard in recitals, and his set of Housman settings, his *Songs from Sussex* and his music to W.E. Henley's 'Love Blows as the Wind Blows' are all remarkably fine.

Before he left for France Butterworth destroyed much of his early music. This seems to have been a sign that he had finally settled on a means of expression and, moreover, decided at last to give himself full-time to music. The finished works that have survived are ones that any composer would be rightly proud of. As a person Butterworth remains enigmatic, finding his way late and losing his life early. The great impact that he had on those around him was often remarked on: Sir Henry

Hadow voiced what many felt when he said of Butterworth that 'he will rank, with Brooke and Julian Grenfell, among the real poets who, in this war, have given their lives for their country'. Butterworth's surviving works are miniature but perfect in form; they speak of the pre-war English countryside before it was torn apart. One can hear the man in his music in a very remarkable way. What E.J. Dent observed when he wrote after Butterworth's death, 'It was his music which helped me to understand the nature which he had such difficulty in expressing in ordinary ways', is still true for us today.

# CHAPTER SIX

# *Holding the Middle Ground*

## BAX, IRELAND, BRIDGE

The three composers in this chapter began their careers before the First World War and, as with all those we have so far considered, the war itself had important effects upon their work. But for a number of reasons they need to be considered separately from other of their near contemporaries. Different things mattered to them and influenced them and they were able to develop their own distinctively different voices in the new world of music that came into existence after the war. We might say of them that they held the middle ground in music – middle between the 'old school' of Elgar and the 'modern' of Bliss and Walton – and as British artistic prejudice always tends to go against those who hold the middle ground these three composers, all too easily regarded just as pieces of national music furniture, have failed to receive the attention they deserve.

Arnold Bax, the most substantial composer of this group, was a man who, like Vaughan Williams, developed into a considerable symphonist in his later days, but it would have been difficult to guess this from his early development. Bax was born in 1883 and grew up in a comfortable suburban world. His autobiography, first published in 1943, gives us a major clue to his personality. Called *Farewell my Youth*, the narrative of the book extends no further than the beginning of the First World War, as he did not consider it of any great interest to write of the inter-war years. It is a short, witty book of the sort written by his brother Clifford

Bax – the type of account that his friends and contemporaries would have expected from that much-admired figure, an 'all-rounder'. The book is concerned solely with his youth. He was a romantically inclined man who lived for the moment and who – as he said – had found that in this respect the ideal age to be was twenty-two. But he was also drawn to the pre-war years for other reasons: his love of Ireland before the Troubles, and of particular women in his youth, and his nostalgia for the musical world that had existed in London then.

Bax came from a leisured class whose members had the time to develop their particular abilities and weaknesses. Bax's father, a barrister, belonged to a solid professional world: presented with precocious musical stirrings in the young Arnold he felt the need to take expert advice and arranged a consultation with the organist and composer Sir Frederick Bridge at Westminster. Bax recalled the incident later in his life: 'It was rather like an interview with a Harley Street specialist. "Do you assure me, Sir Frederick, that my son has really this musical taint in his system?" "I fear that I cannot hide from you, Sir, that such is indeed the case. That will be three guineas, thank you and mind the step."'

It is much to Arnold Bax's father's credit that he accepted the advice and acted on it. Arnold was dispatched to the Royal Academy of Music, where he took piano with Tobias Matthay and composition with Frederick Corder. At that time the Academy was very much the 'other place' and when the young Bax had to visit the Royal College of Music he felt that he was entering the unknown. How should one dress when in the presence of Sir Hubert Parry? Bax, after careful deliberation, decided to be on the safe side and 'to array myself in my seldom worn frock coat and tall hat'.

Bax left the Academy early (his father characteristically returned the scholarship money that his son had won) and went to study in Dresden. There with Paul Corder (Frederick Corder's son), Roland Bouquet and Archie Rowan Hamilton – one might almost call them the 'Dresden Gang' – Bax enjoyed the varied musical life of the place. He is amusing also about his early encounters with women at this time. His love of women, as of cricket, was to be a lasting interest in his life. In 1910 he followed a 'tragic young girl', with whom he was in love, all the way back to her home in the Ukraine. Such passion was not rewarded and although the journey was one that had a certain influence on his music, it was not a happy affair. His marriage the following year was not a success either, and in his later life he was close to two women: the pianist

Harriet Cohen and Mary Gleaves, who in the words of Lewis Foreman, the composer's latest biographer, 'provided Bax's secret retreat from the world'.

Of the musical life in Great Britain before the First World War Bax wrote, 'The decade between 1904 and the beginning of the Great War saw an awakening of interest in and patronage of native music such as had never occurred before.' It was a great period for, among other things, establishing bodies to promote interest in the music of British composers. In 1904 the Patron's Fund at the Royal College of Music was set up, in 1905 the Society of British Composers (Frederick Corder was its President) came into being, and 'in the autumn of 1908 was witnessed the primal blooming of the shrinking violet, Sir Thomas Beecham', as Bax put it. In 1909 the Musical League was born, with Elgar and Delius as its leading figures, although Bax, who met Delius then, tells us that the latter's solitary contribution to the scheme was advice on the proposed eating arrangements for the league's meetings: 'What you want is a Cauld Colleetion!', said Delius in a West Riding voice. Then there were also the concerts given at the expense of Balfour Gardiner, whose patronage of British music at this time assisted Bax as well as Vaughan Williams, Holst, Grainger and many others. And, again in Bax's words, after Gardiner had withdrawn from active patronage of British music, his 'Maecenas role was assumed by a newcomer, Bevis Ellis, one of the De Walden family, a charming man-about-town and an amateur of all the arts'. (The first performance of Vaughan Williams's *London Symphony* in its original form was given at one of Ellis's concerts.) Bax tells us that these were golden days. But, as we have seen, the trumpet of doom sounded all too soon. Ellis, who lived, as did Clifford Bax, in what this social group liked to think of as a 'highly civilized Albany flat', was one of the many victims of the war to end all wars.

In 1914 Bax had written, 'There is a certain amount of talk current at the present time about a young British school – sometimes grouped together under the title of post-Elgarians.' His own feeling was that there was a lack of a 'national base' for such a school to build on. Like Ireland and Bridge, in different ways, Bax was to stress the individuality of the composers of his own generation, and he felt that this did not allow one to speak of a 'school'. But the musical careers of Bax, Ireland and Bridge and many others were, in an important way, built on the achievements of the earlier generation. Bax shared many of the beliefs central to the renaissance of English music. As a further testimony to the

strength of the opinion that one of the keys to a revival of composition
in Britain lay in desisting from profitless adoration and weak emulation
of Continental composers Bax's views of 1928 are of interest:

Those amongst my British contemporaries whom I most respect and for
whose work (notably that of Vaughan Williams) I have the greatest sympathy,
have developed their own personal styles, regardless of any of the heady excite-
ments emanating from Austria or Russia. And I believe that the sincerity of
English composers is one of the most remarkable features of their work. I may
mention too, perhaps, that certain of the younger writers who began their
careers with an attempt to imitate and even outdo the fashionable gamineries
and jocosities of the Continent, have since settled down and are quite likely to
produce works of serious import in the near future.

As a musician it was not until the war years that Bax really began to
make his own mark. At the time his greatest interest was not in the
musical world of London but in Ireland. Contrary to what many people
believed when he was alive Bax was not Irish – not even in the slightest
degree. But he was a Celt in his romantic heart. Like other artists of the
time he turned to the Celtic tradition for inspiration, and his love of
Ireland, and the influence that this had on his music, was to be a major
theme of his life. In Ireland he took on a second personality. Here he
was known as Dermot O'Byrne, and being a friend of the Irish poet
'AE' (George Russell), Padraic Colum, once editor of the *Irish Review*,
and others he was known as a man of letters rather than a composer. He
knew much about the Irish language and history and his stories and
poems were well received in the Anglo-Irish literary world that then
existed in Dublin. The Dublin *Freeman's Journal* once announced that
'Arnold Bax' was a pseudonym, 'adopted solely for musical purposes by
a West of Ireland poet and novelist named Dermot O'Byrne'. They had
it exactly the wrong way round, but one should not be too surprised.
In *Farewell my Youth* Bax told his readers of the process of becoming
Irish:

I worked very hard at the Irish language and steeped myself in history and
saga, folk-tale and fairy-lore. 'Arnold, you have a completely Gaelicized mind',
said 'AE' once, to my pride and delight. By degrees a second personality came
to birth within me, that Dermot O'Byrne who later on was to turn author and
find his books accepted by Dublin publishers. Thereafter I led a double life, for
when I landed at Dunleary or Rosslare I sloughed off the Englishman as a snake
its skin in the spring; and my other existence as a musician – still much under
foreign influence – as an ardent cricketer, even as a lover of women, became

almost unreal. For now I was in love with Ireland and for the while needed no mortal mistress.

The poems speak of youth, love and Ireland – often all three together. They speak especially of the West of Ireland where, like another Synge, Bax spent much time living with the people of the wild fringe of the Celtic world. 'I wake alone and desolate days begin/And angry sea-winds drive the autumn in', he wrote in one of his poems. Bax formed a particular attachment to Glencolumcille in Donegal.

> Ah, mind me well until we meet
> Under the hills again,
> Dear clumsy merry rough-shod feet
> That clatter through my brain,
> O tender wistful country eyes, old roads dim in the rain!

And when in the Ukraine, after his fruitless chase of the Russian girl he loved, his thoughts turned to Ireland.

> I am weary of high-born people.
> Of men with milky hands,
> Of idle malignant women,
> And a life none understands,
> And the mountainless horizons
> Of these burning alien lands,
>
> I will go back to my country
> To life with Ireland's poor ...

Back to Ireland he went. And there in 1916 he set his face against the English soldiers sent into 'his country'.

> And when the devil's made us wise
> Each in his own peculiar hell,
> With desert hearts and drunken eyes
> We're free to sentimentalize
> By corners where the martyrs fell.

Bax's Celtic side was very much to the fore now. The poem quoted above was part of a collection banned by the censor in Ireland. Bax's enthusiasm for Ireland had, however, reached its high-water mark. Many of his friends died in the Troubles and, like other Englishmen, he re-treated from the violence that now ruled in Ireland.

Bax entered the post-war world a disillusioned man. This was not just because of the position in Ireland but also because the new spirit of the age – the 'silly twenties', as he put it – was not one that he felt any sympathy for. New young composers were catching the public's attention with what seemed to many to be tricks and stunts, and composers like Bax found that the rules had been rewritten without reference to themselves. Although there was to be a reaction against the most 'modern' styles of music in the mid-1920s, the golden days of Bax's life were not to return. It was at this point in his life's story that Bax concluded his autobiography. Of the twenty years that separated the end of his account and his writing of it he had nothing to say. The early period was what interested him and the musical works that he wrote during this period were the ones that he was, and still is, best known for – in particular the three tone poems *The Garden of Fand*, *November Woods*, and *Tintagel*.

In 1915 Bax wrote to Philip Heseltine, 'Nearly all my longer compositions, the orchestral works at any rate, are based upon aspects and moods of extreme nature and their relation to human emotion.' The attraction of these works is that they share, in common with other 'programme' works, an immediate appeal, and that they describe in precise terms an atmosphere, mood or feeling well known to all. At the front of the score of *Fand*, for example, Bax gives us a programme for the work and it conveys something of the spirit of the music:

The Garden of Fand is the sea.... Upon its surface floats a small ship adventuring towards the sunset from the shores of Eirinn, as St Brendan and the sons of O'Corra are said to have sailed in later times. The little craft is borne on beneath a sky of pearl and amethyst until on the crest of an immense slowly surging wave it is tossed on to the shore of Fand's miraculous island. Here is unhuman revelry, unceasing between the ends of time, and the voyagers are caught away, unresisting, into the maze of the dance. A pause comes, and Fand sings her song of immortal love enchanting the hearts of her heroes for ever.

There is an equally suggestive programme for *Tintagel*. In the preface of the score Bax revealingly says:

Though detailing no definite programme this work is intended to evoke a tone picture of the castle-crowned cliff of Tintagel, and more particularly the wide distances of the Atlantic as seen from the cliffs of Cornwall on a sunny but not windless summer day. In the middle section of the piece it may be imagined that with the increasing tumult of the sea arise memories of the historical and legendary association of the place, especially those connected with King Arthur, King Mark and Tristan and Iseult. Regarding the last named, it will be noticed that at the climax of the more literary division of the work there is a brief reference to one of the subjects in the first act of *Tristan*.

(The reference to Wagner's *Tristan und Isolde* is a quotation of the so-called 'sick Tristan motive'.) In the music of these two once very well-known pieces one can clearly hear the stories and characters that are depicted there, but one hears above all else the Celtic sea – great blocks of sound which are waves, rocks and the immensity of the ocean, something that can in fact be heard in much of Bax's music.

Bax was and still is held in particularly high respect by pianists. Several of his contemporaries commented on his great technical ability at the piano and he was well known for his abilities as a sight reader, this leading him on a number of occasions to be importuned to play at sight, or with only extremely limited notice, the works of some modern contemporary European composer. At a time when new works for the piano excited an interest quite unimaginable today his were well received. (One of the very first projects that the Lyrita record company – which has done so much for English music – undertook in its mono days was to record Bax's main piano works.)

In more recent years, however, writers on Bax's music have turned their attention to another – and really a much more remarkable – aspect of Bax's music, his seven symphonies. Bax had put much of the obvious influence of Ireland and the Celtic world behind him and although the symphonies are still suffused with 'Irish' feeling and mood, as a musician he now underwent considerable development. Bax's symphonies did not create a major impact when they first appeared and it is only recently that a proper study of them has got under way. It may be that they will have a reasonable chance of being heard by the public in the years to come, as the once fashionable *ennui* with late Romantic music recedes, but it is unlikely that they will ever become popular.

Bax once described himself as a 'brazen romantic', and it is certainly an accurate description as far as it goes. Through his teacher Frederick Corder he was strongly influenced by Liszt and as a young man, like many of his contemporaries, he had worshipped at the altar of Wagner. But Shaw, among others, noted that Bax soon escaped a too strong attachment to these early influences, and his music came to reflect many other things: Celtic twilight and Celtic gaiety, a fascination with the sea, with its moods, atmosphere and immensity, and in later life one can further detect a turning towards Scandinavia, its myths and lore – Bax was powerfully affected by the music of Sibelius. Above all, however, Bax's life and music were influenced by a strong sense of the supernatural. Once, in the company of 'AE', Bax tells us that he was

reading in the window seat near the door, and we had not spoken for perhaps a quarter of an hour when I suddenly became aware that I was listening to strange sounds, the like of which I had never heard before. They can only be described as a kind of mingling of rippling water and tiny bells tinkled, and yet I could have written them out in ordinary notation. 'Do you hear music?' said 'AE' quietly. 'I do,' I replied, and even as I spoke utter silence fell. I do not know what it was we both heard that morning and must be content to leave it at that.

Others have heard similar sounds in Bax's own music. Writing of the second piano sonata Harriet Cohen said that

It has been described as 'the Battle of the Loathly Worm'. There must be something lurid and sinister about this work, for when it first appeared and was often played, Arnold Bax was on one occasion taken aside by a Danish mystic and very seriously warned that he must be extremely careful, as he was temporarily possessed by a devil. Bax told him that he had just written a work (the first symphony) which he feared the Dane would think still more deeply concerned with Demonology: to which he replied that he hoped it would never be performed.

In his last years Bax claimed to have retired – 'like a grocer', as he put it – from being a composer, and he lived in the White Horse Hotel in Storrington in Sussex. His musical life was largely over and it was a surprise when he was created Master of the King's Music in 1941. Wilfrid Mellers, for one, pointed out that 'one cannot help thinking it odd that the creator of this dark universe of primeval gods and satyrs should have become that honoured guardian of British musical respectability', and the musician and broadcaster Julian Herbage humorously noted that Bax 'did not overburden royal ears with occasional compositions'. It was in this last period of his life that he wrote the music for the 1942 film *Malta GC* and the 1948 version of *Oliver Twist*. (With regard to the music for *Malta GC* Bax once made the following observation to Laurence Olivier, who had asked if the composer was displeased with the talking going on simultaneously with the music in the film: 'Yes, I jolly well am – chattering all over my music. Bombs falling in all directions, planes crashing right and left, my music is faded down to make way for some fatuous remark like "an air-raid is in progress; it is a time of danger for the population!"' Bax's reply, while intentionally humorous, serves to highlight, however, a serious problem that composers who wanted to write well for the new medium of the films would have to come to terms with.)

Bax is attractively pictured as an old man by his first biographer Colin Scott - Sutherland: 'He gradually fell into the leisurely life of a country squire, reading (especially detective novels), drinking with the older worthies, playing billiards with his host, acting as president of the village cricket club and every day doing the crossword in *The Times*.'

Bax was a man with a far-seeing eye. Although for him the golden age – the age of his youth – passed with the First World War, his music still had far to develop in the seven symphonies. He persisted in being a 'Romantic' composer long after the tide had left him stranded, but that was typical. In a booklet on 'Inspiration' he once wrote, 'all that can be said with certainty is that the truly inspired artist does not possess a gift, but is possessed by it as by a demon'. His music is eloquent testimony of this. Vaughan Williams described him after his death:

Arnold Bax, like Shelley, seemed to have something of the faun in his nature. One almost expected to see the pointed ears when he took his hat off. This reflected itself in his music. Though no ascetic, he seemed not to belong to this world but always to be gazing through the magic casements, or wandering in the shy woods and wychwood bowers waiting for the spark from heaven to fall.

Such a man had been transformed from a sympathizer with Irish rebellion who had his poems banned in 1916 by the British censor to the Master of the King's Music thirty years later. He had also grown from modest musical beginnings to become an essayist of considerable range. Like Vaughan Williams, Bax had needed much time and room to grow in; but there was about him a lack of inner certainty that separates him from the other composer; for Vaughan Williams always had a clear idea of what he wanted and kept himself at full stretch throughout his long career in order to achieve it. Bax's aims were less ambitious but his achievement was nevertheless considerable and his music has a distinct charm that can still beguile its listeners today.

Another man whose musical ambitions were circumscribed by his surrounding horizons but who, like Bax, was the composer of many works of great skill and beauty, was John Ireland. We can only get as close to

the subjects of our interest as they will allow us – in the case of the
letters and memoirs of Percy Grainger, for example, we are given free
rein in the lumber room of his extraordinary mind – but with John
Ireland there is little information. Ireland left no autobiography and
biographies of him have a tendency towards the anecdotal. You can, for
instance, learn much from these books about Ireland's love of cats or the
arrangements that he made for his washing and darning, but there are
few real clues as to the mainsprings of his life and music.

Outwardly, Ireland's life was uneventful. The influence of his own
sensibilities, however, was much greater than any external force. As a
man he was most affected by two things: first, by a series of complicated
personal relationships, and, second, by his strong sense of place. With
John Ireland we have to look to the more intimate side of the man and
his musical offerings to understand him and his music. As a composer
Ireland was a perfectionist, never allowing anything to be published until
he was completely happy with it, and his output was not enormous. He
tended to write in the smaller, more intimate forms: there is, for example, no Ireland symphony, only one piano concerto and only one
major choral work. Some of his short orchestral works have remained'
popular and he is still well known for his chamber music, songs, and,
especially his piano works, for like Bax in his early days, Ireland was a
keen pianist – a solitary man.

Ireland was born in 1879 in Bowdon in Cheshire. His parents were
both substantial figures in the literary world – his father, already seventy
years old when John Ireland was born, was well known as the author of
*The Book-Lover's Enchiridion* and the editor of a Manchester newspaper,
and had known Hazlitt, Leigh Hunt, Carlyle and Emerson. Ireland's
mother was also a literary figure in her own right, having written a
biography and edited the letters of Jane Welsh Carlyle. John Ireland,
apparently on his own initiative, went up to London at the age of
thirteen and secured a place at the Royal College of Music on the
strength of his ability as a pianist. It seems that he did not meet any
parental opposition to his youthful ambitions and he entered the College
at an early age – in 1893. Within a few years both his parents were dead
and the young man had to make his own way. There was sufficient
money to keep him going and his studies at the College progressed: at
sixteen he became the youngest Fellow that the Royal College of
Organists had ever admitted, and at the Royal College of Music he
became one of Stanford's composition pupils. Ireland, like many others,

found that Stanford could be hurtful and trying, but in later years he looked back on his teacher with gratitude. This was a common experience with Stanford's pupils, for though he was hard on them as students he did teach them a great deal. Stanford was quick to hand back compositions to his pupils with the comment, 'It won't do.' Indeed Stanford once got Ireland to copy out a full set of orchestral parts of one of his pieces and then played it over with the orchestra to prove to the composer that 'it wouldn't do'. Parry was much more encouraging in a kindly way to the young Ireland; but Ireland's hero was Stanford and he admired him all his life.

In much later life Ireland recalled that Stanford had said to him, 'Your music is all Brahms and water, me boy. I shall have to do something with you which I have never done with anyone else', and put him to work on sixteenth-century music for a year. Ireland recalled, 'I think the best quality Stanford possessed as a teacher was that he made you feel nothing but the best would do. He wouldn't let you write in pencil. He held that you would have more respect for what you did if you wrote in ink. He could be severely critical, almost cruel at times.' But Ireland had learnt a great deal from Stanford and looking back he obviously regretted that the rigorous and formal education that he had had at the hands of Stanford was no longer available for young English composers. As someone who had both suffered and benefited from Stanford, Ireland's later summary of his teacher's achievements is revealing:

When I first went to Stanford his most admired pupils were William Hurlstone and Coleridge-Taylor, both of whom unhappily died young. My fellow-students were Holst, Vaughan Williams and, at a slightly later period, though it overlapped, Frank Bridge. I couldn't say which of these Stanford considered the most talented. They all had something individual to say, and with the later years Vaughan Williams grew to be the most powerful personality. Then Cyril Scott was a composer many thought exciting. You see, he was the first to break away from the academic school. Scott, of course, got his advanced training in Germany, not here. In his later years Stanford thought all his students had gone mad.

In later life Ireland taught at the Royal College and held various positions as a church organist and, like Vaughan Williams, was free from the financial pressures that forced other young composers to sell their music quickly. He was thus able to afford an extreme reluctance to publish his works until he felt that they were as near perfect as they could be. Also like Vaughan Williams, Ireland knew that it would take time for him to find an individual style that would satisfy him. He first came to notice with his A minor Phantasy Trio, dedicated to Stanford and published in 1908, which won a Cobbett prize. Ireland was already almost thirty at this time and although he began to publish works in greater number it was not until 1917 when the first performance of his Violin Sonata No. 2 was given that he really became widely known – he was then almost forty. Of this work Colin Scott-Sutherland has written, 'with the success of the Sonata – enshrining a feeling both patriotic and serene, characterized by that fervour associated with the Georgian poets – Ireland's career was assured'.

There were those who saw Ireland as one of the most promising contemporary composers. To Joseph Holbrooke in 1925 he was 'one of our strong men', and Holbrooke looked forward to an Ireland symphony; but this was a measure of how little Holbrooke knew his man. Ireland was to retain for the rest of his life a position as one of the most celebrated English composers but he never experimented with large musical forms. Indeed the time for Holbrooke's 'strong men' was itself passing and most of Ireland's important work was written in the considerably altered post-war world of music. Here Ireland fitted in rather as Bax did, holding the middle ground: he was not one of the new radicals nor was he strongly identified with the pre-war world then held in such disdain. Later he complained that his music was not getting played enough – a familiar enough complaint – but over the years he did in fact receive fairly frequent performance, and there are still many who appreciate his music. The John Ireland Society, which claims to be the first of the, now many, appreciation societies for recent English composers, was founded for the composer's eightieth birthday in 1957, when he was still alive; a true mark of honour.

As a young man Ireland was a curious mixture of confidence and insecurity. In many respects he quickly became firmly set in his ways and changed little during his lifetime, and he was always confident about his music once he had decided that it was fit to publish. At the same time, however, there were many difficulties – particularly in practical matters – that were part of a basic insecurity in his life. Although he had attended the Vaughan Williams student teashop meetings in his youth, he was not at ease in social gatherings. A practical decision could make him ill with worry and he got very depressed when external circumstances interfered with his life. He was well known for being uneasy in female company and his attempts to get close to women frequently ended in disaster. In 1927 he married a pupil of his, many years his junior. One of his biographers, Muriel Searle, wrote of this incident, 'that this incongruous pairing was a calamity became apparent within hours. The union was never consummated'; the marriage was soon annulled. On another occasion he became very attached to a woman for whom two other composers, it seems, were competing, one of them being Arnold Bax, who won the day; Ireland retaliated in his Piano Sonata by writing a theme on the notes C–A–D. (In later years Bax and Ireland were friends: the two men lived close to each other and although there was always some rivalry between them, they both seemed to have enjoyed their meetings.)

Ireland's life had other muddled moments. In 1930 he dedicated his Piano Concerto to Helen Parkin, a pupil of the Royal College of Music, and gave the first performance of the work to her, a great privilege for a young unknown performer, causing much gossip in the College. Ireland seems to have idealized women: he frequently told his close friend John Longmire, 'Helen is like a Madonna!'. But Ireland, thirty years older than the girl, lost her as well and in 1950 he even removed the dedication from the concerto. With other people Ireland liked the trappings of a formal relationship: he was known to many of his acquaintances as 'Doctor', and some of his former pupils retained the habit of calling him 'Sir' long after their formal master-pupil relationship had reached its end. There was indeed about Ireland always a sense of élitism – he said that he agreed with George Moore that 'art is aristocratic, for the privileged few'. There is also a certain 'impishness' about some of his music that seems to represent private references and jokes with his friends, but the surprising thing is that most of his music is quite free from the mawkishness that one might expect from such a man.

Another major influence on Ireland was his strong sense of place. Ireland was drawn to the mystical writings of Arthur Machen and he shared that author's interest in the powers of evocation, of magic and of the strength of ancient ritual. He was particularly drawn to the Channel Islands, which he visited for many years. Here he conceived many pieces including *The Forgotten Rite*, *The Island Spell* and *Sarnia*. His *Mai-Dun* orchestral symphonic rhapsody was inspired by the vast prehistoric earthworks of Maiden Castle. (Ireland followed Thomas Hardy's spelling of the place in the title of his piece.) He was also greatly moved by the Sussex Downs, where he lived during the last period of his life. He gave an example of the effect that places had on him in an interview with the

Canadian composer, writer on music and educationalist, Murray Schafer. Speaking of the 'burial mounds and so forth' on the Sussex Downs he referred to the completion of his *Legend for Piano and Orchestra*:

I was intrigued by an old track leading to the ruins of an ancient church. During the Middle Ages the track was used by lepers. Although they were not allowed to mix with ordinary people they could not be denied the right to worship God, and so they were allowed to enter the church by another entrance and to peer through an opening in the wall called 'The Lepers' Squint'. Things like that would often start up certain thoughts and images and these would be reflected in my music.

Ireland's interest in the supernatural and the influence on him of Arthur Machen's visionary writings were in their turn a source of inspiration for others. There is, for example, a passage in Jocelyn Brooke's *The Goose Cathedral* where we read that 'Ireland's music became one of my *cultes*. I associated it with my own love of certain country-scenes which I felt to be haunted by Druidic memories and the "forgotten rites" of a pre-Christian civilization.'

It was not only 'natural' places that John Ireland had a strong feeling for: he also wrote music about London, which until its invasion by the motor-car was a place he was exceptionally fond of. One of Ireland's best-known pieces is his *A London Overture* with its phrase inspired by a bus-conductor calling out 'Pic-ca-dil-ly'. He also wrote three *London Pieces* for piano: 'Chelsea Reach', 'Ragamuffin' and 'Soho Forenoons'.

Ireland set a variety of English poets to music in his songs. Like many of his generation he was particularly fond of the work of A.E. Housman (his two major Housman cycles were called 'The Land of Lost Content' and 'We'll to the Woods No More'). He also made settings of Christina Rossetti, Thomas Hardy, Rupert Brooke and Arthur Symons, among others. Of Housman Ireland said, 'I have the greatest admiration for A.E. Housman because he managed to say so much in such a condensed way.' Ireland's constant ability to choose good words for his music did much to help improve the standards of song-writing at the time.

Ireland never went in for Vaughan Williams's use of folk-song although there is a clear folk-song tune in one of his works. On the question of national music Ireland said,

I've never been conscious of my music being excessively English. It is true, my past is in this country and the traditions I was brought up on were English, but all that only affects you unconsciously. The rediscovery of Tudor church music about the turn of the century has had as great an influence on my music as anything. This is true of all the composers of my generation.

Ireland's church music has remained popular: his services and his hymn tune 'Love Unknown' are both still often heard.

Ireland then, like Bax, did not belong to the Vaughan Williams group of English composers who sought salvation through folk-song; but they all, nevertheless, shared a common background. It is hard to imagine Ireland discovering his own voice with such confidence without having learnt the lesson of striving for independence from foreign forms and influences; and the growing English musical tradition played an important part in his life. Many people also hear unmistakably English characteristics in his works, suggesting the places, moods, and times in which they were written. His publishers, Chester, made a great point of this in a pamphlet on Ireland they put out in 1927, in which they said that the 'chief interest in his work lies in its being essentially English'.

In some respects Ireland was closer to Elgar's characteristic Englishness than to that of Vaughan Williams. As a young man Ireland had once been put down by the often tetchy Elgar in a conversation highly revealing of them both. Ireland asked a seemingly innocent question, 'What are you working at, at present, Mr Elgar?', to which the great man replied, much to Ireland's surprise, 'Work! work! – did you say "work"? I don't know what you are talking about.' Notwithstanding this incident Ireland had the highest opinion of Elgar: 'Elgar was a serious, first-class composer', he later said. He was very impressed when Elgar went through *Mai-Dun* page by page with him, saying afterwards that this was the best lesson in orchestration that he had ever had.

In Ireland we see a figure placed midway in the history of the musical renaissance in England. His best days were between the wars and the onset of further hostilities in 1939 not only forced him to flee from his haven in the Channel Islands but also completely upset the world in which he had done so well. Ireland also stands in the middle as a pupil of the old generation and a teacher of the new. Many of the new generation of musicians passed through his hands – notably Alan Bush, Humphrey Searle, E.J. Moeran and Benjamin Britten – and in their very different ways, these composers and others learnt much through Ireland's example.

E.J. Moeran has left an account of John Ireland as a teacher that tells us that his view was that 'every composer must make his own technique', as he himself had indeed done. But he insisted on his pupils having a sound grounding in counterpoint. He did not allow any padding in the youthful works of his pupils and got them to think very carefully about all parts of their compositions. He also stressed the need to be able to stand outside the details of a work and see its logical continuity and shape; all these things being the marked characteristics of his own successful style.

Though intensely professional, Ireland knew his own limitations, and he thought he knew those of others also. He believed that all British symphonies, with the exception of Elgar's, were 'absolute backaching poppycock'. He thought that 'you must have a very good opinion of yourself to write a symphony'; in similar vein he also once said, 'What does a composer do when he can't get ideas? He turns to opera!' That was not John Ireland's way. He felt that chamber music was a 'far finer medium for one's inmost thoughts' than orchestral music. Although he never liked to talk about other people's music he once revealingly said, 'look at Roger Quilter. He has had the sense to know his limitations.'

Throughout his life Ireland remained rooted in the Classical/Romantic tradition and, although his use of harmony developed considerably over the years, his style never became obscure to the average listener. His music can be both charming and rugged but it is always inviting and speaks in a language familiar to the listener. Ireland's music, however, is of some technical complexity and for this reason it was unusual for his pieces to reach the average parlour piano of the time (although his setting of Masefield's 'Sea Fever' once had a very wide circulation). Only in those households where there were players of quite a high standard could Ireland be performed. These houses were indeed where much of Ireland's music really belonged. When, after the Second World War, the practice of music making at home underwent a complete revolution, the natural habitat of much of Ireland's works was destroyed. As a man who would never 'concoct' a symphony – to use his word – he left few works suitable for presentation in today's public concerts. Ireland and his music belong to a much more intimate time and world than our own.

The third composer in this chapter, Frank Bridge, was also a rather private man. His father conducted a theatre orchestra in Brighton and the young Frank, born in 1879, learnt to play the violin. It was as a violin student that he entered the Royal College of Music. In 1899 he won a composition scholarship and became a pupil of Stanford's for four years. He became well known as an able viola player and when the celebrated musician Emanuel Wirth was unable to play in the Joachim quartet due to illness Bridge was put in to play in his place. He also made a name for himself in the musical world as a conductor capable of taking on a difficult work at short notice and good at reading modern scores; he was occasionally called on to deputize for Henry Wood. In 1905 his Phantasy Quartet won a first prize in the Cobbett competition and this was followed by other successful works of a similar nature. From this early period there are also piano works and songs which, while of immense appeal and charm, are still clearly rooted in the then prevailing Romantic idiom.

Many influences were, however, still at work in Bridge and were to be for some years to come. The effects of the First World War on him, as we have so often noticed in the case of other composers of his generation, were severe, and his visit to the United States of America in 1923 to conduct his own compositions was also important. (While there he made friends with the great patroness of the arts, Elizabeth Coolidge.) By the mid-1920s there had been a marked transformation of his musical style and in 1929 William Walton wrote an article about Bridge's music under the perceptive heading 'A Modernist in the Making'. Bridge's progress was slow – he could take many years over a single composition – but it seems that even at this stage in his life he was still considered to show real promise as a composer.

Two of his works of the 1920s – *The Sea*, first done at the Norwich Triennial Festival of 1924 and *Enter Spring*, performed in 1927 – met with some success. Of the second of these pieces Benjamin Britten was to say that, on hearing it, he was 'knocked sideways'. Some years later Bridge was to become Britten's teacher and it is for this that he is now chiefly known. Britten had the highest opinion of his teacher. 'His loathing of all sloppiness and amateurishness set me standards to aim for that I've never forgotten', he wrote. 'Bridge insisted on the absolutely clear relationship of what was in my mind to what was on the paper. I used to get sent to the other side of the room; Bridge would play what I'd written and demand if it was what I'd really meant.' Bridge's strong sense of professionalism was widely respected by all sorts of musicians; he was known to be able to get good results from orchestral players, as well as his pupils.

In the 1920s Bridge built a house in Sussex. There he and his wife lived, according to Peter Pears, a 'straightforward, simple but lively and warm sort of existence' until his death in 1941. His love of Sussex went very deep, and Britten could remember Bridge driving him around various parts of the south of England. Bridge 'opened my eyes', Britten tells us, 'to the beauty of the Downs and the magnificence of English ecclesiastical architecture'. Britten further recalled, 'In everything he did for me there were, perhaps above all, two cardinal principles. One was that you should try to find yourself and be true to what you found. The other – obviously connected with it – was his scrupulous attention to good technique, the business of saying clearly what was in one's mind. He gave me a sense of technical ambition.' It is some small justice – although quite inadequate – that Bridge should still be widely known today for the theme which lies at the heart of Britten's popular *Variations*.

Bridge's later works, the product of a great development of style which put him at some distance from popular interest, now attract increasing attention: works such as *Phantasm*, *Oration* and *Rebus*, which tell us by their very titles that they are a world away from the Edwardian scene where Bridge began as a composer. He has won the approval of some contemporary critics because it is supposed that these later works represent the 'real' Bridge; but there were many others who explained the change in a rather different way. Herbert Howells wrote that 'superficially the change was extensive. Actually it was less radical than it seemed.' Howells stressed the points of technical similarity between the two phases of Bridge's music and noted that 'above all, the old warmth and humanity are there, the variability and the abiding technical mastery'. In this change the influence of Berg was important (Bridge would have liked the young Britten to go to Berg for lessons). The fact that Bridge was interested in Berg's work led some English music critics of the 1960s and 1970s to bend their knees in respect, and this led to the danger of over-exaggerating the significance of the change in Bridge's music. Bridge was always a very independently minded man. The development of his technical abilities as a composer, however, inevitably drew him away from the public that had shown interest in his earlier works, works in which one can easily understand the most attractive idiom of this man of Sussex; but he is there also in the later, more personal works, for those who have ears to hear.

# CHAPTER SEVEN

# The Frankfurt Gang

## GARDINER, O'NEILL, QUILTER, SCOTT, GRAINGER

In the 1890s there were a number of English-speaking students at Frankfurt, known collectively as the Frankfurt Group or Gang. This group was made up of four young men from England – Balfour Gardiner, Roger Quilter, Norman O'Neill and Cyril Scott – and Percy Grainger, who was Australian by birth, lived for an important period of his life in England, and died a citizen of the United States of America by naturalization.

If we were to deal with these composers only as individuals and strictly on the grounds of the interest and value of their work we would only include Grainger for certain, and would definitely not cover Gardiner or O'Neill; but there are two real advantages of looking at all five of the composers for their representative value. First we can see there were problems as well as advantages in going abroad for a musical training. Where would they fit into the contemporary English music scene when they returned home? They did not belong to the main line of the great choral tradition nor the folk-song school. Indeed they were cast adrift from their German training as well. It is remarkable that after their Leipzig years none of these men developed into a great opera composer or a major symphonist in the German tradition. Second, we can see here the closeness that existed at the time between the more serious and the lighter, more popular sides of the musical world. This is shown most dramatically in the great friendship between Delius and O'Neill.

With the exception of Grainger, the Gang shared many things in common. They came from fairly well-off families and were not driven to make a living from music. That is not to say, however, that they were not all devoted to their music because, each in his own way, they clearly were. As a group their musical achievement was, however, modest. Gardiner and O'Neill achieved only limited success but both men, while composers of attractive work, knew their limitations, and there are really no works of any great substance from either of them. Quilter, as a song-writer, enjoyed considerable attention, and was widely sung up and down the country, and although some professional musicians have today tended to be rather snobbish about his music, his appeal as a high-class popular composer is well deserved. Both Scott and Grainger were experimentalists and for a while made a considerable reputation for themselves as such. But changing views as to what was 'experimental' put both these men into the shade – a shade out of which Grainger is now emerging as the only member of the Frankfurt Gang likely to retain attention in the long term.

As a group of composers they were all strong individuals, a fact which shows in their work, but they held some musical beliefs in common. They were all young Turks joined, for example, by their disapproval of the music of Beethoven and their sympathy with Delius. They remained close throughout their lives (although it seems that in later days there was no great friendship between Grainger and O'Neill). As a group of musicians they had admirers and critics. The 'Oxford' atmosphere that Gardiner exuded was the focus of some disdain from those who looked at the Gang and their friends as a sort of musical 'smart set'. The identification of their music with a comfortable world that has now disappeared may also contribute in some measure to their present-day lack of success. Our contemporary belief that there is no good music but high-brow music has cut us off from the much more liberal and generous musical world in which these composers lived and worked.

Balfour Gardiner, born in 1877, was a man who never had to work for a living but who laboured hard on behalf of two causes in his life: the first was the music of his contemporaries in England and the second was afforestation. (He combined the two interests to a certain extent by encouraging his composer friends to come and help him plant woods which he then named after them.) He came from a successful family – his brother Sir Alan Gardiner was a well-known Egyptologist. Gardiner first went to Frankfurt between leaving Charterhouse and going up to New College, Oxford. He continued to visit Frankfurt during the vacations at Oxford and when his university course was over he went back there once again. Gardiner, like other prospective composers of his generation, had not had a high opinion of music at Oxford at the time but he later said to Cyril Scott that he regarded his love for Oxford as being his musical undoing, 'because it had put a curb on his flight of creative imagination'. (Vaughan Williams likewise wrote of the 'Oxford manner' in the early days of George Butterworth – 'that fear of self-expression which seems to be fostered by academic traditions'.)

On his return to England Gardiner worked for a brief time on the staff of Winchester College but left in order to concentrate on his career as a composer. From 1900 to the time of the First World War he made something of a reputation for himself as a composer. His style of writing was not innovatory. He had, according to Cyril Scott, a 'robust and rather Byronic exterior', but within himself he was hyper self-critical and quite unable to decide which of his musical ideas were worth pursuing. His doubts finally overcame his ability to develop as a composer and he eventually gave up composing to the disappointment both of himself and his friends.

Gardiner is better known today for his role as a large-handed patron of English music in the exciting years before the First World War. His enthusiasms and generosity were extensive and in a series of concerts that he gave at that time many British composers were brought before the public. We have seen that Delius, Holst and Bax were among many who were particularly grateful for Gardiner's help. Gardiner gave up being a promoter of concerts in the post-war years; he felt that there was no place there for the kind of music that he liked. He told Sir Thomas Armstrong that 'music should be an intoxication – something that carried one wholly out of this world. Gardiner did not share or understand the guilt-laden mood of austerity in which the post-war generation as a whole seemed to find itself.' When asked in 1922 what style of music he composed, Gardiner humorously but revealingly replied, 'Oh, the style of 1902, I suppose.'

As a composer Gardiner was not prolific and much of his early music is now lost. In his songs he set Housman and Hardy and in this and other respects he was closer to the Vaughan Williams stream of music than any other member of the Frankfurt Gang. The work for which he is chiefly remembered today (if at all) is his *Shepherd Fennel's Dance*.

Those who have examined his work in recent years think that this once well-known tune is not representative of him at his best. It is now, however, highly unlikely that we will ever get a chance to judge this question in public performance.

Norman O'Neill is another composer whose works are now never heard although in his day he was well known for his theatre music. He was born in 1875 and his life as a boy was spent in a comfortable house in Kensington - the same house in which Thackeray had lived when writing *Vanity Fair*. O'Neill's father was a successful painter and had good connections in the artistic social world of London. In 1893, on the recommendation of the violinist Joachim, it was decided that the young O'Neill should go to study under Knorr at Frankfurt. His experiences there were similar to the others of the group: he greatly enjoyed himself, and he learnt a considerable amount, but on returning home, aware that he had been rather spoilt at Frankfurt, he had to ask himself the difficult question - what was he going to do next?

The answer to this question was very different for each of the composers of the Frankfurt Gang, but O'Neill, like Gardiner, did not really develop musically. With his wife Adine, he settled in London, and over the years they built up a considerable reputation in polite London society as musicians. She was a well-known pianist and became head music-mistress at St Paul's Girls' School - where she brought Gustav Holst on to the staff. O'Neill, after becoming known at first for his songs, became Musical Director of the Haymarket Theatre, where he worked for many years. He had a special talent for composing music for plays and, at a time when such music was still in demand, he made it his speciality. (He even attempted to develop a system of printing the music for his orchestral players as white notes on a black background, which was supposed to give greater clarity of vision and allow the orchestral lights to be lowered. The timing of the music at the Haymarket was done by electric lights which, according to O'Neill's biographer, Derek Hudson, 'anticipated by many years the appearance of the traffic lights in Piccadilly Circus'.) O'Neill composed music for over fifty productions at the Haymarket. In this sort of work he followed in a fine English tradition of lighter music, a form that composers as great as Elgar had been drawn to, and which was best represented at the time by the figure of Edward German, whose music for the theatre - especially his *Henry VIII* and *Nell Gwyn* - was of a high standard and enjoyed considerable popularity.

*Edward Elgar, thinker and dreamer:*
*a photograph of 1903 by Dr Charles F. Grindrod*

*Elgar boarding an aeroplane in 1933:*
*'there is a delightful feeling of elation*
*in sailing through gold and silver clouds.'*

*A reluctant in uniform: Rutland Boughton*
*served in the army from late 1916 until early 1919*

*Josef Holbrooke:*
*once considered a daring experimentalist*

*Frederick Delius,*
*a photograph taken circa 1907*

*The indomitable Dame Ethel Smyth*
*with her dog Marco*

*Samuel Coleridge-Taylor:*
*music making at home*

*William Yeates Hurlstone: his early death was*
*a great loss to English music*

*Granville Bantock*
*in characteristic Oriental dress*

(left) *Ralph Vaughan Williams and Gustav Holst on a walking tour, circa 1913 (the photograph was taken by their fellow composer and companion W.G. Whittaker) (right) over forty years on: Vaughan Williams and Michael Tippett at a rehearsal of Tippett's Second Symphony in 1958*

*Men of the middle ground:*
*Arnold Bax (far right) and John Ireland (next to Bax) at a function*
*in late 1942 with Granville Bantock (far left), the voice of pre-First*
*World War music and Benjamin Britten (centre), the voice of the future*

*George Butterworth:*
*lost in the Great War*

*Percy Grainger with his mother Rose in 1903:*
*'Your mad side has ruined us' she said*

*The young Cyril Scott: 'my vanity was colossal.'*

*The young Herbert Howells*                    *Ivor Gurney: the asylum years*

*Philip Heseltine (Peter Warlock), standing left,*
*E.J. Moeran, standing right,*
*with members of the Dramatic Society of Shoreham, Kent, circa 1928*

*Arthur Bliss:*
*'part of the stir' in the 1920s*

*Constant Lambert:*
*a portrait taken in 1930.*

*William Walton, photographed by Cecil Beaton*
*in 1926: the Sitwell's 'adopted, or elected, brother'*

*Lord Berners at home at Faringdon:*
*a photograph of 1945 by Bill Brandt*

*Michael Tippett and Benjamin Britten:*
*Tippett said of Britten that he believed him to be*
*'the most purely musical person I have ever met';*
*Britten dedicated his* Curlew River *to Tippett*
*'in friendship and admiration'.*

(German also composed light operas in the Sullivan vein – in one he cooperated with W.S. Gilbert – and in his *Merrie England* of 1902 and *Tom Jones* of 1907 he produced genuinely popular works.)

O'Neill was a particularly close friend of Delius. Eric Fenby once wrote, 'I could see that O'Neill was one of the very few people whom he loved.' Delius would stay with the O'Neills when he came to London and he even stood as godfather to the O'Neill's second child; a highly untypical gesture of regard on the part of this Nietzschean man. When young, O'Neill had been strongly influenced by Delius and aspired to great things for his own music. But, as it turned out, there was no real future for O'Neill's sort of music. It is, indeed, difficult now to imagine how his music can ever be heard again in the context for which it was written. Economic considerations as well as artistic ones have put an end to incidental theatre music of this sort. O'Neill's music, with the rare exception of one of his orchestral suites, is thus hardly ever heard.

The third of the group, Roger Quilter, also achieved notable success in a limited field – that of song-writing; and although both public song recitals and singing at home have greatly declined in recent years some of his songs are still occasionally heard. As a song-writer Quilter belonged to an important school in England. During the period of the renaissance of English music, song-writing – in a number of different styles – was one of the richest of all forms of musical composition. Many serious composers wrote songs that were as suitable for the salon as for the concert hall, and modern critics have been much too dismissive of many of these works. Quilter is considered by some people to be a composer of only light-weight achievement, but a proper acquaintance with his work will modify this view, for while one must admit that much of his work now seems very dated, his best songs are good.

Quilter was born in 1877. His father was a wealthy businessman, landowner and politician and he saw that his son had a conventional upbringing. After Eton College (which he hated), he was allowed to go to Knorr at Frankfurt. Like others of the Frankfurt Gang the problem of what to do when he returned home was a serious one. He began to establish some sort of an artistic reputation for himself but he did not need to earn a living and the story of his life is quite void of public event. Apart from one or two orchestral works – notably *A Children's Overture* and the music he wrote for *Where the Rainbow Ends* – he became known chiefly through his songs. He was helped in this by being taken up and championed in his early days by the celebrated singer Gervase Elwes, a service repeated in his later life by Mark Raphael.

At a time when singing at home was still a thriving concern, to be known as a song-writer was an achievement of some order. Quilter considerably improved the standard of the drawing-room ballad of the Victorian era although there are songs of his which suffer from the most awful choice of words. He set Stevenson, Ernest Dowson, W.E. Henley and May Coleridge and verses of his own (it is interesting, however, that there are no settings of poets such as Housman or Hardy). Quilter's best songs are meticulous and finely detailed and he pleased both the singer and the accompanist alike with his finely wrought and imaginatively composed music. His songs are based on harmonies conventional for the period, having none of the 'experimental' aspects of, say, Scott's music.

Like many other composers of the time Quilter wrote his best works before the Great War; the peak of his career was probably a few years before hostilities began. After the war and especially in the 1930s the public for his sort of songs declined, and those who bought songs to sing at home (and it was still a considerable number) turned to other composers. Quilter never altered the style that he had settled on in the very early years of the century and in this he was one of many who were not able to develop in the new world following the years of the great European conflagration. His choices of text and his musical style, both of which had once seemed so appropriate, became thought of as very limited.

Quilter's life ended sadly. For a large part of it his music ceased to be of great public interest. Stephen Banfield in a recent short biographical notice of the composer referred to Quilter's 'homosexual attachments which must have been a major contributory factor to the draining capacity for intense feeling, inevitably resulting in sorrow, which in the last decade of his life cost him his mental balance'. Quilter died insane in 1953.

Of the Frankfurt Gang Cyril Scott - always a rather precocious figure - first went there for a short time at the age of twelve. He returned a few years later and we can get a good picture of the period from his autobiographical work of 1924, *My Years of Indiscretion* (a work that can now interestingly be read in the light of his second thoughts in his 1969 *Bone of Contention*). These were exciting days for the young men who feature in Scott's memoirs. To Scott, like the others, it was a time to consider possible new developments in music, but, of the Frankfurt Gang, it was only Scott and Grainger who were to be innovators – in some respects, indeed, they were considered to be ahead of the entire musical world in their thinking.

Scott was born in 1879. His father, a distinguished Greek scholar, was not initially enthusiastic for his son to study composition. His mother, however, was interested in music, and Cyril Scott was eventually allowed to follow his desired course. Scott's accounts of his early days reveal that he was a handsome, fun-loving young man. His first most serious concern as an artist was to search for a suitable musical style; he set out his views on this matter in *The Philosophy of Modernism*, a book that helped bring him to the attention of a wider audience. This self-important book has not, however, weathered well: Scott himself later said of this period of his life that 'my vanity was colossal'.

In Germany Scott became a close friend of the poet Stefan George and considered himself to be in the front line of the new movements in art. When he returned home to Liverpool he brought with him some arrogant ideas. He wore his hair long and sported 'curious ties' – the uniform of the 'artist' of the period. He was also a keen follower of certain Pre-Raphaelite customs, creating an ecclesiastical atmosphere in his home by installing 'gothic' windows and burning incense. He was particularly fond of Burne-Jones's stained-glass windows. Some, understandably, called him a poseur.

In Liverpool he began to teach music, but never with any great success. In 1900 his *Heroic Suite* was performed by Richter and his First Symphony was played at Darmstadt. In 1901 his Piano Quartet in E minor was heard in London and Henry Wood conducted his Second Symphony in 1903. Scott was meeting, then, with some success both in England and Germany, and on the Continent he became known, along with Elgar and Delius, as one of the bright hopes of English music. Scott was in fact the only one of the Frankfurt Gang to make his German connections work for him at all, and his reputation there was at one time considerably higher than at home. The high point of his career was perhaps the performance of his one-act opera *The Alchemist* in Essen in 1925. In England he became mainly known, however, for his smaller works and for his stance as a radical young man of music – the 'English Debussy' as he was tagged. He later recalled: 'By the time I had reached my late twenties I was already regarded as the musical *enfant terrible* of the Edwardian age, some music-lovers liking me for my *enfant terriblism* and others scandalized by it and hating me for it.' He thought of himself as part of the generation of Stravinsky and Scriabin but their 'modernism' and that of Debussy has outlived his in England.

Scott was also known for other interests as well as music, interests to which he devoted great energy. These included naturopathy, homeopathy, osteopathy and spiritualism and it is still possible to see copies of his books on these subjects in bookshops – his work on *Cider Vinegar* and *Crude Black Molasses*, for example, as well as *The Initiate*, which he wrote under the name of 'His Pupil', and which was last reprinted in 1977. The relationship of such interests to his music was a curious one. He believed that some composers were inspired by the 'Higher Powers' to mould desirable characteristics of the future through the medium of music. Scott was strongly influenced by Mahatma Koot Hoomi who, in a previous incarnation, was said to have been Pythagoras. This 'Master' was described by Scott as being well over 150 years old. To a certain extent the subjects of Scott's music reflect his interests – his *Lotus Land* or *Sphinx*, for example – but he also believed that music brought thought-forms and colours to the psychic sight of the listener and came to regard composition as a very serious and powerful matter. In 1944 he had considered giving up composition altogether, until an occult sign told him not to. It is indeed impossible to consider his later work out of the context of his spiritual life.

Other artistic influences also acted upon Cyril Scott, especially Stefan George in his early days, and Charles Bonnier, Professor of French Literature at the University of Liverpool. Scott developed a considerable interest in poetry. He translated many of Stefan George's poems into English and wrote verse of his own:

> I see them now – those travailed ones,
> I, glad initiate of death's rare meadows:
> They wander 'mid the cypressed shadows
> To deck with buds the urns of bronze;
> So wearied, yet so mighty in Belief,
> Where but one gleam of Knowledge had disbanded grief.

As a musician Scott could be an innovator. He was in the vanguard of the move away from traditional key tonality towards developed chromaticism; he also threw over conventional regular rhythmic periods at a very early date. His developed musical style was thought to be evident by the time of his Piano Sonata, written about 1904. The works in his later style, however, never had the same appeal for the English public as the earlier songs and piano pieces had enjoyed. But among other composers he had many admirers. In 1911, for example, after the first performance of Elgar's Second Symphony George Bernard Shaw remarked to Elgar that his harmonies were surprisingly modern 'for an Englishman'. Elgar replied, 'You mustn't forget that it was Cyril Scott who started all that.' And Sir Thomas Armstrong once wrote of Scott, 'There is no doubt that Cyril Scott was a musician of truly original mind. His harmonic gifts were altogether outstanding, and greatly influenced those who came into contact with him.' Armstrong (writing in 1958) went on to say that Scott's harmonic idiom was 'now wholly out of fashion' but that he believed the time would come when his work would be revalued.

The *enfant terrible* label is often a millstone around the neck of an artist in his later years. Viewed from today's perspective it is all too easy to dismiss Scott's music on the evidence of his early life rather than listening to the works themselves. In his later autobiography Scott wrote with a mixture of irony and amusement about the earlier exciting days. He recalled how his music had been called 'scandalous' and how 'I was even told that I was ruining people's nerves with my "hideous discords" and that altogether I exercised a very bad influence on all and sundry'. But things changed greatly during his lifetime. Once he had been proud of the 'alien harmonies' that he had introduced into the National Anthem, but his religious life taught him not to seek after effect and fame. His deliberate retirement from the public eye was also, doubtless, partly responsible for the lack of prominence of his music in later life.

Unlike Cyril Scott in his later days, the last of the Frankfurt Gang, Percy Grainger, could never be accused of not trying to promote interest in his life and work. Grainger left behind him ample material for a whole industry of scholars. The collection of the ephemera of his life is extraordinary. Grainger was, however, a builder as well as a collector of what most people would regard as junk. The Grainger Museum at Melbourne University, founded by himself, is a lasting monument to the remains and recordings of his life and career. (It was quite typical of the man that, when time allowed, he even helped out in the bricklaying of this building.) Appalling amounts of material are stored in the museum: Grainger was a prolific letter-writer who in the later days of his life resorted to a copying machine so that he could send lengthy duplicated letters round to his friends. Moreover, in addition to the Melbourne museum, there are also substantial collections of Graingerana both in Britain and the United States of America. His decision to build his museum in Australia reflected his wish to give Australia concrete evidence of its first important composer, but he had in fact spent most of his adult life in Britain or in the United States, and in both he left considerable remains.

To think of Grainger as an 'English composer' is in no way inappropriate – how else could you class the composer of 'Country Gardens', 'Mock Morris' and 'Handel in the Strand'? Beyond this, however, Grainger held a most tenacious 'Anglo-Saxon' view of the world, its history and development. His belief in the Anglo-Saxon and Nordic peoples and their music was extreme: he spoke of being 'at war' with German music. In musical terms one of his great ambitions was to see the 'filthy Sonata-Symphony form' (as he put it) fall into disuse, because it was a German form. Grainger's mind was, by usual standards, muddled: he seems to have considered that Australian/British/North American/Scandinavian – that is, the nations or racial groups that had his approval – were often more or less synonymous (although in the later days of his life he expressed reservations about the ever-growing 'Americanization' of Australia). Grainger's extreme racial views are also important for a proper examination of his own complicated character. Some may consider that in recent times undue emphasis has been put on accounts of Grainger's life to the detriment of his music, but there is no real imbalance here: Grainger himself was responsible for leaving his biographers vast amounts of personal information. This was how he wanted it. There will always be a danger with a man of such extraordinary and forceful character that present-day followers will be accused of over-exaggerating his position in the musical world for non-musical reasons. As a musician, however, Grainger is of real interest. He was, like Cyril Scott and many others of the time, a man who greatly changed his musical style over the years. In pre-First World War England his expertly crafted, tuneful pieces established a reputation for him, and, indeed, it is by these pieces that he is still best known. But he was also an experimentalist and his work in this respect and its reception by the musical public tells us much about the period.

Grainger was born in 1882 in Melbourne of English stock. He underwent formal schooling in Australia for only three months. He studied in Frankfurt from 1895 (an experience he found very unpleasant) and

moved to London in 1901. He stayed in England until the outbreak of
the First World War, when he went to the United States, where, in
1918, he adopted US citizenship. He died in the United States in 1961
and his body was taken back to Australia for burial. At every stage of
his life he travelled extensively and, as a pianist, he kept up a strenuous
and very successful public career until the time of his death. He was a
phenomenally energetic man – hugely prolific in many fields. As with
other energetic people, Grainger was profoundly restless. His writings
also are endlessly discursive, repetitive and often contradictory. Most of
his letters (the correspondence archive of the Grainger Museum alone
recently numbered over 28,000 items) are not of any lasting interest.
There cannot be many of the general musical public, or even specialist
students, who will want to read Grainger's every letter, memo, note,
record of weight, and so forth.

At the centre of Percy Grainger's life lay his relationship with his
mother – Rose Grainger. That she absolutely dominated him until she
committed suicide in 1922 was obvious to all Grainger's friends; while
she was alive he was unable to enjoy close relations with other people.
She was highly jealous where her son was concerned, guarding carefully
both whom he saw and how long he saw them for; she vetted his
girlfriends, and she even tested his love for her by pretending to die, so
that she could see how he would react. Rose felt that nothing should be
allowed to interfere with his work as a musician, and, parting from her
frequently drunk architect husband, who it seems had given her syphilis,
she set out for Germany to ensure that her son had a good musical
training. They were inseparable: the two of them – 'us against the
world', as Percy Grainger put it – lived together until she died, and in
later life Grainger never forgave or forgot a criticism of his mother,
remaining faithful to her memory long after her death.

Grainger was a strange man in many respects. From a very young age
he was a sexual masochist and he recorded his experiences in this respect
in as much detail as any other aspect of his life; even with photographic
evidence. (His mother knew about this side of his character, although it
seems that his wife, at the time of their marriage, did not.) This all
seemed quite straightforward to Grainger: he felt that in his sexual life,
as with his music, he was ahead of the times and that it would only be
a matter of time before the world caught up with him. He believed that
the record of his sexual activities was important evidence that needed to
be carefully preserved for posterity, and human nature is such that much

recent curiosity about Grainger has been fuelled by interest in this area of his life as much as by his music, but not for the reasons Grainger had hoped for. Here the last word belongs to his mother when she said to him 'your mad side has ruined us'.

Percy Grainger held many other unconventional views. He believed in what he called the 'blue-eyed' people: the Anglo-Saxons and Nordic races. Such was this obsession that at one stage of his life he began to take colour-plate photographs of the eyes of leading composers – including Walton, Ireland, Scott, Bliss, and Vaughan Williams – to show that they had blue eyes. A few years after the death of his mother he met and later married his ideal woman: a blonde-haired, blue-eyed, Swedish beauty who curiously resembled his mother. (Their marriage took place in the Hollywood Bowl in front of an audience of some 20,000 people.) His belief in the 'blue-eyed' people did not, however, extend to the Germans, whose musical 'tyranny' he found unacceptable. Grainger completed his racial views with a strong anti-Semitism.

Grainger also believed in the need for a reform of the English language; he wanted to uproot and discard all words of foreign origin. Many of his letters contain strange neologisms that he developed for this purpose: a 'state-thane' for an official, 'he-high-rangesome' for tenor-like in musical range, 'puzzle-wifty' for complicated, 'a-chance-for-all-ye' for democratic. His 'blue-eyed English', as he called it, had few supporters, although he did find one other Australian who had reached similar conclusions to his own and to whom he gave financial support to carry on the good work. In his compositions Grainger frequently gave instructions to the performers in English rather than in German or Italian, thus his scores are familiar for their markings: 'louden lots', 'rollickingly', 'hold till blown', 'lower notes of woggle well to the fore'.

In his musical concerns Grainger was as free from convention as in other ways. He had no interest at all in the sonata or symphony form and almost all his work is on a small scale. At an early stage he became interested in English folk-music. To Grainger, as to many others, folk-songs were proof that England was a musical nation and had a tradition to put beside the Austro/German one. Like Cecil Sharp and Vaughan Williams, Grainger was a keen collector of folk-songs and would travel round England noting down the tunes and words – a practice he also followed in other countries when the opportunity arose. He was among the very first to record songs by recording machine; this was not really approved of in those days by the 'official' folk-song movement. Grainger would delight in all the modifications and variations of tunes that he heard on his collecting expeditions, while other collectors looked for what they felt to be the 'proper version' that lay behind the many variants and would only publish this. Grainger, however, recorded everything that he heard: H.G. Wells is said to have commented on this, 'You are trying to do a more difficult thing than record folk-song, you are trying to record life.'

On the question of using folk-song in his own works Grainger also disagreed with many other musicians of the time. The traditional harmonies and inflexible rhythmic patterns usually given to the tunes were, he felt, quite inappropriate and his own versions are much freer and more variable. Much of his early music is based on folk-song material and, while the structural form that he followed was often strophic, there were continual variations of detail. This he felt was appropriate in view of the variety in the original material itself. In more recent days many leading musicians – including Benjamin Britten – have come to share Grainger's point of view and his early recordings are of inestimable value now.

One should not, however, think of Grainger as belonging to the Vaughan Williams tradition of folk-song music. That there were composers who had an interest in folk-song and who were not part of the Vaughan Williams camp has not been sufficiently realized, and the important part that Percy Grainger played in the folk-song movement has only recently been recognized. His influence on other composers in this respect should also be noted. The most famous of the songs that Grainger collected was probably 'Brigg Fair', which he heard from Joseph Taylor in North Lincolnshire in 1905; when Grainger met Delius two years later he brought the tune to the older man's attention, who later used it as a theme in one of his best-known pieces. The meeting was to have important consequences for both composers and Delius took to Grainger at once. He wrote to his wife at the time, 'I also met Percy Grainger, a most charming young man & more gifted than Scott & less affected.' The two men got on well from the start and Grainger later did much to promote Delius's music in the United States, when he lived and worked there. The two composers also shared many musical beliefs as well as some close similarities of musical technique, especially in harmonic terms. (An entertaining coda to their first meeting was that when Delius's *Brigg Fair* was conducted in 1908 by Beecham at the Queen's Hall, Joseph Taylor, who had been brought to London to hear the work, stood up and sang 'his' tune when he heard it being played by the orchestra.)

Grainger became well known in pre-war England for his folk settings: 'Country Gardens', 'Molly on the Shore' and other pieces written in his years in London were, and still are, the best-known pieces that he ever composed. Other composers of the time thought him a considerable talent: at the end of Grieg's life Grainger enjoyed a brief friendship with him, and Grieg complimented him by saying, 'Your composition of English folk-song is full of genius and contains the seed of a new English style in music.' Busoni once showed his high opinion of Grainger by inviting him to become one of his pupils; Bartók was keen to hear about his music; and Richard Strauss was the first to programme his music in Germany. In England Thomas Beecham offered Grainger a post as his assistant conductor but he would not do it (possibly, as someone pointed out, because Beecham did not have blue eyes). Many must have felt that there was real justification for Grieg's optimism: did not Percy Grainger's compositions contain the seed of a new English style in music?

As a musician Grainger had wide-ranging interests – from the songs of Stephen Foster to the work of Duke Ellington – and there is a great variety in his own music. At Frankfurt Grainger got what he needed in terms of musical training; like Delius his 'formal' musical training was short and with an amateur (he left Knorr and studied with the amateur Klimsch instead). In London Grainger moved in high social circles, numbering among his friends John Singer Sargent and Sir Edgar Speyer; Queen Alexandra was also an admirer of his. He was a good catch at a soirée musicale. But his entrée to this world was as a performer and he was often put upon at social gatherings to provide musical entertainment. Moving in these circles had disadvantages as well as advantages for Grainger. Like many of his contemporaries he was badly hit by the First World War. Before the war some progressive musicians may have thought that Grainger was becoming something of a drawing-room composer, while after the war was over some drawing-room audiences may have felt that he was becoming something of a progressive – both ways he lost. In any case Grainger's and his mother's decision to leave England to live in the United States when hostilities began cut them off from many of their former friends.

In America Grainger had to establish himself again and although he soon enjoyed a wide reputation as a concert pianist the days of his greatest popularity as a composer were over. As a performer Grainger was able to earn a good living for himself, for his relations, and for various poor musicians and others that he generously supported. (This he also felt was part of his 'racial duty'.) As a composer, however, he never successfully came to the fore again. He developed many of his earlier interests and enthusiasms way past the point where the musical public were prepared to follow him. In his later days he acquired new interests in, for example, church music (he enjoyed a friendship with the Nashdom monk Don Anselm Hughes, the secretary of the Plainsong and Medieval Music Society), but his main energies were set on a new form of music which he called 'Free Music', which had interested him since his very early days in Australia. Grainger wrote later in his life of the 'Free Music I've been hearing in my head since a young boy & which only now I am technically equipped to embark on'. After a number of technical and musical experiments, Grainger developed a form of machinery which might translate his ideas into practice.

As early as his days in Frankfurt Grainger had been working on a new system to communicate his musical thoughts to the public, and he came up with the idea – never in fact realized – of an 'orchestral supervisor' to replace the conductor. The main task of this person was to operate a device whereby strips of music would pass across the music desks of the players indicating what was to be played and when. Grainger's desire to find a way of controlling the performance of his music also came out in many other ways. He took enthusiastically to the piano-player, for ex-ample, and made many rolls for the Duo Art Company. But nothing compares to the series of strangely-named machines – such as the 'Kangaroo-Pouch Free-Music Machine' – that he developed himself. 'Free Music' was no longer to be tied to tones and semi-tones, and rhythm was no longer to be dictated by the technical ability of the performer. He developed an early form of 'synthetic' music: by means of lamps and pitch-control photocells Grainger's scores, written in a form of graph notation, could be 'read' by the machines and, through a series of oscillators, transformed into sound. In this way Grainger felt that he at last had a machine for composer's rather than performer's music. He was able to achieve the sort of irregular rhythmical patterns that he believed he and Cyril Scott had pioneered, as well as the sliding tones used by Duke Ellington, intervals closer than a half-tone as used by Arthur Fickenscher, and the revolutionary harmony of Schoenberg. 'No non-Australian composer', Grainger explained, 'has been willing to combine *all* these innovations into a consistent whole that can be called *Free Music.*'

Grainger seems to have achieved a much greater measure of fulfilment in this work than at any other period of his career. Other composers, however, were not convinced: Vaughan Williams, for example, felt that Grainger was working himself into an artistic corner. Only time will tell if, as Grainger himself thought, he was rather working himself out of an artistic impasse. Many of Grainger's present-day supporters believe that his experiments were of lasting importance; but until much more detailed work has been done on both Grainger and other composers of the period their case will have to remain unproven. That Grainger, like Scott, was in the forefront of musical innovation in his day cannot be doubted but the exact position is not yet clear. What is clear, however, is that even with the recent revival of interest in his music with its emphasis on unconventional pieces like *Random Round* and *The Warriors* (about the merits of which even his greatest admirers are divided), the record companies in their substantial releases of Grainger's music have judged the wider public interest to lie with the earlier, more conventional, period of his life and work.

How much the present interest in Grainger's music is sustained by a fascination with his undoubtedly curious life is another question that will also only be settled by time. The Percy Grainger that the public knew in the earlier part of this century was a colourful character, the 'Siegfried of the Piano', as he was known. He was equally celebrated for his love of physical exercise. When on tour in Australia he would sometimes walk considerable distances in between concerts through rough countryside in order to keep fit. He appears in Eric Fenby's book on Delius in this eccentric light, jumping out of a window in order to meet Delius in the street because the window was closer to him at the time than the door. His part in helping to carry the infirm Delius up a mountain so that the nearly blind man could see the sunset is well known. He also achieved notoriety for his unusual behaviour in public: he would, for example, demonstrate a glissando on the piano by wrapping a handkerchief over his fingers which, by dint of being attached to his clothes with a length of elastic, would return itself to his pocket when released. His notoriety was further increased by such events as his public marriage (his wife doesn't seem to have been aware of what was involved when he proposed the venue).

Grainger extended his personal athletic regime to all seasons of the year and in cold weather wore little or no overclothing and no hat; he was more than once arrested on suspicion of vagrancy in the United

States. There was another period of his life when he became a keen advocate of the wearing of towelling clothing. These were not just the harmless musings of a crank: the implications of some of his views could be dangerous if carried out in practice. Since the appearance of the biographical work of John Bird, we know that Grainger extended his extreme athletic enthusiasms right into his private life. To Grainger love was pain to be endured rather than a pleasure to be enjoyed. Grainger believed that 'a man cannot be a full artist unless he is manly, & a man cannot be manly unless his sexlife is selfish, brutal, wilful, unbridled'. He said that he believed also that music should agonize rather than entertain; that art, like life, should be a struggle. Grainger truly remarked of himself, 'I am full of violence.' And yet, listening to his charming music, so skilfully and sometimes so delicately orchestrated, one can often hardly match the words of this man to his music.

It is tempting to think that a psychoanalyst might make a better judge of Grainger than a musical biographer. His was certainly a very contradictory character, often disappointed with his life. As a young man, for example, he said that he would 'hold back' his music for a number of years, whereas in later life he explained that he had dried up as an artist at twenty-five. The appeal of his music is, however, undeniable and he is the only one of the original Frankfurt Gang whose work has lived on in any appreciable way. His admirers are spread throughout three continents. Grainger thought of himself as the first Australian composer of importance (when he spoke of the 'Australian contribution' to music he usually meant his own), and slowly Australia is beginning to realize the musical legacy that he left his native land. But he was also an important figure in the history of English music and his place in a gallery of English composers of this century is both appropriate and secure.

# CHAPTER EIGHT

# The Shock of the New

## BLISS, WALTON, LAMBERT, BERNERS, WARLOCK, MOERAN

The major change that came over English music in the period after the First World War has been referred to frequently in previous sections of this book. All the composers from Edward Elgar to Percy Grainger who had flourished before the war found the profoundly changed circumstances of the post-war world unsympathetic, to one degree or another. There were many reasons for this: the vast social and economic change that had taken place during the war years (although few saw this clearly at the time); the enormous changes in music on the Continent, changes that were already beginning to affect English composers before the war; the profound emotional and spiritual influence that the war had had on individual composers; and the rise of the radio and the vastly increased interest in popular music from America. The new modern composers of the post-war period – establishing themselves with extraordinary rapidity in a world of huge spaces crying out to be filled – also played their part, deliberately emphasizing the apparent differences between themselves and their immediate musical forebears in England. In order to underline this difference many younger musicians turned again to the musical developments on the Continent; France and Russia were now the main areas of interest, not, as before, Germany. But, like their immediate English forebears, they did not look to the Continent as mere imitators. The success of the English musical renaissance hitherto had given these younger composers a strength and confidence from which they could judge which developments in European music they wished to adopt or reject.

For the first half of the 1920s to be 'modern' was everything, and many more 'traditional' composers went under. Somewhere around the middle of the 1920s, however, a reaction set in and slowly but surely the young musical poachers began the transmutation into their generation's gamekeepers. The composers in this chapter include the most *terrible* of the post-war *enfants* while those of the next chapter were composers whose musical interests and careers were not marked with such a reputation but who equally belonged to this new world.

Arthur Bliss's life and work as a composer most clearly show the changes that took place in music in England from the years of the First World War to those after the Second. That is not to say Bliss was an 'average' composer, but, rather, that his great humanity and wide vision allowed him to see and contribute to what was alive in each succeeding period. Even as an old man Bliss was still full of the zest for living he showed in his early days and which is always apparent in his music.

Bliss was born in 1891; his father came from the United States and was to return there to die. Arthur Bliss himself married an American but his connections with that country were not important musically. He went to school at Rugby, where the facilities for music were quite inadequate at the time. While at school he first developed a fervent admiration for the music of Elgar, especially *Gerontius*. From Rugby he went to Cambridge where he fell under the influence of Charles Wood and E.J. Dent. At Cambridge Vaughan Williams was then the magical name: Bliss tells us that 'his *Songs of Travel* were on all pianos'. Bliss had a great capacity for enjoying himself and at Cambridge he was a member of a mutual admiration society for composers, The Gods. He had, at that time, as he himself put it, a reluctance to concentrate on music. There were no financial constraints preventing Bliss from going on to study composition seriously, so from Cambridge he went to the Royal College of Music where a group of young musicians – which included Herbert Howells, Eugene Goossens, Arthur Benjamin and Ivor Gurney, all to do well as composers – recalled the exciting days of the 1890s. The great new influence was that brought by Diaghilev's ballet company to London and change was in the air. But this was the generation whose young lives were to be so cruelly torn apart by the First World War and Bliss spent only a brief time at the College before joining up at the start of hostilities.

From 1914 to 1919 Bliss served in the army. He was mentioned in dispatches, wounded on the Somme and gassed at Cambrai. One of his brothers was killed. While in France Bliss continued his musical life as far as he was able. He had with him a portable gramophone and he would send home for records, although it seems incredible that such fragile objects could undertake the perilous journey from the genteel drawing-rooms of London to the thunder of the Western Front. He corresponded with various musicians, including Parry and Elgar, and he treasured in later life a miniature score of Elgar's *Cockaigne* which had been sent to him by the composer during the first week of the Battle of the Somme. In his autobiography *As I Remember* Bliss tells us that he later noted that this score still carried 'the mud marks of the trenches on its pages' and had the composer's inscription 'Good luck' scrawled across it.

During the war a few early works of Bliss's were performed at home but once the war was over he gathered together the parts of these and destroyed them. 1919 was to see Bliss, now aged twenty-eight, make a fresh start, and it was in the early years of the 1920s that he briefly made a reputation for himself as the new *enfant terrible* of English music. Bliss was thought of as eminently modern at roughly the same time that William Walton was coming to the public's attention. These two figures, later to be so firmly respectable, aroused passionate controversy in the 1920s. In the early years of this decade the place for an aspiring composer to be was Paris, where the young hornets of the day were gathered; there Bliss went to become 'part of the stir'. His early works received attention by the avant-garde of the time at home. In describing *Rout*, one of his 'modern' works of this period, the composer wrote, 'the voice part is given a string of syllables corresponding to the scraps of song that might reach a listener watching a carnival from an open window: musically, the soprano is just part of the orchestra'. Originally written for voice and ten instruments *Rout* was later rescored as a musical interlude for the Russian ballet of Diaghilev.

In retrospect this all seems rather less than 'shocking' to us today. Some of the techniques that Bliss used were not, in fact, particularly modern even at the time. But with the advantage of hindsight we must not underestimate the effect that Bliss had; his notoriety as an experimental composer pre-dated that of Walton. Bliss, however, always had a steady head, as we can see from a talk he gave in 1921 to the Society of Women Musicians entitled 'What Modern Composition is Aiming At'. He was not a man to grind an axe: in his talk he attempted, rather, to explain what he felt his generation was trying to do. Bliss felt that with composers such as Vaughan Williams, Holst, Goossens, Bax, Ireland and Berners England had an important part to play in the new musical world. The English composers were not a 'school' like the modern French composers known as Les Six in Paris; Bliss spoke of the national distrust of such musical cliques in England. In more general terms he felt that modern composers were working towards a new state of simplicity and were attempting a far more direct mode of expression, although he added, 'I fear I cannot say a good word of German music.' He was keen to investigate more fully the individual timbres of the various musical instruments and urged the case for ridding sound of 'all its obligations to non-musical elements'. In a cry for the 'music of the future' he took *The Rite of Spring* as a model. This was the voice of the new young men, for whom Stravinsky, above all, reigned supreme.

The early years of the 1920s were exciting days in the musical world both in England and overseas, but the modern wave broke quickly on the sea-wall of English musical life and by the middle of the decade a reaction was clearly under way. Bliss's development was quite different from that he had, with such characteristic liveliness, outlined in his talk. In his autobiography he later wrote a much more considered summary of his views. 'I believe that through whatever changes and transformations music is passing it must unswervingly keep its idealistic aim; otherwise, it may cease to retain its mysterious power of healing and of giving joy, and just dwindle into an excitant aural sensation, and nothing more.'

In the 1920s Bliss, however modern his views, still continued to learn from those around him in England – he was an admirer of Parry although, like many others, he did not get on well with Stanford. At Cambridge the influence of Vaughan Williams was important and after the war Bliss took one of his pieces for advice to Holst, whom he greatly admired. It was, in fact, another composer, Elgar, who helped him to become really established in the English musical world. In 1920 Elgar hosted a lunch at the Royal Societies Club for young musicians and from this occasion came the commissions for works for the 1922 Three Choirs Festival at Gloucester: Herbert Howells's *Sine Nomine*, Eugene Goossens's *Silence*, and Arthur Bliss's *A Colour Symphony*. It was through this work that Bliss really began to be properly appreciated. Explaining the idea for this work later, Bliss said that he had first thought of it when looking at a book on heraldry. He said then, in sharp contrast to his earlier view:

I have always found it easier to write 'dramatic' music than 'pure' music. I like the stimulus of words, or a theatrical setting, a colourful occasion or the collaboration of a great player. There is only a little of the spider about me, spinning his own web from his inner being. I am more of a magpie type. I need what Henry James termed a 'trouvaille' or a 'donnée'.

(A visual impetus was, half a century later, to provide the stimulation for another of Bliss's works, the *Metamorphic Variations* of 1972.)

The *Colour Symphony* is an episodic work of four movements based on purple, red, blue and green. It was received with mixed feelings after an inadequate performance; familiar problems, such as badly copied parts and insufficient rehearsal time, were to blame for this. Bliss was disappointed: he had worked hard on the symphony in Vaughan Williams's London house, where he had found the companionship of the other composer and his friends very helpful. The symphony did however suggest that Bliss was going to be a composer to be reckoned with in the future and that he would not long be saddled with the unenviable label of being the 'latest thing' in music.

A settled pattern began to emerge in Bliss's life, a pattern supported by his private income. His time was given over to either his family or his music, for composition did not claim him at all times. He later wrote, 'I know the rhythm of my musical life very well, and can judge the intervals during which my extrovert side must exert itself.' Bliss liked to mix his music, which he felt he had inherited from his mother, with his practical abilities, which he thought came from his father. (During the Second World War he worked for a while for the BBC in London, where he was able to show his administrative powers to the full.) Bliss also greatly enjoyed travelling and for two years after the *Colour Symphony* he lived in the United States. Here he met his wife Trudy, with whom the rest of his life was to be closely bound. (When George Moore once asked her in a loud voice at the Tate Gallery 'Do you admit many lovers?', all he managed to do was amuse Bliss.) The young man who had lived it up in Paris, who had dashed across Europe after a young dancer with whom he was having a love affair, who had been the bright young thing of English music, who had once composed a piece of music entitled *In the Tube at Oxford Circus*, was now settling into the more graceful role which was to carry him through his career.

Returning to England Bliss and his wife embarked on a life that was busy and successful. Like Delius, Bliss numbered among his friends some of the leading artistic lights of his day and was especially interested in contemporary painting and sculpture. This interest he shared with his close friend Bernard van Dieren, who introduced him to Epstein. (Van Dieren was a Dutch composer who lived for most of his adult life in London and whose work was for a while much admired by writers and musicians, particularly Philip Heseltine.) Bliss was also friends with Ben Nicholson, Barbara Hepworth and a multitude of other artists. He later wrote, 'for me, visits to the studios of painters act as a greater incentive to work than any amount of talk with fellow-musicians. In looking at the struggle for realized form in a sculptor's or painter's work I find something that instructs me in my own art.' Bliss was also interested in modern architecture, as the house he had built in Somerset by the architect Peter Harland shows. In addition Bliss's letters reveal the fruits of wide reading: his favourite authors were Dostoevsky, Chekhov and Henry James. His was an artistic family. His wife compiled a selection of the letters of Jane Welsh Carlyle (curiously, John Ireland's mother had also done an edition of her letters), and both his daughters took to the stage: one as an actress, the other as a ballet dancer. At the end of his life Bliss looked happily back on the life of his family and on 'fortune' which 'has permitted me to work at what I best love, music'.

Bliss became something of an ambassador for English music. In 1922 he travelled with Boult to Prague to do a concert of British music there (which included works by Elgar, Butterworth and Vaughan Williams). His interest in the International Society for Contemporary Music brought him into touch with many of the leading musical figures of the Continent, German as well as French (he grew to have a great respect for Hindemith and also Schoenberg). Later he visited many other countries, including, after the Second World War, the Soviet Union, where he established close relations with contemporary composers. He acted also on the juries for international competitions and, on the death of Arnold Bax, was made Master of the Queen's Music. The occasional music that he produced for this post, in the best Elgarian tradition, was among his most popular work.

Bliss's musical output covers a very wide range. He wrote an opera, *The Olympians*, to a libretto by J.B. Priestley, which was put on at Covent Garden in 1949. Insufficient rehearsal time and the fact that relations between the producer Peter Brook and conductor Karl Rankl deteriorated to such a point that they were unable to speak to each other contributed to the mixed reception that it received. Bliss's music for the ballet was treated much more kindly and *Checkmate* (1937), *Miracle in the Gorbals* (1944) and, to a lesser extent, *Adam Zero* (1946) proved to be great successes. Early in his career he wrote incidental music for the theatre; unlike some other composers Bliss was later able to develop this talent for dramatic music in a very different way in his music for films; especially in his well-known score for the film of H.G. Wells's book *The Shape of Things to Come*. Bliss also wrote good music for brass bands.

One musical form that Bliss was to make his own, and which was later also taken up by Benjamin Britten with great effect, was the anthology choral piece. The detailed history of English choral music remains to be written but there can be no doubt of the close relationship between the festival cantatas of the Parry/Elgar world and the anthology choral pieces of the new generation. The first of Bliss's works in this form was his *Pastoral: 'Lie Strewn the White Flocks'* of 1928, a setting of words from Ben Jonson, Fletcher, Poliziano, Theocritus and Robert Nichols. This piece, which was dedicated to Elgar, grew from Bliss's wish to depict 'a Sicilian day from dawn to evening'. Elgar, who had been afraid that Bliss would turn out to be a mere 'paragraphist', was generous in his praise of this work: he wrote to Bliss of its '*large* and *fine* scale, and I like it *exceedingly*'. Another striking anthology work was Bliss's *Morning Heroes* of 1930. The composer later explained that he had written this work, 'as a tribute to my brother and all my other comrades-in-arms who fell in the Great War of 1914-18. Each of its five movements describes an aspect of war common to all ages and to all times.' The texts were taken from Homer's *Iliad*, Walt Whitman, Li-Po, Wilfred Owen and, as Bliss wrote, 'finally the chorus sing a poem by Robert Nichols in which, as the sun rises over the "scarred plateau" of the Somme, the words "Morning Heroes" occur, from which this symphony takes its title'. Although Bliss called the finished work a symphony it is, like the *Colour Symphony*, more episodic than a traditional example of that form. Bliss's other choral works included settings of single poets, as in *A Song of Welcome* from C. Day Lewis (1954), and the *Golden Cantata* with words by Kathleen Raine. Bliss got on well with Kathleen Raine, who later wrote to him, 'the words were like tacking stitches in the sewing (useful while working), but the work is all yours'. In his later years choral compositions became especially important to him, especially in collaboration with the poet and librettist Christopher Hassall (*Book of Tobit*, *The Beatitudes* and *Mary of Magdala*).

Bliss's works also include orchestral pieces, notably the *Meditations on a Theme of John Blow* of 1955, a Piano Concerto, a Violin Concerto and a Cello Concerto. (This last was first performed at the Aldeburgh Festival in 1970 where it was conducted by Britten with the English Chamber Orchestra: of this work Bliss wrote 'there are no problems for the listener, only for the soloist'.) Bliss also composed some important chamber music, which he turned to as a welcome change from the demands of the larger forms. In this field his inspiration often came from a specific individual: Frederick Thurston (clarinet), Leon Goossens (oboe), Lionel Tertis (viola), Soloman (piano), Campoli (violin), and Rostropovich (cello). The emphasis in Bliss's *oeuvre*, unlike many earlier English composers, is not on the world of domestic music: there is little piano music and few individual songs. (This, in some part, is a measure of the new musical world that was then coming into being.) His works taken as a whole show a sure command of technique and a lively imagination. Bliss himself wrote, 'If my music is to make any impression it must move on, and not be static; that is the very essence of my own character', and this feeling of movement is a marked and attractive aspect of his work. His catalogue of works is impressive, and it is interesting that his output was high in the later years of his life: many of his orchestral and choral works date from the 1950s and 1960s. He chose to spend much of his time away from composing but the works that he did produce all have a great confidence and certainty about them that confirms that as a composer he knew himself well. If we take him as a further central figure in the renaissance of English music, Bliss's confidence is most revealing. He stands in the middle of a process whereby preceding English composers had built sure foundations for younger musicians, who were in their turn to give an inheritance of yet greater worth to those who followed them.

It was typical of Bliss as a man that when he got caught in the United States at the outbreak of the Second World War he determined to get back to England as soon as possible, because 'whatever growth I had attained I owed to that country's traditions of thought and design of living'. Both as an individual and as a composer Bliss was recognizably English. Thinking of the immediate post-First World War period when Stravinsky's music set the pace throughout Europe, Bliss later said, 'I got bored with this musical Esperanto. I prefer infinite variety in all aspects of life, whether in cooking, language, architecture or music. I hope the distinctive and refreshing flavour of regional genius will always have a welcome.' Bliss was not the kind to folk-dance round the English village green but his music is as markedly English as many of those who did go in for the folk style. His musical energy and the range of emotions his work betrays also clearly belong to an English tradition.

From the early days of providing a piece for the great choral festival at Gloucester to writing *Tobias and the Angel*, an opera for television in 1959, Bliss was keenly interested in the music of England. At the end of 1935, for example, he went on a tour of 'Musical Britain' for the *Listener* magazine, and one can tell from reading his articles that this was an experience he greatly enjoyed. He also cared deeply about bringing music to a wide public, and during the war, as Musical Director of the BBC, he strove to uphold high standards. His travels to play British music overseas were also important to him. His life and works bear testimony to the strength of the great tradition that grew up in the days of Parry and Elgar and was carried forward by the generation of pupils of the 1890s. In his early days as a composer Bliss openly broke with all the obvious traditions of pre-war music, but this was not a phase of his life that lasted long. He soon returned to one of his first loves, the music of Elgar, and became himself a central thread in the mainstream of English music running from Elgar to Britten. From a mix of the traditional and the advanced in music Bliss made a style all his own. His contemporaries – like John Ireland, who referred to him as 'one of the few really authoritative and representative voices of British music' – knew his musical worth. Like Walton and, in a different way, Vaughan Williams, Bliss's music has yet to be given its proper value by present-day audiences; but the great pendulum of public interest that so surely swings away from all major English composers shortly after their death will, in his case, as surely one day swing back again.

Bliss's work is above all suffused with Bliss himself: a man of great charm who drew the best out of himself and those around him, and who knew how to draw the best from his own native musical traditions. In a recorded discussion in 1974 Bliss neatly summarized his musical beliefs when he said, 'I demand from music not what I demanded as a young man, which was sound and sound only.... I now demand enhancement of life, which means that I must feel behind this music a great personality telling me something about experience that I haven't had before. That's what I want.'

Arthur Bliss's failure to sustain his role as the *enfant terrible* of English music in the 1920s concentrated attention on to another composer, William Walton. Walton seemed to have all the necessary qualifications for the post: he was very young, he was untouched by the musical styles of the pre-war period, and – this was thought to be a great bonus at the time – he had had no formal musical training in any of the London music schools. The Sitwell family fell upon Walton with relish, but this was not perhaps to the composer's advantage. Osbert Sitwell later wrote that he regarded the influence of himself, his brother Sacheverell and sister Edith as the reason why Walton did not attend one of the London music schools, and he came to realize that this had not been an entirely wise move. Walton's extreme youth at this period, however, allowed him time to rework his musical style, to emerge from the various associations of the 1920s, and to develop as a composer of important musical works that could stand firmly on their own. And this later development of Walton as a major composer is really much more remarkable than his notoriety in the 1920s.

William Walton was born in Oldham in 1902; his father was a choir-master and singing-teacher who had been trained at the Royal Manchester College of Music. The composer thus belonged to the second generation of the renaissance of music 'made in England'. Moreover his family lived in Hallé territory. It was a reasonably promising beginning. Walton was entered for and won a place at Christ Church Cathedral, Oxford as a chorister and here he was able to acquaint himself with the great traditions of English cathedral music. Walton was lucky in the support that he received at Oxford, especially from Thomas Strong, then Dean of Christ Church, who helped with the financing of his education. Parry also took an interest in Walton at this stage. Strong encouraged the sixteen-year-old Walton to become an undergraduate of his college but the young musician was not able to pass the necessary examinations in Greek and algebra and left the university in 1920.

For the next decade or so Walton joined the Sitwell circle in London, living with them for much of the time. Osbert Sitwell's account of this relationship can be found in his *Laughter in the Next Room*, where Walton is shown as a withdrawn hard-working young man. Sitwell wrote, 'we already possessed among our friends an undoubted and more mature musical genius, Bernard van Dieren', but on the urging of his brother he took up the young Walton, whom the Sitwells soon regarded as an 'adopted, or elected, brother'. Osbert's impression of Walton was that he was shy and silent:

most of the summer days he appeared to spend in his room at the top of the house, where he sat by the window for long periods, eating black-heart cherries from a paper bag, and throwing the stones out of the window, down on to the smooth brown-tiled pavement outside the door. Swan Walk was so quiet that there was only to be heard a distant booming of traffic, and nearer, this dry, staccato rattle of cherry stones.

Sitwell goes on, 'soon a piano was hired for him, and in consequence he remained in his room for longer periods even than before ...'.

Without any formal training in composition but with an obvious talent that had already been noticed by many people, Walton worked hard on his own. It took him a while to fit into the Sitwell world. Osbert's musical friends included Bernard van Dieren and Lord Berners, and soon Constant Lambert, who was still, like Walton, very young. Sitwell noted that Walton also made friends of his own, especially Philip Heseltine (not a favourite of Sitwell's) and George Gershwin. At this time Walton also met Ernest Ansermet and Busoni, who gave him advice on, and encouragement with, his early works; he had made a promising start.

Walton first came to a wider musical public's attention in 1923 when a work of his was performed at the first festival of the International Society for Contemporary Music (ISCM) at Salzburg. He travelled there with the two Sitwell brothers, and in the company of Lord Berners was taken by Alban Berg to visit Schoenberg. Berg greeted Walton, according to Sitwell, as 'the leader of English atonal music', a curious description not borne out at all by later developments, but interesting as it reveals the sort of reputation that Walton was then acquiring. There followed the first performance in London of Walton's music for Edith Sitwell's *Façade*. The story of this is told in a colourful account by Osbert: the sense of outrage that the first public performance created is vividly conveyed. Even the fireman at the Aeolian Hall, asked for his opinion, said that 'never in twenty years' experience of recitals at that hall had he known anything like it'. The audience were surprised that neither the reciter of the poems nor the musicians were visible, and that all they could see was a painted curtain with an open mouth in it through which the reader recited with the aid of a Sengerphone – a loud-speaking device originally devised by a singer to help his performance of the role of Fafner in Wagner's *Ring*. The primary purpose of the work was to 'exalt the speaking voice to the level of the instruments supporting it'; it provided a wonderfully effective vehicle for Edith Sitwell's experiments with the rhythm, speed, colour and rhyme of words:

When
Sir
Beelzebub called for his syllabub in the hotel in Hell
      Where Proserpine first fell,
Blue as the gendarmerie were the waves of the sea....

That this might be a taste of the music of the future was, however, too dreadful a thought for many of the critics. 'Surely it is time this sort of thing were stopped', one of them wrote. The incomprehension, even hostility, between the old and the new generations was profound. In 1927, for example, Walton and Osbert Sitwell travelled down to the music-loving financier Frank Schuster's house for a private performance of one of Elgar's works. Two musical worlds stared at each other over the gulf created by the First World War. Sitwell wrote of the 'gathering which, apart from Arnold Bennett and Dorothy Cheston Bennett, and a few others, was chiefly made up of people who were strangers to me'. To Sitwell these were the 'floccose herds of good-time Edwardian ghosts, with trousers thus beautifully pressed and suits of the best material, carrying panama hats or glossy bowlers, or decked and loaded with fur and feather. ... The glossy motors waited outside to carry them home, like the vans drawn up to take the fine beasts away from an agriculture show.'

The 1920s was the period *par excellence* of the vogue for modern French music, of ceaseless experimentation, of breaking away from the forms that had dominated musical life before the First World War. That Walton was an important part of this movement is certain but, unlike many others of his generation, Walton escaped from it. As a musician he went on to develop his talents fully and he produced a steady succession of good musical works. Unlike Lambert and Heseltine, Walton was not blighted with a despair of the world and he was able to see a way forward for his music at a time when many of his contemporaries had turned aside from composition or had burnt themselves out. Walton's generation was, after its initial impact, something of a 'lost generation'. But Walton himself, like Bliss, was able to concentrate his powers on his music and he made considerable headway in his career. And, also like Bliss, Walton lived a much quieter life than that enjoyed by many of his contemporaries. He was helped in this by the generosity of friends and admirers – notably Mrs Samuel Courtauld and Lady Wimborne. He later met and married Susanna Gil, an Argentinian many years his junior, with whom he lived on the island of Ischia until his death in 1983.

Throughout the 1920s and the 1930s Walton produced a number of works which received attention in England, in Europe, and in the United States. After *Façade* he engaged in a study of contemporary jazz; he tried writing pieces in the jazz style but he abandoned this 'in a fit of disgust'. His next important works were *Portsmouth Point*, an overture based on a print by Thomas Rowlandson, and *Siesta*, a short work for small orchestra, full of Mediterranean atmosphere. Neither of these works marked any further experimentation for Walton: indeed, the wind had changed and was beginning to blow the other way already. *Portsmouth Point* owes something to Philip Heseltine's interest in early English dance music, with its sections titled 'Sarabande', 'Corante' and 'Brawles'. At this time also Walton had begun work on a ballet score for Diaghilev, but the great impresario turned it down on the grounds that he thought Walton would write better things in the future. The work that he did for the projected ballet was, however, used instead in his *Sinfonia Concertante* for orchestra and piano, which was completed in 1927. (Walton revised this work in 1943.) It is dedicated to the Sitwells, with Osbert, Edith and Sacheverell being the inspiration of a movement each.

This ballet score that became a symphonic work with its salute to the Sitwells marks the end of one phase in Walton's career. His next work, the Viola Concerto, belongs to a period of Walton's life when, slowly but surely, the popular view of him as a modernist changed and he came to be regarded as one of the conservative pillars of English music. Throughout the 1930s, however, Walton was still thought of as an important modern composer, albeit now a widely 'acceptable' one. Osbert Sitwell recalled an occasion in 1941 when he returned to the Aeolian Hall for a performance of *Façade* and found that even the fireman 'seemed to have reconsidered his original aesthetic estimate of the entertainment'. By the 1950s – after a second world war, as damaging as the first to the traditional patterns of musical life – there were many who came to regard Walton's music in the sort of light that the bright young things of the 1920s had reserved for Elgar and the 'Edwardian ghosts'.

Had there been a great change in Walton's life or music that explains the shift in the reception that his new works came to be given? Walton was a very reserved and private person who worked steadily at his music, and he gave only a few non-musical clues as to how we might answer this question. In 1926, however, he said, 'When I sit down to write music, I never trouble about modernism or anything else. I certainly never try to write for today or even for tomorrow, but to compose something which will have the same merit whatever time it is performed.' Walton's head was, in fact, never seriously turned by the great excitement which surrounded him in his early days. Nor did the later reverse in his public reception seem to unduly worry him. In 1939 he rightly observed that 'today's white hope is tomorrow's black sheep'. Neither the plaudits of the 1920s nor being shunned by later generations of fashion-mongers seriously interrupted his music.

Walton's musical flow was steady, but the number of works produced was not spectacular. His Viola Concerto of 1929 was followed two years later by *Belshazzar's Feast*. The years of the 1930s saw his Symphony No. 1, and in 1940 he produced his Violin Concerto. The post-war years continued this pattern of infrequent but major works with the appearance of an opera, *Troilus and Cressida*, a chamber opera, *The Bear* (1967), the Symphony No. 2 (1960), a cello concerto, *Variations on a Theme by Hindemith* (1963) and *Improvisations on an Impromptu of Benjamin Britten* (1970). There is virtually none of the piano music and songs that so fill the catalogue of other composers' works. Walton stuck, in fact, to the major forms that belonged to the mainstream Classical/Romantic tradition. He was also quite capable of composing impressive choral works – as *Belshazzar's Feast* shows. Here Walton took on the most traditional of all forms of English music and did so on one of its strongest home grounds – the work was first performed at the Leeds Festival of 1931. It was greeted by many as the most important English choral work since *Gerontius*. There must have been those in the early 1920s who thought that the advent of such works as *Façade* spelt the disappearance of works like *Belshazzar's Feast*; how quickly things had changed.

Walton was, in fact, developing into a quite recognizably Elgarian figure in other ways also. Elgar's mantle as the musician of important state ceremonial occasions fell in part on Walton. Walton's own contributions to this sort of music included *Crown Imperial, Orb and Sceptre*, the *Spitfire Prelude and Fugue* and *March, A History of the English-Speaking Peoples*. Walton was a composer who, like Elgar, could write works that were keenly anticipated by a wide general public. His output in this field was small but in his choral works he achieved importance. His concertos and symphonies were also well received and, compared to the works of other contemporary composers, frequently played. Like Elgar he also wrote for brass bands and occasional music for the stage. It is interesting to see the number of parallels between the works of Elgar and Walton – even down to the orchestrated version of Walton's *Music for*

*Children* which in some ways resembles the *Wand of Youth* suites – parallels which show, in some part at least, how much of the traditional English musical background Walton had picked up in his very early years; especially, as he himself pointed out, as a chorister at Oxford and from the Professor of Music there at the time, Hugh Allen.

Like Elgar, Walton was first and foremost a writer of major music not, like so many other of his contemporaries, a miniaturist. Frank Howes wrote of Walton, 'He thinks in themes, textures and structures rather than in transcripts of visual and verbal images and concepts.' That Walton belonged to an Elgarian tradition of English concerted music became more and more obvious as the years went by. Walton, for all Berg's greetings in 1923, never developed an atonal style, sticking firmly within a conventional – if very fluid – tonality. The 'bitter-sweet' quality in his music that is frequently remarked upon is also a marked characteristic of a kind of developed Classical-Romanticism; but while he could be as mellow as many of the more tender traditional Romantics he could also be as sharp as a modern wit when he chose.

In an interview that Walton gave to Murray Schafer (one of an important series of interviews with modern British composers published in 1963) he was asked if he would object to being called a 'Romantic' composer. The composer replied, ' "Romantic" can mean so many things. If anything, I would say I am a classical composer with a strong feeling for lyricism. I'm probably one of the few composers who dare admit their liking for such unfashionable composers as Brahms or Sibelius.' Walton went on to say that his music had, however, never been consciously inspired by nature. His inspiration came from other sources. Like Bliss a visual image could inspire music in him. Two of his works took their starting-points from drawings: *Portsmouth Point* from a drawing by Rowlandson, and *Scapino* from one by Callot. As with Bliss, and also later Britten, Walton responded well to specific commissions; the Violin Concerto was for Jascha Heifetz and that for cello for Gregor Piatigorsky.

One area where Walton became very well known to a wider audience was film-music. Like Bliss he began writing for films in 1935, producing the music for *Escape Me Never* while Bliss was working on *Things To Come*. Walton's music for *Richard III* and *Henry V* showed, in particular, how much he was able to write in an obviously 'English' musical idiom if he chose to do so. He also wrote appropriate music for the 'patriotic' films he worked on during the Second World War. These scores became popular outside the immediate context of the films for which they were written, although Walton himself said that he was 'inclined to doubt the value of film-music on its own' as the music was so bound up with visual cues from the film itself.

Through a number of musical forms, then, Walton kept in touch with a wide musical audience, although he actually lived in Italy from the time of his marriage in 1948 until his death in 1983. Walton told Schafer that he believed living in Italy had 'possibly made my music more British than it might have been had I stayed at home. One sometimes feels a great deal of nostalgia when one is absent from England for long. I don't think there is any escaping the background and tradition one was born into.' Walton also felt that composers in the 1960s were relying on only a 'small audience of trained musicians' to appreciate what they were doing and that there was 'too much dogma surrounding music today – too many "isms" and all taken too seriously. I feel it is like living under Oliver Cromwell or any puritanical dictatorship. Now it is time for some Charles II with his mistresses and drinking and general relaxing qualities.'

The image of Walton of the 1920s – particularly of the *Façade* episode – still lingers in some people's minds. Too often he is still thought of as an English extension of Les Six. But, as Hugh Ottaway, the writer and lecturer, has recently pointed out, Walton was never really one of the intellectual modernists of the 1920s. From the letters and memoirs of Walton that have been published (we wait eagerly for the promised major biography of the composer) we can see that his life was perhaps not a simple one in emotional terms. As a composer he was in many ways a very lucky man. Through the generosity of those around him he escaped the financial privations and the need to take on uncongenial work that affected many other English composers although he did not really begin to earn any substantial sums from his music until he began to write for films in 1935. Walton was also fortunate in the conductors who championed his work: initially Sargent and Harty, then Szell and Previn. His usual speed of work was extremely slow: at one point in *Belshazzar's Feast* he got stuck on one specific passage for around seven months. (He could, however, also work at an almost unbelievable speed on occasion: in its earliest form *Façade* was composed in three weeks.) There were also considerable gaps between major works in his composing career – gaps sometimes of many years.

Like Arthur Bliss, Walton acted as a kind of ambassador for British music in his later days: he toured Australia in 1964 and the Soviet Union in 1971. Walton, like Bliss, shared also much of Elgar's mantle as the 'national' composer at home. But for all the similarities that we have observed, comparison between Elgar and Walton can easily be overdone. Walton knew the real value of Elgar's music. In 1942, when popular opinion of Elgar was very low, Walton proclaimed, 'I have unbounded admiration for Elgar.... There's no other English composer to touch him. He's bigger than Delius, bigger than Vaughan Williams. He's becoming bigger all the time. Consider his *Falstaff*. It's much finer than any of Strauss's tone poems. Some day that will be generally accepted.' But Walton was a very different man and a very different musician. The most important lesson he learnt from Elgar's example was that a composer should not be a slave to any school of composition but, rather, should turn in on himself and listen carefully to his own voice.

As an older man Walton pointed out how much easier it had become for a composer to make a living through composition and how much more of an affluent business contemporary music now was. But because things were getting easier it did not necessarily mean that they were getting better. Walton saw composers who now wrote 'diatonic music for films and ultra-modern music for themselves; one kind for the élite and one kind for the mob'. The secret of the success of the major English composers of the main period of the renaissance had been that they never adopted this dual approach. In Walton's music one can always hear the meticulous craftsman's care that he took to ensure that while his music would mean something to his audience it was also of the very best. This was a remarkable talent and, as the music critic Felix Aprahamian rightly wrote, 'The public has never had any doubt about Walton.'

Walton and Bliss, then, both escaped their early reputations as rebels to establish themselves as considerable figures in the English musical renaissance. Others who came to notice at roughly the same period did not fare so well, either in their lives or their music, although each of the four composers in the remaining part of this chapter wrote music of some importance. The concerns, beliefs and ideas that went to make up the musical life of the new young men of the 1920s in England can be seen to no better advantage than in the life and work of Constant Lambert. Writing in 1934 in his celebrated book *Music Ho! A Study of Music in Decline*, Constant Lambert felt that he had reached a position where he was able to pull together the various strands of the post-war musical world. (This, of course, was the self-same year that saw the deaths of Elgar, Delius and Holst.) The 1930s were a period when various music writers sharpened their pens to keen points as van Dieren's *Down among the Dead Men* and the music writer and critic Cecil Gray's *A Survey of Contemporary Music* show. But of this group Lambert could not only write very sharply, as some of his music criticism shows, but he also had an unusually acute understanding of many of the developments then taking place in music. *Music Ho!* is one of the very few books on music of the period that is still worth reading today.

Lambert's view was that music always had to be seen in its social context. He gave examples of how the music of the past had been linked to its period in history: Mozart's *The Marriage of Figaro* and eighteenth-century aristocratic classicism, for example. He pointed to the great modern revolutionary period of music in Europe which had begun before the First World War and which was associated especially with the names of Debussy and Schoenberg. He believed that the years in which he lived and worked were part of an age of consolidation and he turned his attention to considering the various solutions offered by contemporary composers. Lambert was critical of Stravinsky, Hindemith and Honegger and of the coteries that gathered round these composers. He felt that the hope for music lay, rather, with men like Sibelius, Busoni and van Dieren.

*Music Ho!* caused great interest when it was first published and as a picture of the musical life of the 1920s it is invaluable. (Lambert wrote in the preface to the reprint of 1948 that he felt it was not the sort of book that could be brought up to date. It is a period piece and especially valuable as such.) To many people, however, Lambert is only really known as the composer of *The Rio Grande* and of ballets for the Sadler's Wells Company. Those who know something about the wild artistic life in London at this period might also be aware of the many personal problems that Lambert faced. But it is a mistake to underestimate him. His achievements were substantial and both his music and his writing have remained alive and interesting, which is much more than can be said of the output of many of his contemporaries.

Constant Lambert was born in 1905; as a child he had poor health. His schooling was at Christ's Hospital, and in 1922 he won a scholarship to the Royal College of Music. Here Lambert became a pupil of the new generation of teachers who had taken over since the First World War. The pupils of the 1890s had become the teachers of the 1920s. So

Lambert's teacher for composition was Vaughan Williams, who recognized real talent in the young man. Lambert was, however, subject to very different influences from those which existed at the turn of the century. He loved jazz and the prevailing vogue for the exotic (he fell passionately in love with the film actress Anna May Wong, for example). As a student he was particularly interested in French and Russian music, and like many of his contemporaries turned his back on the Austro-German tradition. One of Lambert's college pieces, *Prize-Fight*, shows us the direction he was taking. This 'Realistic Ballet in One Act' had a synopsis written by the composer which clearly reveals a strong French influence:

A boxing ring (in confusion). A noisy group enters. The referee attempts to announce the programme and to obtain silence (in vain!).... He introduces first the white man (a popular figure), then a Negro (a man of sullen disposition).... The bell sounds. The boxers proceed gingerly from their corners. (NB during the round the blows on the stage are registered off-stage by machines making the sound of breaking glass, horses' hooves, motor horns etc. ad lib.)

Lambert was a man for his times and was recognized as such by the lions of his day. He was friends with the Sitwells and their group. He was thought of as one of the men who would take a brush to the old musical world and claim the new. During the 1920s and early 1930s Lambert was regarded as one of the most exciting and promising composers of the day, as fashionable society turned its back on Elgar and the other composers who were considered to be Germanists or Romantics.

Like other composers of this period Lambert came to public attention at a very young age. At twenty he was invited to compose a ballet for Diaghilev, a notable honour at the time. Lambert worked hard on *Romeo and Juliet* with the painter Christopher Wood, who was to design the sets and the costumes, but there was trouble in staging the work and Diaghilev dropped Wood's designs in favour of others by Max Ernst and Joan Miró. This greatly angered Lambert and he tried to withdraw the music. This was a brave step for a young composer and it caused a breach with Diaghilev. The trouble did not end there, however; in Paris Louis Aragon and André Breton – the vanguard of the Surrealist movement – incited a riot at the first night because of Ernst and Miró's 'defection' to the 'capitalist' Diaghilev, as they saw it. Lambert was learning to swim at the deep end.

After his dispute with Diaghilev a rather barren period ensued, in which Lambert had no regular income. He earned what he could by playing for dancing classes and by occasional journalism. He continued to write music and in 1929 he enjoyed a second moment of fame when *The Rio Grande* was first given in concert performances in Manchester and London. This setting – of a poem by Sacheverell Sitwell – was especially championed by the composer and conductor Hamilton Harty. It was greeted by the popular press as 'jazz changed into music of genius', and the work became a favourite at once. But, as Lambert's biographer Richard Shead has pointed out, 'to hail a man not yet twenty-five as a genius is not necessarily to do him a service'.

As a composer Lambert was highly thought of at this time but, unlike Walton, he was not able to sustain this interest. This was in part because of the many other activities that he undertook – especially his work in the early days of the Vic-Wells Ballet as conductor and musical director. During the 1930s and the 1940s the Vic-Wells Ballet and a variety of other similar organizations (such as the Carmargo Society, of which he was musical director from 1931-47) were at the centre of Lambert's life and work, and at this time he wrote considerably less music than before. With Ninette de Valois and Frederick Ashton he formed the basis on which the Vic-Wells Company was to grow and become one of the most successful of all musical ventures of the inter-war years. Lambert stayed with the company through the difficult years of the Second World War and when it was impossible to have proper orchestras he would often play the piano himself or act as the reciter for the performances that were put on.

After the war Covent Garden became the home of Sadler's Wells Ballet, as the Vic-Wells Company had become, but Lambert did not long survive there. There were a number of reasons for his break with the company, not least his frequent excessive drinking. Lambert had never enjoyed perfect health and he had lived a highly active life. Following his departure from the ballet company in 1947 his decline in health continued and he died in 1951 at the age of forty-six. Many of life's major events had come too early to Lambert.

As a composer Lambert never achieved the early promise that he once seemed to show. He knew his limitations: according to the painter Michael Ayrton, Lambert 'described himself carefully as a good second rank composer'. The years before the attachment to the ballet company were the most productive of his life in terms of composition and ensured for him a lasting reputation; but the composer himself came to regret the great popularity that one of his works of this period – *The Rio Grande* – had over all his others. One result of his early popularity was the public's reluctance to listen properly to his later, more ambitious works such as *Summer's Last Will and Testament*, a 'Masque' for orchestra, choir and baritone solo to words by Thomas Nashe, which received only a lukewarm reception. The composer of slick ballet pieces was not really expected to turn out serious works.

Lambert belonged to the hectic world of 'Old Bloomsbury (district of laughter, district of tears)', as he once referred to it. His friendships extended in many directions. In the musical world he belonged to a group which included William Walton, Bernard van Dieren, Philip Heseltine and the music writer Cecil Gray. He knew most of the Bloomsbury literary figures well and was highly thought of by them. Many painters were his friends, particularly Christopher Wood and Michael Ayrton (Lambert's father had been a well-known portraitist and his brother was a sculptor); he also knew several writers (he shared a house for a while with Peter Quennell), and politicians – notably Tom Driberg. The author Anthony Powell was also a close friend and the figure of Moreland in Powell's *A Dance to the Music of Time* owes much to Lambert.

Lambert was known both as an exuberant man and a melancholic one. His many friends attest to his great charm; but there was a dark side to him as well. It became increasingly apparent over the years that he – like Heseltine and van Dieren – drank far more than was wise. His drinking never interfered with his musical performance but in his later years his health began to decline seriously and with it his good humour. His was, in many respects, a sad life. A man who Osbert Sitwell thought was 'the most lively, quick, well-informed and in general most intelligent young man I had ever met' destroyed himself with a style of life that ill-served his talent.

As a musician and the author of *Music Ho!* Lambert's place in the history of twentieth-century English music is, however, secure. He was the most articulate of the new young English composers. Lambert's generation had much greater opportunities to share in the general life of European music than earlier English composers had had. His association with Diaghilev brought him into touch with contemporary musical events in Europe, as did the festivals of the International Society for Contemporary Music. (E.J. Dent, a moving spirit behind the society, was a great admirer of Lambert's.) *Music Ho!*, unlike, say, Elgar's or

Vaughan William's written work, ranges widely over the music of the Continent. But we should not imagine that a man whose horizon stretched from Russia to Spain did not also have a very special interest in English music. *Music Ho!* shows that Lambert had thought carefully about what an English composer should be, and although in many respects his views are utterly different from Vaughan Williams's, whose *National Music* was published in the same year as *Music Ho!*, one also notices many points of similarity.

Lambert, as the voice of the new generation, saw the dangers of the 'narrow critical outlook' that can come with nationalism in music. He agreed with Vaughan Williams that the contemporary view of music as an 'international language' was 'obviously untrue'. (To illustrate what he thought of as an 'international language' in music he pointed to the composers of the eighteenth century as possessing a common musical language 'comparable to the Latin in which medieval savants carried on their arguments'.) Lambert held the view that, 'It is fairly easy for the modern composer, reacting against the passionate nationalism of recent musical movements, to rid himself of parochialism not by intensifying his thought but by denuding it, and to reach universality through nullity.' Having sounded this clear warning Lambert went on to point out specific problems with the use of folk-song in composition, problems which were resolved by a composer of the stature of Vaughan Williams during his career but perhaps by few of his imitators in theirs. 'To put it vulgarly, the whole trouble with a folk-song is that once you have played it through there is nothing much you can do except play it over again and play it rather louder', Lambert observed with dry humour.

For all such views, however, Lambert subscribed to two of the basic beliefs held by Elgar and Vaughan Williams. First, that there was a 'positive influence of a tradition that is in our blood', and, second, that there was also a 'negative stimulus of something that has deliberately to be fought against'. The 'stupider composers', when faced with contemporary circumstances, 'escape from the situation either by an empty and wilful pastiche of an older tradition or by an equally fruitless concentration on the purely mechanical and objective sides of their arts'. Lambert is sometimes portrayed as something of an iconoclast (this is probably to do with his rather 'racy' image) but his book shows no great evidence of this. Like Vaughan Williams and Elgar in their own ways, he wanted to see young English composers cease to ape the form and style of past masters of the Continent and he thought that the best way for them to do this was to draw on their own tradition, being careful to distinguish the real from the humbug.

Lambert was not himself at all drawn to the folk-music school in England *per se*, although he believed that there was a real case for the use of folk-song in Russian music. He felt that folk-song meant something very different to an average Russian than it did to the English: he could imagine a Petrograd coachman singing tunes of the type found in *Boris Godunov* while not being able to picture a London bus-conductor singing the type to be found in Vaughan Williams's *Hugh the Drover*.

At the same time Lambert was able to see the virtues of the English folk-song movement in providing 'an excellent *pied-à-terre* for those who not unnaturally wished to rid English music of the intolerable accretion of German clichés that had been strangling its growth for a hundred years or so'. By the time of writing his book, however, he felt that the folk-song revival had run its useful course: 'this rustic arbour is now showing signs of imminent collapse, and since the Shropshire Lad himself published his last poems some ten years ago it may without impertinence be suggested that it is high time his musical followers published their last songs'. Lambert also rejected the German tradition that he felt was personified in England by Elgar and he explained why Elgar's music had lost much of its appeal for young musicians:

> It is more than probable that, but for the social and spiritual changes brought about by the war, Elgar would have been a more potent influence on English music than Vaughan Williams.... Much of Elgar's music, through no fault of its own, has for the present generation an almost intolerable air of smugness, self-assurance and autocratic benevolence.

Having cleared himself a space in the dense undergrowth of English music Lambert faced the problem of how to find out what was 'genuinely vital in English civilization at the moment'. He believed that to be honest the artist must 'accept a work like Eliot's *Waste Land* as symbolizing the essentially negative and bleak spirit of post-war intellectual England. Yet what a rejection of lyrical impulse this acception involves!' But Lambert's main anxieties about music were also wider than this. He wrote, in one of the best passages of his book, of the 'appalling popularity' of music: how music was invading every area of life and how the more music one heard the less one paid attention to. The gramophone and, especially, the wireless – 'the loud speaker is the street walker of music', he wrote – were spreading music everywhere and at all times. 'In the present age it is impossible to escape from Culture, and the wholesale and wholetime diffusion of musical culture will eventually produce in us, when we hear a Bach concerto, the faint nausea felt towards a piece of toffee by a worker in a sweet factory.'

Lambert's own music did not, however, really set out to solve any of the problems that he so ably outlined in his literary work. He never pretended that he had the answers and pointed to other composers as possible leaders towards a better future. He had a deep concern about the music of the future: for a time when music would be completely taken for granted and the 'high-brow' in music would go off on its own away from a mainstream national musical life. This was not what he wanted to see. When he staged Purcell's *The Fairy Queen* he thought, for example, that 'the greatest and most intelligent tribute I received was not from any academic source but from my local greengrocer'. Making a similar point he wrote that in Elgar, 'we get an example of a composer in touch with both his audience and his period', and this was a central concern of Lambert's. He was keen to keep music as alive and as widespread as possible. Like many other serious musicians of the time he was also interested in first-class popular music: Chabrier and Sousa were among his favourites.

Below the surface glitter Lambert lived a muddled life. By all accounts he was not a good father to his son, nor a faithful spouse to his wife. Below the exciting fast rhythms of his music, his art also was not what it seemed. Hubert Foss wrote of an 'elegiac nostalgia [that] pervades the whole of Lambert's work and has at times a poignancy that is almost unbearable'. This is well summed up in lines from Nashe's *Summer's Last Will and Testament*, the work whose poor reception deeply disappointed the composer:

> Queens have died young and fair;
> Dust hath closed Helen's eye:
> I am sick - I must die.
> Lord, have mercy on us!

It was inevitable that Lambert should be dubbed the 'English Diaghilev' and, turning to one of Lambert's associates as a composer of ballet music, it was perhaps equally inevitable that Lord Berners should have been called the 'English Satie'. Like Lambert, Berners's artistic interests were wider than just music and his musical horizons further distant than the shores of England. Berners also never really fulfilled himself as a musician.

Gerald Hugh Tyrwhitt (Tyrwhitt-Wilson from 1919), later the four-teenth Baron Berners, was born in 1883; he was educated at a preparatory school in Cheam and at Eton. His accounts of his early years, *First Childhood* and *A Distant Prospect*, furnish us with a vivid and at times moving account of the loneliness of a sensitive boy at boarding school during the decade before the turn of the century. These charming works deservedly retain a certain popularity today. The Tyrwhitt family had a variety of objections to the boy going into the army, the navy, the church, the law, or into banking so it was decided to put him into the diplomatic service. He served at Constantinople and then in Rome. In 1918 he succeeded to the Berners title and, leaving Rome in 1920, he returned to England, settling at Faringdon House in Berkshire where, living the live of an eccentric English country gentleman, he remained for the rest of his life. He died in 1950.

In his writings, his paintings, and especially in his music Berners left much of interest. He was a much gifted man: the description of Lord Fitz-Cricket in his novel *Far From the Maddening War* is autobiographical:

Lord FitzCricket ... was always referred to by gossip-column writers as 'the versatile Peer', and indeed there was hardly a branch of art in which he had not at one time or other dabbled. He composed music, he wrote books, he painted; he did a great many things with a certain facile talent. He was astute enough to realize that, in Anglo-Saxon countries, art is more highly appreciated if accompanied by a certain measure of eccentric publicity. This fitted in well with his natural inclinations.

Berners was notorious in his day for his peculiar behaviour, 'a superb instance of *real* eccentricity', as Edith Sitwell noted. Among his better-known antics were dyeing his fantail pigeons all colours of the rainbow, having a spinet fitted inside his motor-car and driving round the countryside wearing strange masks. He also built what is said to be the last folly in England. Literary memoirs of the period often contain anecdotes about Lord Berners. Edith Sitwell, for instance, recalled an occasion when she was lunching with him:

His stately, gloomy, immense butler Marshall entered the dining-room, bear-ing a huge placard. 'The gentleman outside says would you be good enough to sign this, my Lord.' Gerald inspected the placard and wriggled nervously. 'It wouldn't be of any use, Marshall,' he exclaimed. 'He won't know who I am – probably has never heard of me.'

It transpired, eventually, that the placard was 'An appeal to God that we May Have Peace in Our Time.'

From such accounts one might be tempted to believe that Berners was a superficial man; but that would be quite wrong. His autobiographical writings show that, while he possessed a sharp wit, he could also be a serious, sometimes rather a sad, man. Constant Lambert, with a fine disregard for mixing metaphors, wrote of Berners that 'though his tongue was often in his cheek his heart was just as frequently on his sleeve'. This side of Berners can also be seen in novels and short stories of the period where he was the original for various characters: Nancy Mitford's *The Pursuit of Love*, for example, where he is Lord Merlin, or Osbert Sitwell's short story 'The Love-Bird', where his 'character' Robert Mainwroth is referred to as a 'moneyed nomad'. Sitwell also said of Mainwroth, 'when he was alone he seemed more alone than anybody I knew'.

As a composer Berner's published music is of a high technical standard: he was no mere musical playboy. His work was considered to be in the avant-garde of his day – he was popularly known as 'our futurist peer'. While in Rome he was encouraged in his musical endeavours by Stravinsky and Casella. Stravinsky regarded Berners very highly and once referred to him as 'the best twentieth-century English composer'. Berners wrote music for the piano, songs and ballet scores, for which he became well known. His sense of humour is visible throughout his work – no more so, perhaps, than in the titles to his small piano pieces and songs – *Valses Bourgeoises: Trois petites marches funèbres* ('For a Statesman', 'For a Canary', 'For a Rich Aunt'), *Dispute entre le Papillon et le Crapaud*. These are all, to one degree or another, parodies, but in all of them there is also a strong element of self-parody as well. As the musical scholar J.A. Westrup wrote of Berners's orchestral *Fantaisie Espagnole*, 'the composer pokes fun at all the Spanish capriccios that ever were, and yet takes an obvious delight in playing with the idiom himself'. Berners found it hard to take anything seriously – even himself.

Of Berners's larger works his ballet *A Wedding Bouquet*, still in the repertory of the Royal Ballet, has fared best. It is a lively piece with a 'futurist' libretto by Gertrude Stein, of which the following is an example:

> Arthur Julia Arthur Julia Arthur
> this would make a dog uneasy dog uneasy

Guy would it be possible to believe it of three
All of them having come to the door
this is now scene four.

Of his other ballets. *The Triumph of Neptune*, from a book by Sacheverell Sitwell, was first performed in 1926 by Diaghilev's Russian Ballet in London with choreography by George Balanchine. (On the first night Berners refused to take a curtain call with Sacheverell Sitwell, claiming that his aunt had threatened to disinherit him if he ever went on stage.) *Luna Park*, also with choreography by Balanchine, was produced by C.B. Cochran in 1930; *Cupid and Psyche* (1938) and *Les Sirènes* (1946) were both choreographed by Frederick Ashton and conducted on their first performances by Constant Lambert. He also wrote a one-act opera *Le Carrosse du Saint Sacrement*, which was first staged at Paris in 1923.

Berners was well aware of the tendency of the English to 'judge art by size and weight', as he wrote in one of his novels, and his short piano works and songs have only appealed to a very small minority. All his works display his great abilities as a satirist, a master of parody and caricature; they are witty, clever and serious by turn. (Of the three funeral marches it has been rightly observed that the only genuinely sad piece is for the canary; the statesman is presented with excessive pomp and the demise of the rich aunt is greeted with hilarity.) None of his works contain musical 'padding' of any sort, and the music itself undergoes little development. Writing for the ballet was ideal for such a composer, for here was a form where he could build episode on episode without necessarily having to develop his musical ideas at any real length.

It is of interest in terms of English musical history to observe that Berners was born in the same year as Bax, and to ask briefly what the two composers had in common and how they differed. Both were serious composers, and although neither of them needed to compose in order to pay their bills they were both deeply committed to their art. Berners, however, lived at a much more exalted social level. At first sight one might think that he would have enjoyed considerable advantages over Bax. But there is a real irony here, for it was Berners who was actually in the disadvantaged position when it came to realizing his strong desire to be a composer. Bax, like many contemporary English composers, came from a family that had, over the years, developed a broad interest in music. His father was a subscriber to the Crystal Palace Sunday Concerts and his uncle, a colleague of George Bernard Shaw, was a well-known music critic. Berners had no such advantages.

In comparison, the world into which Berners was born was, particularly in musical terms, something of a cultural desert. His mother, unlike many of the other mothers of English composers at the time, did nothing to encourage his real talents. She was herself fond of the country life, especially hunting, a pastime for which her son had no sympathy. His early attempts at music were not encouraged in any way. On the extraordinary occasion of being visited by his father (a distinguished naval officer) when he was at Eton, Berners recounts the story of how he was given a sum of money for 'a book'. The 'book' he wanted was a vocal score of Wagner's *Das Rheingold*. Berners later related:

I was overwhelmed with gratitude. At the same time my conscience pricked me. Ought I confess the nature of the book I wanted? If it had been my mother, I should have felt myself obliged to tell her that it was a musical score, and it would probably have been denied to me. But my father asked no questions, and I appreciated the advantage of having to deal with a parent whom I cared for less and whom I felt less compunction in deceiving.

Such an incident forcibly reminds one of Shaw's observation on the position of music in an upper-class English house: a 'complete gentleman', he observed, was

forced to spend his boyish leisure at cricket and football before he enters an adult society in which he cannot escape hunting, shooting, bridge and billiards, though he can go through life ... without hearing a Beethoven sonata in any form than that of a disagreeable noise which he forbids his daughter to make in the schoolroom except during the hours when he is usually out of doors. If you eliminate smoking and the elements of gambling, you will be amazed to find that almost all an Englishman's pleasures can be, and mostly are, shared by his dog.

Berners did not fit into the life of hunting and riding which went on around him and there was little encouragement to follow any other course. He stuck to his artistic interests and later Osbert Sitwell wrote of him that, 'in the years between the wars he did more to civilize the wealthy than anyone in England. Through the darkest drawing-rooms, as well as the lightest, he moved ... a sort of missionary of the arts.' This is, perhaps, an over-dramatic view but it is true that Berners cuts a lonely figure against his background.

Like Lambert, Berners had both a strong European perspective and also a marked English streak. His novels abound in a sense of humour that is utterly foreign to those who have not been trained in the old English public-school tradition. Many of Berners's musical jokes will likewise escape those who do not share his general background. As a young man interested in music he was deeply attached to the music of Wagner, an interest that he shared with many, if not most, English composers of the period. But, like many others, he worked out his escape from his early hero's style. His own developed musical style is, however, not in itself innovative for its period; he makes his best musical points with his keen wit rather than through experimental techniques.

In his later years Berners completely dropped from public view. In 1943 Osbert Sitwell wrote 'Dear Gerald is here. God, he is a bore now, bless him, with all his little *diableries*. But I am very fond of the old boy, very sweet and pathetic, but those stories of his are like flies circling round one on a summer day.' By the years of the Second World War the age that had fêted Berners, and indeed Sitwell, had passed, and as the world tired of them they tired of each other. John Betjeman once sympathetically remarked of Berners, 'like anybody very cheerful, he was also very gloomy, and we who had the privilege of knowing him can remember how sad it was when he just turned his face to the wall and died – died, I think, because he felt there was nothing more he could do'. Berners wrote his own epitaph:

> Here lies Lord Berners,
> One of the learners,
> His great love of learning
> May earn him a burning
> But, praise to the Lord,
> He seldom was bored.

Two other composers – Peter Warlock and E.J. Moeran – while having much in common with those we have already looked at in this chapter were separated from them, as we shall see, by important musical differences. Constant Lambert was the figure who most easily crossed from the Walton world of music to that of Warlock, and both Lambert and Warlock were hard-livers, given to excess. While a general description of them and their friends as a 'lost generation' is perhaps too dramatic it is true that some of them lost their way.

The composer Peter Warlock was really the man Philip Heseltine, and adopted this sinister pseudonym for his published music. He said later in his life that he had ceased to be Heseltine, having completely 'become' Warlock. He died by his own hand. The composer's biographer, his friend Cecil Gray, set the area of debate for Heseltine/Warlock in his

unusual biography which, whatever its merits, has so coloured the popular view of its subject that it must be briefly considered. Gray suggested
that the life of Heseltine/Warlock was cast in sonata form and thus,
given the original exposition of themes and their development, the re-
capitulation and coda – his subject's suicide – followed naturally enough.
The argument further ran that Heseltine turned into Warlock and the
latter killed the former when the unhappy man gassed himself. Gray's
interpretation has been disputed by many and it is clear that the picture
given in his book is an over-simplification. But it is equally true that in
some way or other the Warlock side of Philip Heseltine did come to
completely dominate his life and lead to his death. It is also true that he
had a notable musical talent and merits our attention.

Philip Heseltine was born in 1894. His father, a solicitor, died when
his son was only two; Heseltine was educated at Eton and Oxford. At
Eton his interest in music was encouraged by his teacher Colin Taylor
and through him Heseltine came, at the early age of sixteen, to discover
the music of Delius, which was to become a passion with him for many
years. Coincidentally, Heseltine had an uncle who lived close to Delius
in France and he soon met that composer at Grez-sur-Loing, from which
meeting a friendship, well recorded in their correspondence, began between the two men. Heseltine's interest in Delius was a remarkable
thing, for Delius was known to few at the time. Heseltine did much to
help establish Delius's reputation, especially by writing a book on the
older composer, first published in 1923, and by helping to organize the
1929 Delius Festival in London.

As a young man Heseltine turned to Delius for advice and here the
older man showed himself at his best. Delius could be very difficult and
selfish but in the letters which he wrote to Heseltine at this time he is at
his most attractive. Delius's complete lack of rhetoric and humbug was
valuable to the younger man. Delius advised Heseltine on all aspects of
musical craft, as the following shows: 'Your songs are beautiful. In one
or two I have made slight alterations – only a suggestion, mind – you
come back so persistently to E flat in one of them. It is of no importance
whether you write at the piano or not as long as you feel you want to
express some emotion. Music is nothing else.' Heseltine also put to Delius
the general problem of what he should do with his life. It was proposed
that he should follow a career on the Stock Exchange or in the Civil
Service and Heseltine wrote to Delius, who was now clearly something
of a father-figure to him, for advice. As we have already seen Delius

replied, 'I think that the most stupid thing one can do is to spend one's life doing something one hates, or in which one has no interest; in other words it is a wasted life.' Delius encouraged Heseltine to study music and even visited the young boy's home to urge the case for allowing him to take up a musical career, much indeed as Grieg had done for Delius himself some years before. Heseltine's replies to Delius already show two sides of his character that were to war within him throughout his life. He was bursting with enthusiasm for music, but he also realized that he was not able fully to achieve the object of his enthusiasms. In 1913 he wrote:

> My strongest joy lies in *expectation* – in looking forward to things, especially if they are unknown, mysterious, and romantic, full of possibilities. That is what keeps me going; perhaps it is but a vain illusion, a dream – but it is all I have. I have often felt myself to be a mere *spectator* of the game of Life: this, I know to my sorrow, has led me to a positively morbid self-consciousness and an introspectiveness that almost amounts to insincerity, breeding as it does a kind of detachment from real life.

In terms of immediate musical training Delius advised Heseltine, who had already stayed for a short time in Cologne, to go to Germany; but the advent of war made this impossible. Heseltine went up to Oxford, where many of his life's passions began really to develop. One of his contemporaries, Robert Nichols, later recalled that while at the university Heseltine read Havelock Ellis, Carpenter and Otto Weininger and that together they would discuss ' "sex" after a manner now common among "modern" flappers but in those days rare'. They shared a mutual interest in Whitman and Nietzsche. Heseltine was also known for his verses and limericks, frequently in priapic style, and was keen on motor-cycling. In a calmer and more musical vein he showed an interest in English folk-tunes and had a great admiration for Vaughan Williams, although the two men were never close friends.

Heseltine, although he had done very well there, had been unhappy at Eton; he now found Oxford 'just one foul pool of stagnation'. He left the university and having considered the idea of studying music with Holst, suggested to him by Balfour Gardiner, he went to London University to read English instead. This didn't last long either and he moved on again to a job as music critic with the *Daily Mail*, this time through Beecham's influence. This lasted only six months. Heseltine explained his departure when he wrote to Delius, 'It is only doing harm to praise what one knows to be bad.'

It was to this period of his life that Heseltine's friendship with D.H. Lawrence belongs. Heseltine, with typical enthusiasm, threw himself into working for his new friend's cause: he paid, for example, for 600 circulars to be sent to supposedly suitable people in an attempt to raise money for a private printing and circulation of *The Rainbow*. Heseltine also helped promote Lawrence's idea of a 'colony of escape', even asking Delius if his ill-fated Florida orange grove would be suitable for the venture. The friendship with Lawrence did not last either. Heseltine came to the opinion that 'Lawrence is a fine artist and a hard, though horribly distorted, thinker. But personal relationships with him are impossible – he acts as a subtle and deadly poison.' On his part Lawrence recalled Heseltine as Halliday in *Women in Love* and Heseltine's wife, Minnie Lucy (who had been an artist's model) appears in that novel as Pussum. Heseltine was furious and his complaints forced the publishers to withdraw the book. (Heseltine was a good model for writers: he also appears in Aldous Huxley's *Antic Hay* as Coleman.) About this time his friendship with Cecil Gray also began to come unstuck due, Gray thought, to Heseltine's marriage, which, in its turn, did not last long. These dramatic events took place against the backdrop of the First World War and in 1917 Heseltine spent the year in Ireland, partly to escape the conscription board, although he was almost certainly unfit for active service, and partly because, following his usual way, he wanted to turn his back on his muddles – this time the 'great cesspool of London'.

In musical terms, however, this was the beginning of the most fertile phase of Heseltine's life. Delius had never ceased to urge him to get on with his music. He had written to the young man, 'Turn to music, dear boy, that is where you will find the only real satisfaction.' Delius still had great belief in Heseltine: 'wait a bit, prepare, gather works', he advised him. And in Ireland Heseltine began seriously to follow this advice. Like many other English people who went to live in Ireland – Arnold Bax, among musicians, for example – Heseltine was quickly captivated by the country and its people. He studied Celtic languages, and took a great interest in occultism and horoscopes. Dressed in the robe of an African medicine man and wearing a large, untidy beard, he once delivered a lecture at the Abbey Theatre in Dublin on 'What Music Is'. His talk was followed by a group of folk-songs from Ireland and India showing, so Heseltine thought, the fundamental similarity of the two traditions.

One could be forgiven for thinking that Heseltine was developing

into a lost cause; it was clear – even to him – that the audience at his
Abbey Theatre talk could not make much of his theories. But the end
of the war saw him back in England and beginning to publish his music,
under the pseudonym of Peter Warlock. (He had originally adopted this
name for some of his literary work but used it now to submit works to
the publisher Winthrop Rogers as a subterfuge, for the two men were
not on good terms at the time.) Much has been made of this change of
name as the sign of a new departure in Heseltine's life, but we must be
careful not to accept too easily Cecil Gray's over-simplified view of a
complex man. Heseltine himself wrote in 1929, 'I am now officially
Peter Warlock for all public communications – it saves trouble and
confusion and keeps one's name in people's minds: they cannot remember two at a time.' But it is important to note that he signed the letter
in which he explains this point 'Phil'. For public musical purposes, in
concert programmes and on the sleeves of his records, he must be referred to as Peter Warlock, but Philip Heseltine should not be allowed
to escape us for that reason.

The next few years of Heseltine's life were his most active musically.
He re-entered the lists of musical criticism in 1919 when he engaged in
a public dispute with Ernest Newman and it was clear that his genius
for controversy was unimpaired. In 1920 his magazine the *Sackbut* came
into existence. The issues he edited are lively and still of interest – he
got Delius and Arthur Symons to write for him as well as printing an
Augustus John drawing and poems by Roy Campbell. He did this only
for a year, however. (He was later to edit *Milo*, the magazine of Beecham's Imperial League of Opera; but this only lasted for three issues.)
Heseltine continually moved around: travelling once to Budapest to visit
Bartók, whom he greatly admired. In 1925, however, he settled in Eynsford in Kent, where he lived for three years in a cottage shared with
E.J. Moeran. From time to time he also lived in London and Wales. In
December 1930 he died of gas-poisoning in his London flat, and although
the coroner's jury was unable to determine whether it was suicide or
not, few have ever doubted that he died by his own hand, having first
carefully put his cat out of the door.

The social life of Heseltine during the 1920s is well recorded for he
had become a figure of some popular interest. Heseltine, hidden behind
his beard and his new name, was able to indulge many parts of his
character previously held in some sort of check. He frequently appears
in both the celebrated and the more mundane anecdotage of the period,

whether in the memoirs of Augustus John or in the pages of the writer Jack Lindsay and the artist Nina Hamnett. Life at Heseltine's cottage was presented as one long carousal. He was looked after by his 'man', Hal Collins – also known as Te Akau – a part-Maori, who boasted a cannibal grandmother. (Collins was an interesting man in his own right: he was an effective artist, as his woodcuts show, and also, it seems, a self-taught musician who once played Cecil Gray a whole act of an opera from *Tristram Shandy* which he had in his head. Collins did the illustrations for Heseltine's anthology of poems on drink and drunkards by Rab Noolas: 'saloon bar' spelt backwards.) Much beer was drunk at the local pub, and Heseltine acquired a reputation for womanizing. It was as such a character that Warlock developed in the public eye. One could almost be forgiven for thinking that Peter Warlock, as well as Philip Heseltine, was now a lost cause. But that would be unfair: the music that came from the composer at this time marked him out as a man of real talent.

In his earlier period Heseltine's music was close to that of Delius, giving rise to the joke that, following Delius's 'first cuckoo in spring', Warlock was the 'second cuckoo'. Heseltine then discovered the music and ideas of Bernard van Dieren and in 1916 wrote to him saying that his music had been a revelation and that he would begin again *ab ovo*. Shorn of his Delian phase, Heseltine began to publish, although his work is not noticeably like van Dieren's as a result. Van Dieren, who had brought a lively personal view to contemporary music in England, showed Heseltine above all how to 'see clearly'. During this later period of his life Heseltine achieved much notable musical work. He became well known for his researches into and knowledge of the music of Elizabethan England. He frequently transcribed original scores and, in collaboration with Philip Watson, was responsible for six volumes of *English Ayres, Elizabethan and Jacobean* and many other similar works. His literary output also blossomed at this period with his Delius book (1923), then *The English Ayre* (1926), *Carlo Gesualdo, Musician and Murderer* (1926) with Cecil Gray, and *Giles Earle, His Booke* (1932), a work described by Heseltine as a 'good specimen collection of the favourite songs of a Jacobean musical amateur'.

Of his own compositions the vast majority are songs, although, iron-ically, he is perhaps best known today for his orchestral *Capriol Suite*. (In today's musical world it is, of course, much easier to hear an orches-tral suite in a concert than a song cycle.) Warlock's *The Curlew*, a cycle of four linked songs for tenor, flute, English horn and string quartet, once enjoyed a wide reputation. Most of his works, however, are in the single song form and this has led to his gaining a reputation as a 'charming miniaturist'. Such a description can all too easily be made into a slightly sneering criticism; but this is not how it should be. Some of the best English music of this period is in the smaller forms, and composers like Heseltine were able to achieve much in this way. Heseltine himself saw both sides to this question. In 1920 he wrote to van Dieren:

> sometimes I feel that this exiguous output of tiny works is too futile to be continued – though I have neither the impulse nor the ability to erect monuments before which a new generation will bow down. And then when I think of some of the 'monumental' composers in present-day England alone, I feel that I would rather spend my life trying to achieve one book of little songs that shall have a lasting fragrance, than pile up tome upon tome on the dusty shelves of the British Museum.

Heseltine had a strong sense of English literature and set poems by many authors, some sixteenth-century and others modern. Of the modern he set words by Bruce Blunt, Hilaire Belloc, Arthur Symons and W.B. Yeats (it was typical that after a good start in his personal relations with Yeats, Heseltine argued with him and fell out). His work ranges widely, reflecting his interests and character, from the intense bleakness of *The Curlew* through to the almost light-hearted music of 'Chopcherry' and 'Rutterkin' from Set 1 of the 'Peterisms' (a word taken from a well-known brewers' advertisement of the pre-war period).

From an article written by Gerald Cockshutt about E.J. Moeran's recollections of Heseltine as a composer we learn that

> Warlock's methods as a composer were dictated by the peculiarities of his temperament. For weeks he would be sunk in gloom, unable to think of a note. He would alleviate his melancholy by transcription, until of course the time inevitably came when there was nothing more in the British Museum that he wanted to transcribe. When the black mood passed he would write a song a day for a week. According to Moeran, 'he went to the piano and began fumbling about with chords, and whistling', quite undisturbed by conversation from the next room.

In his later days Heseltine/Warlock lost his earlier enthusiasms for both the music of Delius and that of van Dieren. Gerald Cockshutt tells us that towards the end of his life Warlock 'thought seriously of resuming his technical studies and in 1928 contemplated taking a course of lessons in counterpoint with R.O. Morris'. Heseltine was no idle iconoclast; indeed, he had a marked respect for the established English musicians around him. His description of Vaughan Williams's *Pastoral Symphony* as 'Just a little too much like a cow looking over a gate' is a good joke but this should not cover the fact that Heseltine went on to say of Vaughan Williams, 'he is a very great composer and the more I hear the more I admire him'. Heseltine also made a piano reduction of Vaughan Williams's *Pastoral Symphony*, showing his real professional interest.

Heseltine's own musical style has a strongly individual English character. He was clearly influenced by his love of earlier English music. Constant Lambert was one of the English composers that Heseltine in his turn influenced – especially through his reviving interest in the music of sixteenth-century English dance forms. In his earlier days Heseltine had taken up Delius's views about the cosmopolitanism of music: in 1914 he had attacked what he saw as the insularity and chauvinism of Joseph Holbrooke. In his own music, however, he later showed that he was not only firmly part of an English musical tradition but one of its most individual and valued heirs.

Following his death, Heseltine's many friends and acquaintances soon stirred up the dust of debate over the merits or otherwise of the dead man. That he was a wit and that he had a great talent for friendship as well as enmity was widely known; but he was also on occasion overcome with utter dejection and the interpretation of his character has been an area rich in speculation. Reading the early correspondence with Delius we can still see that he was one of the rare people who was really on Delius's wavelength when it came to talking about composing. Delius for his part knew that Heseltine understood him and tried to urge him to follow his inner convictions – as Delius had himself. This was a great testimony to Heseltine's early talent.

Of the various tributes and assessments of Heseltine that appeared after his death the most illuminating is one written by the celebrated musician, Sir Richard Terry. Terry described what he thought of as a musical 'ring' dominating English music at the time. This 'ring', he believed, was based on an understanding between the 'universities' and the 'conservatories' to 'raise the tone of the musical profession'. Talented technicians were the people most likely to benefit from this system, and posts in the chief musical institutions of the country tended to go to their own alumni. In a bitter phrase, Terry wrote of Heseltine, 'He did not realize sufficiently early the subtle freemasonry that exists between mediocrities.' While it is perhaps an overdramatization to follow Terry in saying that the 'ring' hunted Heseltine down, there is no doubt that a distinction between supposedly worthwhile and not worthwhile composers had grown up in the 1920s. The 'establishment' looked down on the unusual. It was not altogether unlike the 1890s when Shaw had described how Parry, Stanford and Mackenzie constantly wrote in praise of each other, thus making a magic circle from which others were excluded. Terry wrote of the new academicians who were talking and writing about each other in a similar way, and rightly pointed out that it would be British music that would suffer most from this in the long term. Heseltine, Terry thought, got much more out of music than the 'aloof academicians'. 'The music sprang to life on the page before him. ... To Heseltine the cult of Elizabethan music was not a medium for obtaining the distinction and rewards which might come to so important a person as one who studies impressively abstract subjects.' As with Arnold Dolmetsch, old music was only interesting to Heseltine as long as it could be made into living music once again. Heseltine was too much his own man to belong to any institution of music and, between the wars, music in Britain was becoming more institutionalized.

Many people remembered Heseltine as a man who was modest about his own talents. His behaviour was frequently outrageous but he never made any marked claims for his own music - rather the opposite, in fact. Heseltine's songs have, however, kept much of their appeal long after those of most of his contemporaries have vanished for ever. *The Curlew* is among the very best of all the works of the English musical renaissance and the acute sense of desolation it so painfully evokes puts it way above most of the works of the Shropshire Lad school. Of this work Cecil Gray wrote, 'I do not know of any music more utterly desolating to hear than *The Curlew*', and Eric Fenby wisely said, 'it is the saddest music I know'. Heseltine does full justice to Yeats's words: 'No boughs have withered because of the wintry wind; the boughs have withered because I have told them my dreams.'

Another close friend of Heseltine's and another underrated composer of the period was E.J. Moeran. Born in 1894, Moeran was the son of an Irish Protestant priest who lived and worked in Norfolk. At Uppingham School Moeran (he was always known as Jack) developed into a fine pianist and string player and began composing music. He entered the Royal College of Music before the First World War but in 1914 he enlisted as a dispatch rider and in 1917 was badly wounded in the head.

He resumed his studies at the College in 1920 with John Ireland as his composition teacher, and although by this stage he could no longer be regarded as one of the new young men, he was thought to show real promise.

It was at this stage of his life that he was close friends with Philip Heseltine, and between 1925 and 1928 they set up home together in Eynsford. The two men clearly shared something in their approach to life. Stephen Wild has written in a brief biography of Moeran that Warlock was 'a person with whom he [Moeran] shared many common personality and character traits, both laudable and regrettable', and Arnold Bax, who knew Moeran well, also spoke of 'a certain instability in his [Moeran's] character'. As a composer, however, Moeran was widely different from those immediately around him. Although he picked up much from Elizabethan music through Heseltine and was also strongly marked by the harmonic language of Delius, Moeran's music reminds one most of Vaughan Williams and the English Romantic pastoral tradition. Such a description might seem to imply that his style was highly eclectic and that he was a mere imitator of other English composers of his time; but this impression would be quite misleading. Moeran drew from many sources for his musical style but his music was clearly his own: he wrote in a style both personal and distinctive. He was one of the very few closely affected by Vaughan Williams's music who was able to develop his own style without being a weak or slavish imitator.

The folk-song influence on Moeran really originated in his knowledge of the area where he had been brought up. Because of his great knowledge of the Norfolk area he was able to win the confidence of those local people who still remembered the old songs. He is credited with collecting 150 or so songs and his folk-song interests were therefore based on first-hand experience - like Vaughan Williams and Butterworth - not on books or other compositions. J.A. Westrup rightly wrote of Moeran that 'he is one of the comparatively few composers who use the idioms of folk-song not artificially but as if it were their native language'. Moeran was no straight copier of tunes: he rather used the folk-song idiom to fashion his own original melody and on this basis developed an individual musical language. His *Lovely Waters*, for example, was based on a fragment of a song, 'still frequently to be heard on Saturday nights at certain inns in the Broads district of East Norfolk', Moeran tells us.

Moeran also often spoke of the influence of nature and natural sur-

roundings on the music that he wrote. He said, for example, that parts
of his symphony were written, 'among the mountains and seaboard of
Co. Kerry', while the second movement was 'conceived around the
sand-dunes and marshes of East Norfolk'. These influences are clearly to
be heard in Moeran's music. He was, as Arnold Bax pointed out, 'one
of the last romantics. All his work from first to last is characterized by
a deep love of nature.' With Bax, Moeran also shared a deep and
enduring love of Ireland and the Irish. Moeran found a sympathetic
place in Kenmare in County Kerry and it was there that he died in
1950.

Moeran's later musical works – especially his Symphony in G minor
and Violin Concerto – show that he continued to develop as a composer
and was turning to the larger forms (he was working on a second
symphony at the time of his death). The orchestral rhapsody form had
been valuable to him as far as it went but Moeran was looking for
something more than that. Vaughan Williams had shown what could be
done symphonically and Moeran's own symphony was a landmark in
his career as a composer. Like many other British composers he turned
to the example of Sibelius when he came to consider writing a symphony, but the end result is free from any excessive outside influence.
Some found the Symphony in G minor too discursive, but others
pointed to it as a further example of how Moeran was still a composer
with a promising future.

To be thought of as a composer of promise in one's forties is doubtless
better than not being thought of as a composer of promise at all, but
E.J. Moeran – like Butterworth who died so many years before him –
was never really to develop much further than this in the public mind.
Moeran was remembered by those who had known him as a friendly,
straightforward man, a man without pretensions who was able to get
on with a wide variety of his fellow-men. He was a frank man with a
certain brusqueness of speech which some thought concealed shyness.
Above all he disliked artificiality in people. He married the cellist Peers
Coetmore, whom he first met at the home of their mutual friend
Augustus John, and a fine Concerto, Sonata and Prelude for Cello
followed.

To his fellow-musicians Moeran was a byword for meticulously composed pieces and for precise technique: it was only in his symphony that
some saw technical problems. If he was not able to find a place as
a major composer of his time, he did achieve a substantial reputation

for developing a voice of his own when so many around him had long given up any hope of finding an individual style. Like his teacher John Ireland, Moeran was satisfied to do what he could do and to do it well.

CHAPTER NINE

# Traditions – New and Old

## GURNEY, HOWELLS, BUSH, RUBBRA, FINZI, ORR

We have seen that one of the major developments in English music after the First World War was the self-conscious intention to shock by appearing to be utterly 'new'. But there were other composers of the period who followed the pattern of the traditions – new and old – of English music rather more closely. Ivor Gurney, once thought of as one of the most promising of English musicians, was one of these. Having slipped into near-total obscurity after his early death in 1937, he has only recently been re-established in his rightful position. As both a musician and a poet much of his work has now been published and he is the subject of a biography by Michael Hurd. Mr Hurd (to whom all interested in Gurney are indebted), and the latest editor of Gurney's poems, P.J. Kavanagh, join a succession of people who have over the years worked towards the proper establishment of Gurney's reputation: Ralph and Adeline Vaughan Williams, Herbert Howells, Gerald and Joyce Finzi, the poet Edward Thomas and his wife Helen, Walter de la Mare, Edmund Blunden, Marian Scott, the poets J.C. Squire and Leonard Clark, and various others have spoken up on Gurney's behalf and many years of such endeavour have finally borne fruit.

Stanford is said to have thought that, of all his pupils, Gurney was potentially the most gifted, while also being the least teachable. Gurney's unhappy life, however, did not allow him to develop his talents in any ordered way. His main period of creative activity was relatively short and his long descent into madness effectively cut him off from the outside world. It is always difficult to try to consider the work of an artist without some reference to his life and in the case of Gurney this is especially true.

Ivor Gurney was born in Gloucester in 1890; his father was a tailor with a shop of his own. Music was part of the respectable Gurney home and from an early age it was evident that Ivor had musical talents. A local priest began to help out with his general education and Gurney won a place in the cathedral choir. He was determined to become a professional musician and, following a traditional route of those born in major country towns, he became an articled pupil to Dr Brewer, the organist of Gloucester, who had both Herbert Howells and Ivor Novello under his care at the same time. It was a promising start for a career in local music and when Gurney set off in 1911 for the Royal College of Music Brewer was upset, believing that Gurney could do just as well with him in Gloucester.

At the Royal College Gurney was not one to let Stanford trample over him. On one occasion, when Stanford made a few alterations to a work by Gurney he told his pupil, 'There, me boy! That puts it right.' Gurney replied, 'Well, Sir Charles, I see you've jigged the whole show', and was thrown out of the room. There was, though, no doubt that Stanford was fond of his pupil: whereas some people flatter others to their faces and malign them behind their backs, Stanford did the opposite – he was rude to their faces and kind behind their backs. (He once sent some of Gurney's poems to the Poet Laureate of the day, Robert Bridges, for his opinion.) Among his contemporaries Gurney was close friends with Herbert Howells and the young Australian, Arthur Benjamin. They shared similar interests in music, being greatly struck, for example, by Vaughan Williams's *Sea Symphony* in 1913. Gurney also kept abreast of the latest developments in English poetry. This was a time of great activity in the poetry world with the emergence of the 'Georgians' and Gurney himself was experimenting with a new sort of poetry. It was an exciting time for him.

As a musician Gurney's aims were, as they remained throughout his life, ambitious. Like many other composers of the time he turned to the very largest-scale works for a solution to his artistic problems. In the period immediately before the war Gurney was considering a cycle of operas from the plays of W. B. Yeats and a music drama about Simon de Montfort. In 1917, in a letter to Howells, Gurney himself mocks this sort of music. In a 'biography' of Howells which is, of course, of his own invention, he pretends that his friend's 'record is one blaze of great works and huge accomplishments. The first 14 Symphonies, the great Sanscrit Te Deum, for the opening of the new lavatory in the Dead Language Section of the British Museum; the noble setting of the genealogies in the Old Testament; of the great Bradshaw Opera, the epic of railway life ...' (These were, of course, the very years of Holbrooke and Boughton's greatest activity.)

The outbreak of war threw all the plans of the young men into confusion, however, and in 1915 Gurney went into the army. He was in France by May 1916, wounded and gassed in 1917, and sent home for hospital treatment, suffering, in the army's view, from shell-shock. We are now able to see much more clearly than was possible at the time what was really happening to Gurney. Although at the war's end he was able to return to some semblance of his pre-war life, taking up again his scholarship at the Royal College (where he now studied under Vaughan Williams), and although he held down various jobs from time to time, we can see from his letters and other evidence that the madness that was to render the end of his life useless and barren and keep him in confinement for years was already upon him. Indeed, traces of the symptoms which he displayed as a man were with him as a child. The war had obviously had a most profound effect on Gurney but the view that his insanity was directly caused by his experience at war is too neat a solution for so complex a man.

From an early age Gurney suffered from forms of behaviour that in themselves were quite harmless: he ate very irregularly, sometimes stuffing himself with cakes, sometimes eating nothing at all; he was very fond of long walks in the country and often slept rough in the hedgerows (while in London he would sometimes, in a similar way, sleep on the Embankment); he was obsessed with physical fitness and with his health. Taken together and greatly exaggerated, however, such pressures built up within Gurney and began destroying his mind. The conventional medical wisdom of that time diagnosed 'neurasthenia'. Gurney himself believed that neurasthenia was worse even than the fears of war; that a neurasthenic was full of unsatisfied longings and had an inability to concentrate; he also wrote, revealingly, 'You know how a neurasthenic has to drive himself, though he feels nervy and his heart bumps in a disturbing but purely nervous fashion?' This is how Gurney saw himself. While he was in the company of other men, either training in England or on service in France, Gurney envied their apparent self-sufficiency and confidence. He too, wanted to be 'strong in himself, set fast on strong foundations. Not likely to be troubled with neurasthenia', as he wrote of somebody he admired. He never felt master of his own life.

By 1918 Gurney had deteriorated to such a point that he wrote farewell letters to his friends, including Howells and Parry, telling them of his decision to take his own life: 'I am afraid of slipping down and becoming a mere wreck – and I know you would rather know me dead than mad, and my only regret is that my father will lose my allotment.' This and other attempts to kill himself failed to succeed but it ushered in a period in which Gurney began living in an asylum, at first only temporarily and then, from 1922 until his death in 1937, permanently at Stone House, Dartford in Kent. In his later life his insanity developed into a mania that 'electrical tricks' were being played on him, and that 'machines' under the floor were torturing him; he saw faces and heard voices and suffered 'a twisting of the insides', as his medical file put it. His file also pathetically added, 'with regard to suicide he has had such pains in the head that he felt he would be better dead'. His condition was diagnosed as 'Delusional Insanity (Systematized)'. His obsession with big artistic works remained with him: he felt that he had written the works of Shakespeare, Beethoven and Haydn and there is no doubt that the works of his own which he had achieved, small-scale as they were, were a real disappointment to him.

Gurney's output of both poetry and music is, for obvious reasons, not large but what there is has so impressed itself upon other poets and musicians that his talent is now recognized as genuine and important. His poetry speaks of Gloucester and the countryside in which he was brought up, and is close at times to the spirit of Gerard Manley Hopkins.

> There was such beauty in the dappled valley
> As hurt the sight, as stabbed the heart to tears.
> The gathered loveliness of all the years
> Hovered thereover, it seemed, eternally
> Set for men's joy. Town, tower, trees, river
> Under a royal azure sky for ever
> Up-piled with snowy towering bulks of cloud
> A herald-day of spring more wonderful
> Than her true own. Trumpets cried aloud
> In sky, earth, blood; no beast, no clod so dull
> But the power felt of the day, and of the giver

> Was glad for life, humble at once and proud.
> Kyrie Eleison, and Gloria,
> Credo, Jubilate, Magnificat:
> The whole world gathered strength to praise the day.

Gurney first rose to the public's attention through his two volumes of war poetry, *Severn and Somme*, published in 1917, and *War's Embers* (1919), in which the grander rhetorical style of Rupert Brooke – 'Now, youth, the hour of thy dread passion comes;/Thy lovely things must all be laid away' – combines with his almost visionary memories of home:

> The elms with arms of love wrapped us in shade
> Who watched the ecstatic west with one desire,
> One soul unrapt; and still another fire
> Consumed us, and our joy yet greater made:
> That Bach should sing for us, mix us in one
> The joy of firelight and the sunken sun.

But to Gurney music had a higher place than poetry. He once wrote of poetry that its 'chief use' seemed to him, 'one perhaps mistaken musician, to stir the spirit to the height of music'. He also recorded of himself, 'the brighter vision brought music: the fainter, verse or mere pleasurable emotion'.

As a young composer Gurney soon made progress. A letter written by A. E. Housman to his publisher, in 1908, indicates that Gurney had approached the poet for permission to set his poems to music. Housman had no objection but wrote, 'Mr I. B. Gurney (who resides in Gloucester Cathedral along with St Peter and Almighty God) must not print the words of my poems in full on concert programmes (a course which I am sure his fellow-lodgers would disapprove of).' While at the Royal College before the war Gurney also composed his 'Eliza' songs, settings of Elizabethan words. In 1912 Gurney wrote to his friend Will Harvey:

Dear Willy,
It's going, Willy, It's going. Gradually the cloud passes and Beauty is a present thing, not merely an abstraction poets feign to honour.

Willy, Willy, I have done 5 of the most delightful and beautiful songs you ever cast your beaming eyes upon. They are all Elizabethan – the words – and blister my kidneys, bisurate my magnesia if the music is not as English, as joyful, as tender as any lyric of all that noble host.

Gurney kept up his composing in the trenches: his choice of lyrics included Masefield's 'By a Bierside', Sir Walter Raleigh's 'Even such is

Time', F. W. Harvey's 'In Flanders' and 'Severn Meadows' a setting of
his own words:

> Only the wanderer
>   Knows England's graces,
> Or can anew see clear
>   Familiar faces.
> And who loves joy as he
>   That dwells in shadows?
> Do not forget me quite,
>   O Severn meadows.

The main period of Gurney's musical activity, as also of his poetry, was,
however, after the war, in the brief years between coming home and
entering an asylum (roughly speaking, 1918–22). Once he was inside the
asylum he had moments when he composed again but the music from
this period is judged to have really lost its coherence. He continued also
to write poems and long prose-poem 'memoirs' and letters which tell
more clearly than anything else of the unhappy world in which his life
was locked. Many of these were addressed to the 'English Police' at Scotland Yard. Of the time after the war when he tried to earn his living as
a farm labourer he wrote, for example,

> Employment came, but not long kept – the expected
> Body-labour, the cleansing work, directed
> Controlled, till work-end came, once more I was free
> For thought, and writing, and free artistry
> Denied. Denied must be content; on twelve
> Shillings and odd earnings I must serve.

(The twelve shillings is a reference to his army pension: the letter shows
that while Gurney's mind was capable of recalling events in their correct
order and detail he was falling apart from within.)

As a composer Gurney was responsible for some instrumental music
including one complete string quartet, two piano sonatas, violin sonatas,
five choral works and two pieces for orchestra, a coronation march and
the *Gloucester Rhapsody*. Little attention has been paid to these works and
about two thirds of his songs are judged to be of little interest. But the
remaining songs – some eighty to ninety of them – are regarded as
among the very finest of all English songs. Michael Hurd rightly places
Gurney in the company of Dowland, Parry, Warlock, Finzi and Britten.
Vaughan Williams in particular saw Gurney's importance in the revival

of song-writing in England. Pointing out the change that had come with Parry and Stanford and their 'meticulous observance of accent and stress', he referred to Gurney's 1917–20 settings of the Georgian poets. 'These writers', Vaughan Williams judged, 'had just rediscovered England and the language that fitted the shy beauty of their own country. Gurney has found the exact musical equivalent both in sentiment and in cadence to this poetry; he and his contemporaries have at last discovered that English poetry cannot be forced into the procrustean bed of German, French or Russian musical formulas.'

Both as a man and a musician Gurney was one of the most deeply English of all contributors to the musical renaissance. Here was a man who, in a story told by Herbert Howells to Michael Hurd, once left off playing the organ for morning service in Gloucester Cathedral because the great east window was 'aflame with light'. Gurney cried 'God, I must go to Framilode!' and walked out of the cathedral to stay away for three days. The countryside of England, like the verse of her poets, drew out the best in him. He once wrote enthusiastically to Howells, 'What of the Forest of Dean Symphony? What of the opening pages of the sight from Newnham-on-Severn looking out across the Valley to the hills? An A major beginning, surely?' It was Gurney's view that England had been 'poorly off for musicians', but that 'the country that produced the men who wrote such a speech as "Ye elves of hills, brooks, standing lakes and groves" could produce anything. Our young men must write on a diet largely composed of Folk Song and Shakespeare.' Gurney knew, however, that it was a hard task to make English music. Just before leaving for the Front in France in 1916 he wrote to Howells, 'Little Howler, continue in thy path of life, blessing others and being blest, creating music and joy, never ceasing from the attempt to make English music what it should be, and calmly scornful – heedless of the critics.'

As a poet Gurney was drawn to the very best seam of English verse for his own musical settings: there are no dreadful sentimental Victorian ballads or feeble, mawkish rhymes in Gurney's songs as there are in the works of so many of his composer contemporaries. Gurney chose Yeats and Walter de la Mare, Robert Bridges and Edward Thomas, Robert Graves and Thomas Hardy, John Masefield, Hilaire Belloc, A. E. Housman and Francis Ledwidge. He also went back to Shakespeare, Ben Jonson, Walter Raleigh and the mad poet John Clare. The texts chosen cover a great diversity of subjects and emotions but throughout we can see Gurney's deep love of nature and of people close to nature. (One of the reasons why he wanted at one stage to take up labouring jobs that kept him out of doors was, he said, so that he might get ideas for his artistic work.) The music for his songs often truly seems to come out of the words themselves and the close relation between the voice and the piano further binds together his songs as a whole in a remarkable way. His music was certainly influenced by folk-song but it is a broad rather than a specific debt. Above all he was a melodic writer, and he was quite opposed to the 'new' music of the period, rejecting as he did its aesthetics.

Michael Hurd, following Edmund Blunden, has written that there is a 'gnarled' quality to Gurney's music as there is in his poetry; both are the works of a man full of quirks. And others, noting the 'struggle-in-making' of some of Gurney's work, have felt that, at times, it lacks fine finish. While there is a certain truth in this it is also true that, in performance, Gurney's songs are very effective. Howells observed that they were fine songs for singing, and many celebrated singers have indeed enjoyed singing them. Howells added, illuminatingly, 'All union of music to words is based on compromise. It is the mark of genius that it does not stress that compromise. At his best Gurney nearly eliminates it.'

Although the composer of many fine smaller-scale works, one of Gurney's major musical concerns, as we have seen, was his desire to write large works. In this respect he was very much the child of his time: we have seen that a similar challenge faced many other contemporary musicians, and that most of them, casting their eyes back to the Elizabethans, developed into excellent song-writers and miniaturists. It was not given to all to work out the visions of grandeur of, say Rutland Boughton or Joseph Holbrooke. But that his achievement did not match his ambition was something that greatly worried Gurney. At an early stage of his troubles Gurney felt that the spirit of Beethoven had visited him and told him that 'I should probably not write anything really big and good; for I had started much too late and had much to do with myself spiritually and much to learn'. (The letter in which he mentions this incident ends with the following ambiguous passage in which the full horror of madness has not yet descended, and one can still feel that a humorous intention lies behind his remark: 'I could not get much about Howells off L van B: (the memory is faint) he was reluctant to speak; whether Howells is to die or not to develop I could not gather.')

Gurney felt that because he had experienced such great pain in his life he deserved success and notice. He was, in his later years, pathetically proud of being a 'War Poet'. Recognition finally came in the very year he died: preparations were being made for the publication of two volumes of his songs, and articles about him were to appear in the journal *Music and Letters*. It was, however, as the composer and poet said himself, too late.

One should not think that Gurney was utterly neglected in his last years. Many people did what they could for him: Adeline Vaughan Williams for example tried a Christian Science practitioner, and Helen Thomas visited Gurney and went over maps of Gloucester with him (this he greatly enjoyed). Gurney, even when quite well, was not in any case always an easy man to deal with. He was quite an abrasive character with a teasing streak that some found difficult. He does not seem to have enjoyed very close relationships with other men or women, falling in love only once as far as we know, and that with a girl who was considered to be 'unattainable'. Many have worked hard to establish Gurney's proper reputation, especially Gerald Finzi, who persisted in his desire to get Gurney's best songs published; a desire that involved Byzantine negotiations with Gurney's close friend of many years Marian Scott – who had the manuscripts until her death – and the Gurney family. In recent years Gurney's reputation has become assured in the literary world, where much attention is paid to his work. It is, however, a measure of how little the English musical world loves, or even understands, its own best artists that scant regard is really paid to Gurney's equally remarkable songs by today's musicians.

Of the many composers who were struck deeply by the early works of Vaughan Williams few developed such a strong and individual style of their own as Ivor Gurney's friend Herbert Howells. Gurney and Howells attended the first performance of Vaughan Williams's *Fantasia on a Theme by Thomas Tallis* in Gloucester Cathedral in 1910. Howells later recalled how this work had kept 'the *Gerontius* audience ... impatiently waiting for twenty minutes'. The two young men, however, had come to hear the *Tallis Fantasia* and after leaving the cathedral neither could sleep: 'we spent the night pacing the streets of Gloucester'. But Howells was no mere imitator of Vaughan Williams; he possessed a very real ability of his own. Howells later came to know Vaughan Williams very well and said, 'Ralph and I felt and reacted to things musically in a very similar way, and if some of our works are alike in any respect, it's not, I think, merely a question of influence but also of intuitive affinity.' In particular, like Vaughan Williams and many others of his generation, Howells was drawn to Tudor music and folk-music 'more for the modal colouring than for its human associations', as he himself put it.

The strongest associations in Howells's music come from the part of England that he knew best and loved so much. Born in 1892, Howells, like Gurney, grew up in the Gloucester area and his early musical talent was assisted by the interest and financial help of a local family, the Bathhursts. (Howells's own father was a builder and decorator who went bankrupt.) Like Gurney, Howells was an articled pupil of Brewer at Gloucester Cathedral. Like Gurney also, Howells went on to the Royal College of Music where – and this, as we have seen, was a rare occurrence – he got on well with Stanford. This great teacher, but difficult man, found in Howells his 'son in music'. Howells understood the language that Stanford talked; he realized that the advice his teacher offered was almost always indirect advice, and that his bark was far worse than his bite. Stanford had a high opinion of Howells and got him on to the first list of works to be published by the Carnegie Trust along with himself and many other well-established composers of the time: Vaughan Williams, Bridge, Holst and Boughton, for example. Stanford also conducted the first performance of Howells's Piano Concerto at the Queen's Hall in 1913. Howells was obviously getting somewhere and he followed up his success with *The B's* in 1914, a work which bears obvious resemblance to Elgar's *Enigma Variations*. Howells found employment for a short time as sub-organist at Salisbury Cathedral but between 1917 and 1920 he suffered ill-health. In 1920 he went to teach composition at the Royal College in London.

In his letter of 1917, which has already been quoted above, Ivor Gurney teased his friend about the many and mammoth works that he might be expected to produce. It was a good joke but in neither respect – in number nor in scope – was it right. Howells was never, in fact, to write more than a few large-scale works and although in 1922, through the influence of Elgar, he was commissioned to write a major piece for the Three Choirs Festival – *Sine Nomine* – this was not really a typical piece for him at the time. His early work, rather, was in the smaller forms: between 1916 to 1923 he produced a number of fine chamber works including a Piano Quartet (inscribed 'To the Hill of Chosen and Ivor Gurney who knows it'), a Rhapsodic Quintet for clarinet and strings, three violin sonatas, a Phantasy String Quartet and the string quartet *In Gloucestershire*. Various pieces for piano and organ date from this period also, as do some songs and anthems. Although his debt to many of the prevailing musical influences of the time is obvious, Howells developed neither into a late Romantic composer of the sort of large-scale music fashionable in the pre-war world nor did he become a disciple of the new post-war music. Rather, like Vaughan Williams and others, he worked at his own vein of expression in the way that best suited him.

As Howells's professional career in music developed he spent less of his time in composition. Like Walford Davies, Howells, in his own way, was concerned with spreading the love and practice of music. He spent much time adjudicating at competitions, examining and teaching (he followed Holst as a teacher of music at St Paul's Girls' School and was later King Edward VII Professor of Music at London University), and there were periods of his life when he hardly seems to have composed at all. In the 1920s a few orchestral works came from Howells and some keyboard works – especially the remarkable *Lambert's Clavichord* of 1927. A key work was, however, the *Hymnus Paradisi* which, although not first performed until 1950, was inspired by the death of the composer's only son in 1935. The work was finished in 1938 but, in his own words, 'for twelve years it remained what I had always wanted it to be – a personal, almost secret document'. In 1950, however, on the urging of Vaughan Williams, the work was released and Howells conducted the first performance at the Three Choirs Festival in Gloucester. The score is headed with lines from the early Christian poet Prudentius:

> Nunc suscipe, terra fovendum
> Gremioque hunc concipe molli

which was translated by Helen Waddell:

> Take him, earth, for cherishing,
> To thy tender breast receive him.

Following *Hymnus Paradisi* Howells wrote other works for chorus and orchestra: *A Maid Peerless* of 1951, the *Missa Sabrinensis* of 1954 and a *Stabat Mater* of 1963. By the mid-1960s, then, Howells had come to be thought of as a choral composer of the old tradition, and, among choirs, he had a good reputation although his music was considered difficult to sing. This was due in part to the very private nature of much of his work: the 'distinction of his mind and sensibility', in the music writer

Christopher Palmer's exact phrase, are not qualities that have ever achieved great success with a wide musical public.

As a musician Howells is not easily categorized. In his youth he was a fellow-traveller with Vaughan Williams; in old age, he still held that his first encounter with the *Tallis Fantasia* was the vital determining factor in his musical life. He nevertheless followed his own distinctive path. It is interesting that his favourite poet was that most individual of men, Walter de la Mare. Howells's music has a sense of flow about it that came in part from Delius but, in his own words, the difference between them was that Delius 'thinks in terms of blocks of sound, I think polyphonically, in lines'. The spirit of Tudor music was strong in Howells. Of the *Tallis Fantasia* he said, 'It all seemed incredibly new at the time, but I soon came to realize how very, very old it actually was, how I'd been living that music since long before I could even begin to remember.' The spirit of English poetry is also evident everywhere in his work. Howells's description of how he searched for the right words to set in the last part of his *Hymnus Paradisi* shows how much care went into such a selection (in the end he chose 'Holy is the true light' from the Salisbury Diurnal, suggested to him by Sir Thomas Armstrong). Howells never sought a wide public for his work: his music is written entirely on his own terms. At the time of Howells's seventy-fifth birthday Hugh Ottaway accurately wrote that the composer was 'both neglected and taken for granted', and this is a sad if true reflection of the present fate of all too many of the most interesting of recent English composers. Howells's voice is never likely to have a wide appeal but those who consider that they can appreciate music coming from composers of fine sensibility would do well to give Howells and the tradition to which he belongs more careful attention.

A man whose musical career has been undertaken in a deliberately much more public way than Howells's is Alan Bush. His beliefs have made him seek wide publicity for his political views, whereas Howells's personal sensitivity sought privacy. Bush's life and work has mixed music with politics. When the German composer Hanns Eisler greeted him in 1950 as the chief representative of 'progressive music' in England he meant something quite different from Richard Strauss's similar comment on Elgar: 'progressive' had come to have political connotations which were not there in Elgar's day.

Bush was born in 1900 to an 'ample Victorian middle-class family' as he himself has put it. As with many other young artists of the time the artistic encouragement that he received at home came from his mother. Bush later looked back to his early family life with a degree of discomfort: the family's dietary fads, teetotalism and nudism seemed, from the viewpoint of a life dedicated to communist ideals, to be attributes of the petty-bourgeois that were to be regretted. Most regrettable of all was his family's interest in occultism: Bush tells us that spiritual messages once even induced members of his family to undertake a round-the-world trip in search of hidden treasure. As a young man he too had been a member of the Theosophical Society and had cast horoscopes. But he regarded himself as saved from such a wasted life by the private reading he undertook in public libraries and his interest in philosophy and politics.

It was in music that Bush especially shone, however, and in 1918 he went to the Royal Academy of Music where he studied under Frederick Corder for composition and Tobias Matthay for piano. Between 1922 and 1927 he had private composition lessons with John Ireland and piano lessons with Benno Moiseivich, Mabel Lander and Arthur Schnabel. In 1929 he decided that he wanted to know more about the world in general and he entered Berlin University as a student of philosophy with musicology as his second subject. Berlin at that time was a hotbed of radical ideas and music was part of the battleground between the political left and right, both sides making use of it for propaganda purposes. While in Germany Bush lived for a while in a house next to Bertolt Brecht and Hanns Eisler, and he began to move towards joining the Communist Party. (He had become a member of the Independent Labour Party in 1924 and was to join the Communist Party in 1935.)

Politics and music then became so bound together in the life and work of Alan Bush that it is impossible to deal with one without the other. In the 1920s, before theories of communism completely influenced his artistic output, Bush was thought of as a young composer of modern leanings with a possibly interesting future. His String Quartet of 1924 won him a Carnegie Award, and *Dialectic*, also a string quartet (1929), was well received being played at the Prague ISCM festival in 1935. Other pieces followed including a pianoforte concerto, first performed in 1938, and a symphony, first performed in 1942. These early works were based on a form of composition that he later referred to as the 'thematic' method: a system in which every note is intended to be thematically significant (many writers have observed the close similarities between this and twelve-note composition). In the works following the Second World War, however, a great change occurred in Bush's approach to music and in other people's attitude to him. This change was brought about by Bush adopting ideas about art which were broadly similar to those current at the time in the Soviet Union, and which were to lead, in 1948, to the Conference of Russian Composers and Musicologists where, with Zhdanov, the Minister of Culture, presiding, resolutions in favour of greater simplicity in music and more emphasis on nationalism were passed.

Alan Bush was obviously under no direct compulsion to follow this line away from 'formalism' towards 'social realism' but he seems, in any case, to have decided on his own that this was desirable, and his music had already begun to show signs of 'simplification' by this period. Bush's later work is much more didactic in purpose. His four operas date from this time: *Wat Tyler*, *Men of Blackmoore*, *The Sugar Reapers* (or *Guyana Johnny*, as it was known in Germany), and *Joe Hill: The Man who Never Died*. The first three operas, about 'the struggle of peasants, industrial workers and colonially oppressed people against the ruling class at different periods in the history of my country', as Bush put it, were to librettos by his wife. Bush had worked as Rutland Boughton's assistant at the London Choral Union and succeeded him there. As with Boughton, Bush felt that the mainspring of music should be choral. He said that he believed that music began with singing and that instrumental music was a technically elaborated representation of vocal music. He further believed that as different nations had different languages, each with its own peculiarities of rhythm and accentuation, so different nations would have different musical languages; as a corollary he felt that in a perfect international world, when national groupings had finally been done away with, these differences of musical language would also disappear.

In the years after the Second World War, then, Bush believed in a very specific form of national music. The irony was that in taking the position that he did he caused his compatriots to completely lose interest in him. As with Boughton before him, it was felt that Bush's political beliefs inhibited promoters from putting on his works. The first of his operas was one of the four Arts Council prize-winning works of the Festival of Britain opera competition but it was not staged in Britain. Instead Bush's works were in high demand on the other side of the Iron Curtain – especially in East Germany.

In holding the views that he did with such passion and conviction Bush probably damaged his musical career in Britain beyond repair. That many of his contemporaries among English musicians admired Bush's musical talents is shown from a publication of the Workers Music Association of 1950. Here John Ireland, Ralph Vaughan Williams and Herbert Murrill (one of Bush's pupils), while stating their dissociation from his views, sent him their sincere respects. Vaughan Williams, for example, wrote of Bush's 'rather fantastic notions of the nature and purpose of the Fine Arts'. But during the war Vaughan Williams had once threatened to sever his relations with the BBC unless that organization withdrew a ban on broadcasting Bush's works, and there were many others who followed Bush's progress with interest and supported his right to hold his own views. E.J. Dent, for example, wrote in praise of certain aspects of *Wat Tyler*, an 'opera of a whole people', as he called it, comparing it to Mussorgsky's *Boris Godunov*.

Bush's music is now almost never heard; his particular idea of national music is not one that has caught on at all. His *Nottingham Symphony* gave some people the hope that in the future, as patronage became less the donation of the rich few and more the gift of representatives of 'the people', more music for the 'community' would be commissioned. Such works, it was held, would have to be of subjects that were 'fitting', for some specific occasion and easily appreciated by an 'ordinary' person. Examples of such music are to hand but there is no indication at all that the future of English music lies along that path – rather, as was seen with Bush, this way has been rejected. Many people, while holding a high opinion of Bush's music, have seen the problem that Bush's views present in relation to the English musical public. The music critic Colin Mason, for example, wrote of Bush in the fifth edition of *Grove's Dictionary of Music and Musicians* that,

He is surpassed only in melody, as are all the others, by Walton, but not even by him in harmonic and orchestral richness, nor by Tippett in contrapuntal originality and the expressive power of rather austere musical thought, nor by Rawsthorne in concise, compelling utterance and telling instrumental invention, nor by Rubbra in handling large forms well at a rather domestic level of intensity, without dramatic excitement. Yet he has not achieved a comparable popularity or respect which would undoubtedly have been his if he had not handicapped his works with propaganda.

Bush appears from his writings and the interview he gave to Murray Schafer as a man keenly concerned with the world about him. His personal interest in the ordering of both the very smallest of life-forms and the very largest of political organizations betrays a man who, by his own account, was a refugee from the genteel battiness and muddle of a particular type of middle-class family at the turn of the century. His later work to classify and organize his own art on behalf of the people left Rubbra convinced that he was writing better music than ever before – but there are few who agree with him. His vision of national music was quite out of step with contemporary events.

Whereas Alan Bush was part of one broad tradition in English music – a tradition associated with left-wing political aspirations, of which Rutland Boughton had previously been the leading figure and with which Benjamin Britten would also have links – a contemporary of his, Edmund Rubbra, followed a very different course. The broad tradition to which he belonged – with its associations of mysticism and the supernatural – stretched back rather through Cyril Scott and Gustav Holst. While Bush was going to a public library to drink in the wonders of modern political philosophy and escape the spiritualism of his family, Rubbra was doing the exact opposite. He found Madame Blavatsky's *Isis Unveiled* in the Northampton Library and his interests turned towards Oriental philosophy and religion. One lesson that Rubbra learnt from such sources was to regard chasing after fame as futility, and during his life nobody worked less hard to promote himself and his music than he did. In this respect he was not, of course, unique among the composers of the musical renaissance, but he was a special case in the sense that he had no private income and needed to earn his living from music.

Rubbra was born in Northampton in 1901. His father had been an apprentice watch and clock repairer and worked in a factory that made wooden lasts for boots and shoes. As can be seen his background was somewhat similar to Havergal Brian's. In artistic terms the young Edmund got encouragement from his mother. At the age of fourteen Rubbra had to leave school in order to start earning money to help out the family budget: he worked first for Crockett and Jones, the boot and shoe manufacturers, and then as a correspondence clerk in the Permanent Way Department of the local London and North Western Railway station. Rubbra's interest in music developed at an early age and he was able to practise the piano on instruments which were kept at his parents' house by an uncle who had a piano and music shop. The young Rubbra, in return for the use of the instrument, had to give demonstrations to prospective customers. If the piano was sold, he would be given a new one in its place, and the whole procedure would begin again. The opportunities for active music making at the time were, of course, still substantial, and Rubbra, at the age of seventeen, decided to stage a concert given over entirely to the works of Cyril Scott. This unusual event brought him to Scott's attention and he took Rubbra on as a pupil. Rubbra also won a composition scholarship to University College, Reading, where Gustav Holst taught, and from there he went on to the Royal College of Music. Throughout his musical training a local music enthusiast helped find the money required to pay for his studies. (It is interesting to note that Rubbra's brother also distinguished himself; he was chief designer of aeroengines for Rolls Royce and was part of the team that made the Merlin engine used in the Spitfire.)

In later years Rubbra worked as a teacher and musical journalist. For over twenty years he lectured in music at the University of Oxford and was also Professor of Composition at the Guildhall School of Music in London. He was also a frequent performer and the Rubbra Trio was well known in its time. During the Second World War he joined the army, and as a sergeant in the Army Classical Music Group he entertained the troops in concerts of 'Trios, Quartets and Songs by the Great Masters', as the advertising bills proclaimed. He was also involved with the Dance-Drama Group, under the direction of Margaret Barr, who had studied technique with the influential dancer, choreographer and teacher, Martha Graham, in New York. His was a busy and distinguished career in music.

Rubbra was taught composition by Cyril Scott, Gustav Holst and R. O. Morris, and the influences of all three men can be seen in his music, although Rubbra's style of composition is very much his own. He did not, however, really emerge as a composer of interest until the late 1930s, when he wrote his first symphony. When others were despairing of this form of composition Rubbra took it up with zeal, and over the years he wrote ten symphonies, works, although infrequently heard, by which he is probably best known. He also published three full-scale concertos, various other orchestral works including *Improvisations on Virginal Pieces by Giles Farnaby*, three string quartets and other chamber music (including an important contribution for the recorder), and vocal music. Among his works certain titles remind us of his great interest in mystical thought: for example, a choral work from St John of the Cross, *The Dark Night of the Soul*, another from Hopkins called

*Inscape*, *The Morning Watch* by Henry Vaughan, and a setting from Whitman, *The Mystic Trumpeter*, a text which had also been set by his teacher Holst.

Rubbra's output is impressive. Many critics have considered that behind his instrumental and orchestral music the vocal origins of his style can be discerned, and a melodic language was certainly important to Rubbra. He was never tempted by the latest Continental fashions. He told Murray Schafer, 'I don't mind being called "traditional" for that expresses continuity.' He objected however to his music being called 'reactionary': 'my music is not the result of reaction on my part, but an effort to build on basic principles as I see them. The real reactionaries are the revolutionists who react against tradition!' Rubbra's sense of tradition was underlined by his ties with Oriental philosophy and religion. He spoke of the 'oneness' of music and in his work we do not hear any attempt to shock or show off. The voice that can be heard is rather a voice sufficient to itself.

Formal aspects of music were never a problem for Rubbra – he did not like divorcing technical problems from purely musical ones. He once said, 'Frankly I don't give form much thought at all. I never know where a piece is going to go next.' Although Rubbra did not know where each bar was going to lead he said that he had a feeling that the next bar was there to be discovered as he needed it. Like a sculptor working on his block of stone, Rubbra felt that writing a piece of music was a discovery of something that already existed rather than the creation of something new. The links between the various parts of his music became evident when the work was finished. He said, 'My imagination discovers the architecture for me.' Rubbra also revealed that his musical ideas often came to him at unusual times or places: the opening of his Fifth Symphony, for example, came to him while he was in a bus queue. He also added, revealingly, that 'music often presents itself to me in a visual way ... I mean, I see it written down before I actually hear it.'

Such views were based on Rubbra's deep understanding of the philosophies of the East, with their continual contemplation of the higher purposes of life. But Rubbra was a man whose artistic abilities were not exclusively dominated by his personal beliefs. He was the composer of some fine English church music, still much valued by church and cathedral musicians. Indeed, Rubbra's work has had its greatest appeal to professional musicians, who recognized in it a high technical and musical ability and saw in the composer himself another fine product of the

English musical tradition. Rubbra, like many of his contemporaries, stressed order and unity in a period of fragmentation and, although his music is not easy to get to know, those who have done so and have understood his particular idea of the order of the world, and his belief that the interior of music is more important than its exterior, have become firmly convinced of his lasting worth.

Among other traditional forms of English music still attracting able composers in the inter-war years was song-writing; and one of the composers of that time cast in the Parry/Vaughan Williams/Gurney tradition was Gerald Finzi. Finzi, like many of his contemporaries, looked back to the previously undervalued works of earlier periods of English music (he was responsible for editions of Boyce, Stanley, Mudge, Garth and Charles Wesley). He was, as we have seen, Ivor Gurney's great champion: with typical generosity Finzi laboured for many years to get proper recognition for Gurney's music – although he had never actually known the man himself.

Finzi was born in 1901; his father's success as a shipbroker ensured that he would never have to rely on his music to make a living. While Finzi was still young his life was touched by the death of his father, three of his brothers and his first serious music teacher, Ernest Farrow; and many people noted that Finzi seemed aware that his own life too would be cut short. (Indeed, in 1951 he learnt that he was suffering from a form of leukaemia and had, at most, ten years to live.) He underwent no formal institutional training but took private lessons from R. O. Morris in London. He came to know Ralph Vaughan Williams well and greatly respected him: in 1921 he even made a 'pilgrimage' to the older man's birthplace. From 1930 to 1933 Finzi taught composition at the Royal Academy of Music, but his life changed in 1933 when he married Joyce Black, an artist. The Finzis went to live in Ashmansworth, south of Newbury. (Among Gerald Finzi's interests at this period was the growing of apple trees and he had many varieties which had become all but extinct elsewhere.) By the standards of some of the other composers of the period Finzi led a quiet life. During the Second World War he worked for the Ministry of War Transport, judging the war a 'damnable necessity', although he was a man of pacific temperament. He died in 1956.

Finzi was another composer who was especially close to Vaughan Williams and he dedicated one of his most important works to Vaughan

Williams's first wife Adeline. One of the last expeditions that Finzi made before his death was in the company of Ralph and Ursula Vaughan Williams to Chosen (or Churchdown) Hill. Ursula Vaughan Williams's account gives us some idea of the man:

> Gerald described how he had been there as a young man on Christmas Eve at a party in the tiny house where the sexton lived and how they had all come out into the frosty midnight and heard bells ringing across Gloucestershire from beside the Severn to the hill villages of the Cotswolds. Gerald's Festival work, *In Terra Pax*, was a setting of a poem by Robert Bridges about such an experience.

The work which brought Finzi to public notice was his *Severn Rhapsody*, a short orchestral work, which was published by the Carnegie Trust in 1924. There are obvious parallels with Butterworth in this work but Finzi was not happy with it and later withdrew it. That did not mean that he had ceased to be a believer in the English rhapsodic vein - quite the opposite in fact. The post-war period was one when many composers who had tried their hands at the Vaughan Williams style, often with disastrous results, opted for a more modern style and followed more closely the examples of Continental composers. Finzi, however, stayed within the broad tradition in which he had begun.

Finzi was very critical of his own works and he often waited some years before committing them to paper. As a young man he had been uncertain of the details of his music and the practical experience that he gained with the Newbury String Players - a band that the music critic and writer Diana McVeagh has called Finzi's 'instrument', for he was neither a good pianist or singer - was very helpful in this respect. It is impossible not to speculate on what Finzi - while probably losing something of his own particular freshness - would have gained from a proper musical training.

Finzi wrote a few orchestral pieces, including a concerto for clarinet and one for cello, but his major work was for voice. He was very interested in the English choral tradition and his best-known works are those he wrote for chorus or solo voice. He was a great admirer of the works of Parry, Elgar and Gurney. His *Dies Natalis*, first heard publicly in 1940, is a setting of words by Thomas Traherne (whose work was almost completely ignored until the early years of the twentieth century). 'The corn was orient and immortal wheat.... I thought it had stood from everlasting to everlasting.... And young men glittering and

sparkling angels and maids strange seraphic pieces of life and beauty!
... I knew not that they were born or should die. But all things abided
eternally.' Finzi's music is contemplative, inviting the listener to join in
its contemplation. The author who Finzi most enjoyed setting was
Thomas Hardy and in his choice of Hardy's poems we can see Finzi
sharing both in the poet's deep love of the countryside of western England and in the bleakness that was part of Hardy's own world-view. It
is also interesting that Finzi made a setting of Wordsworth's *Intimations
of Immortality*. His choice of texts tells us much about the sort of man he
was. His settings are simple enough in one way: he set the texts word
for word with great care and his musical style is a basically traditional
one. But while there is no grand architecture to his music it is nevertheless beautifully constructed.

When people first met Finzi they often remarked that he was an
energetic man with a good sense of humour and of fun; but as they got
to know him better they became aware of his introversion. These two
sides to Finzi are clearly shown in his music, where there is work that
is vigorous, fun and charming as well as work that is slow and deeply
reflective; and it is in this slow work that many think he really excelled.
Edmund Rubbra once pointed out that Finzi had prefaced one of his
works with the words of Heraclitus, 'Life is flux'. Finzi's best songs bear
out this sentiment with great but serious sweetness.

Another composer who worked within the tradition of the English song
was C. W. Orr. Of all the composers in this book none have a more
slender output. Orr mainly wrote songs and of these there are only
thirty-five. Unlike Finzi, Orr was devoted to the poems of A. E. Housman and twenty-four of his songs were to texts by this poet. Orr would
scarcely merit a place in such a survey, however, were it not for the
outstanding quality of these few works. He lived at a time when many
people, both professional and armchair composers, tried their hands at
song-writing. The total number of settings from the period of works by
Shakespeare and Housman alone is enormous. The number of pastiche
folk-songs written also beggars thought, and there was good reason for
the frequent complaint that there was far too much of this sort of work.
Constant Lambert's view that it was time that the Shropshire Lad's
musical followers published their last settings was well placed.

C. W. Orr, however, stands so far above the routine in his work that
he merits attention as an example of an amateur composer of real value.

He was born in Cheltenham in 1893, and like many other composers of the English musical renaissance he was strongly influenced by the countryside which he knew and loved as a young man. He joined the army but was discharged in 1917 for medical reasons and his life was thereafter marred by ill-health. His musical training was at the Guildhall School of Music and as a young man he had a special admiration for Delius's music. Delius, in turn, offered encouragement. Philip Heseltine, Arnold Bax and Eugene Goossens also admired the work that Orr was producing at this time.

In 1930 Orr moved away from London to the Cotswolds, where he lived for the rest of his life. He sadly developed a form of deafness that effectively closed his composing career and his works date from an early period (most were written in the 1920s). Along with the obvious influence of Delius in music and of Housman in poetry can also be seen a passion for German *Lieder*, especially the songs of Hugo Wolf. It has been suggested, indeed, that Housman was to Orr what Mörike was for Wolf and, although there are many obvious differences between the two relationships, Orr did get closer to the heart of Housman's poems than most others. Of all the English musical miniaturists none can have been – in terms of output – more miniature than Orr, and as Orr's piano accompaniments are not easy to play his songs are heard only rarely these days. But there were many highly respected musicians who knew and loved Orr's songs and his appeal is still strong to those few who have had a chance of hearing his work in recent times. It was not only with such massive figures as occupy the next chapter – Michael Tippett and Benjamin Britten – but also with such small, but significant talents as C. W. Orr that the English musical renaissance was concerned.

# CHAPTER TEN

# Rebels and Heirs

## TIPPETT, BRITTEN

The fact that this last chapter has been given a title which deliberately reverses that of an earlier one is not meant to indicate that the movement which we have been looking at ended where it began; or that it was chasing its own tail. I have, rather, tried to suggest that, while great changes had taken place, many interests, concerns, beliefs and attitudes – although often in a different arrangement – were shared by composers widely spaced in position and time, and what Elgar and Vaughan Williams left as their heritage was a real asset to the musical world of Tippett and Britten, the subjects of this chapter. Many of the musical interests of these two men were also those of the English composers who immediately preceded them. The rediscovery of the music of Purcell, for example, and the search for an artistically viable way of setting the English language were concerns close to the hearts of many earlier composers, as we have seen. But Tippett and Britten did stand on their own in one very different way, for they were really the first English composers to be free from the shattering effects of the great changes in music that took place around the time of the First World War and the often overdramatic reactions of the generation that immediately followed it. Tippett and Britten, and others of their times, had another war to face, a war whose effect on musical life was as profound in its way as the earlier one had been.

And, to a certain extent, history repeated itself with these two composers, for, like many of the composers of the period around the First

World War, Britten and Tippett did not really come into their own until the musical world in which they had been brought up and in which they had grown had undergone great and fundamental change. The brave attempt, after the hostilities of the Second World War had ended, to reassure a nation that all would be well again – the Festival of Britain in 1951 – marked a new scrutiny of the national health of music, and it was evident that a further fundamental change had taken place. The optimism of the Festival and of the New Elizabethans was the optimism that greets the false dawn. Following the initial post-war revival (when, as after the First World War, a determined attempt was made to re-establish pre-war conditions), it became clear that the mood and spirit of the composers and their works had markedly changed again. So many aspects of the musical world had now come to be taken for granted; so much of the music of the earlier part of the century had come to be seen as dated or jingoistic; so much of the confidence of the earlier years had come to be assumed, that a new spirit came to dominate the scene – a new professionalism, a new sort of internationalism, and a new response to a vastly changed form of patronage for the arts. No force for change, however, was greater than that of the now fast-growing new mass-media of communication. From the early days of wind-up gramophones and experimental wirelesses a complete revolution in general musical life was set in motion. This was an utterly different world of music from that in which Tippett and Britten had learnt their craft and found their voice in the 1930s, and this difference often shows in their work and in their approach to music.

These two composers deserve to be treated together, as did Elgar and Delius, as the outstanding figures of English composition of their day, although neither are natural pairings if one considers the men involved either as individuals or musicians. In terms of the history of English music, though, the linking is helpful, for Tippett and Britten came to public notice at about the same time, although the latter was some years the younger. Tippett's reputation as a composer came very slowly. Up to the end of the Second World War his was a name known only to a specialist few and his music was hardly known at all. Tippett made his way on his own: he has never been part of any group or movement. And few other composers have journeyed so far and kept going throughout a long career in music in the way that Tippett has. For he has always been young at heart. Writing of the 'extraordinary possibilities' of contemporary opera, he once said, 'my motto will tend also always to be the simple one of Ezra Pound's: "Make it new". Adventure will in the end take us further.'

Tippett was born in 1905. His father had been a successful lawyer and was able to retire early. Unlike many of the other English composers of the century it was Tippett's father who was the parent interested in music; but Michael Tippett inherited much from his mother also. Mrs Tippett was an ardent suffragette, and had, like Ethel Smyth, gone to prison. She was also a theosophist and spiritual healer. Tippett's mother was artistic: she was fond of singing Quilter's ballads and, in her later days, painted a great deal. Tippett's early upbringing was in the country, and we are reminded vividly of the vast changes that have taken place in the world of music in recent years when we see how little opportunity there was for someone not born within range of London, or in the net of a major festival area, or in an area which boasted a fine orchestra, like Manchester, to hear good music regularly. Such was Michael Tippett's position.

Like Bax's father, Tippett's sought professional advice about his young son's leanings towards a life of music. Mr Tippett approached Malcolm Sargent who advised firmly against the idea. Michael Tippett's desire to study music, however, overcame this initial disappointment and it was agreed that he should go to the Royal College of Music for a proper training. The musical life of London was a revelation to him. The music writer Eric Walter White said that, 'during his first summer in London, he rarely missed a night at the Proms; and some people remember how he was usually to be found on the same spot of the Queen's Hall floor, dressed in white flannels and laden with miniature scores'. Tippett, like so many English composers immediately before him, had, however, a long way to go before he could consider that he had found his own musical voice based on sound experience of the great music of the past. After leaving the College he continued studying – composition with Charles Wood and C. H. Kitson, and conducting with Malcolm Sargent and Adrian Boult. Tippett did not particularly distinguish himself at the time and, in order to supplement his modest income, he took an appointment teaching French at a preparatory school. (One of his colleagues there was Christopher Fry.) Tippett taught for a while but found the experience unsatisfactory, and he decided to leave and, instead, live and work at his music in a small cottage that he had had built for him. (Like many other English composers Tippett is passionately attached to the countryside, and he has lived in a succession of country houses.)

Tippett now became involved with a local choral society and in the Barn Theatre, Oxted, he put on various works including Vaughan Williams's *The Shepherds of the Delectable Mountains*, Stanford's *The Travelling Companion* and his own realization of an eighteenth-century ballad opera *The Village Opera*. He also performed the *Messiah* in a new edition, a work that was to have an important influence on his *A Child of Our Time*. His interests at the time, if we compare him with say Constant Lambert or William Walton, were conservative. In 1930 a concert made up entirely of his own works was given at the same theatre and, although the reviews were not unkind, hearing his own music convinced Tippett that he was still a long way off his ambition to be a composer. (Meirion Bowen, his biographer, tells us that the composer designed the printed programme for the occasion; it is highly characteristic of Tippett that, while he packed the notice full of information about the concert, he managed to leave his own name off it altogether.) Tippett then took the unusual decision of going back to the Royal College of Music, where he made a private arrangement to have lessons with R. O. Morris and studied fugues for eighteen months. More music came from this renewed period of study but it was again rejected by Tippett, and it was not until the second half of the 1930s that he began to write works that have been allowed to survive. It was not indeed until 1939 that he was to find a publisher who would publish his music and, as this firm was Schott's (based at Mainz), publication of his works was delayed for yet more years due to the onset of hostilities between Germany and Great Britain. At the outbreak of the Second World War, then, Tippett was still largely unknown.

Tippett had been busy in the 1930s in other ways, especially working for a variety of left-wing organizations. He was at the time a Trotskyist, and joined and left the Communist Party in quick succession because he was not able to convert his fellow-members to Trotskyism. As a conductor his political beliefs also influenced the kind of work that he undertook. Tippett had been the conductor of the South London Orchestra, a body which consisted of unemployed musicians who had largely lost their jobs through the advent of the 'talkies'. He also worked for the Royal Arsenal Co-operative Society's Educational Department and, for the ironstone miners at Boosbeck in Cleveland in Yorkshire, he wrote a ballad opera, *Robin Hood*, which was performed in 1933. Tippett's musical record to date had not really been distinguished; in one sense, his wide-ranging interests obviously distracted him from composing. But in another sense – and this was all-important – Tippett was developing towards a position where he could begin on the composition that was to announce to the world at large that an important composer, with something very much of his own to say, was at hand.

The inspiration for this work, *A Child of Our Time*, came from a Nazi pogrom against the Jews in 1938. The resulting work of Tippett's – certainly one of his best known and most appreciated – was begun in 1939 but not first performed until 1944. During the war Tippett worked at Morley College and in terms of public musical activity this was his golden period. To Morley had come a number of refugees from Central Europe – Matyas Seiber, Walter Bergmann and Walter Goehr were among them – and Tippett's interest in Purcell brought Alfred Deller there also. Benjamin Britten and Peter Pears became known to Tippett at this period as well, and they performed with him at Morley. Tippett was a worthy successor to Holst at Morley College in the best English tradition of making music. He once wrote of the 'valuable English custom, that the professional never disregards the amateur who makes so much of the music at the grass roots', and at this period Tippett's enthusiasm for good music swept many along with him. Among other interesting performances at Morley College Tippett arranged and put on the first performance in Britain of the complete Monteverdi *Vespers*, which he had edited with Walter Goehr.

Tippett was still, however, largely unknown to a wider public and if he was known at all it was probably not for his music but for his pacifist views. He had long held opinions that meant that he could state a conscientious objection to war service as a soldier. He was granted exemption conditional on his doing some form of work on the land or in hospital. He refused to do either, arguing that the best way that he could serve the community was through his musical work. *The Times* reported the subsequent hearing of his case, and from its account we can see that Vaughan Williams – then the 'senior' figure in music – spoke up for Tippett, calling his compositions 'a distinct national asset'. Vaughan Williams said in Tippett's defence, 'I think Tippett's pacifist views entirely wrong, but I respect him very much for holding them so firmly.' Tippett was sentenced to three months' imprisonment, much to the delight of his mother, who spoke of this time as her proudest moment. Tippett's life in prison was enlivened by a visit from Britten and Pears who came to give a concert. On his release he returned to his work at Morley College. Imprisonment had, by all accounts, been a very important experience for Tippett, a man whose music had always been closely bound up with his philosophy of life, and many people date the full maturity of the artist in him to these months. Following his release Britten encouraged him to put on *A Child of Our Time*, and its first performance, in 1944, confirmed that Tippett was coming into his own as an artist. It was also an important work because Tippett had written the libretto as well as the music, and this was to become his usual practice hereafter. T. S. Eliot had originally said that he would try to write the libretto, but on being shown Tippett's detailed sketch for the work he encouraged him to finish it himself.

Since the war composition of new works has become all-important to Tippett and he has lived a quiet life concentrating on his music. Following *A Child of Our Time* he enjoyed a slow rise to a point where he could command general public interest in his latest musical work. At the same time, his philosophical and artistic views became known to a wider public through radio broadcasts. Many of Tippett's later works reflect in some part his philosophical interests, so his ability to put across his point of view in such a way was important. Much can be learnt from the two books that have been published containing the texts of these broadcasts and other commentaries by the composer, *Moving into Aquarius* and *Music of the Angels*. Tippett once compared the relation between his essays and his musical compositions to that between Shaw's prefaces and his plays, and a reading of Tippett's thoughts relating to a specific composition gives the listener a decided advantage when it comes to hearing the music. Tippett covers wide ground in his writings: his reflections on the theories of Jung, the history of the patronage of music, and many other subjects. It is clear, however, that certain major themes dominate his thought; one such, which was to be central to his life and work, is best expressed in his introductory remarks to the earlier book: 'all the material is concerned in one way or another with the question of what sort of world we live in and how we may behave in it'.

Tippett's writings show us his great scope and the multiplicity of areas where his interests lie. A man's main interest – as we have already seen in the case of Holst – can sometimes be quickly gauged from the books he keeps on his shelves: in a charming article contributed to a symposium published by Faber and Faber for Tippett's sixtieth birthday, David Ayerst wrote as if he was casting his eye over the composer's bookcase.

The favourite books to be seen there – the backbone of Tippett's intellectual life – were the works of Samuel Butler, Bergson and Whitman, Yeats, George Bernard Shaw, Christopher Fry, Goethe (Tippett learnt German in order to read Goethe), Romain Rolland's *Jean Christophe*, Frazer's *The Golden Bough*, T. S. Eliot's *The Family Reunion*, and 'among the most-thumbed books', C. G. Jung's *Psychological Types*. Tippett's reading has been wide and profound.

The musical works for which Tippett is best known today are his operas. A successful form of English opera – the quest of so many of the subjects of the earlier part of this book – did not really take off until the years following the Second World War, the key work in this respect being Benjamin Britten's *Peter Grimes*. Tippett's operas were produced at a period, then, when both promoters and audience were better disposed to the idea of English opera than they had previously been, and composers were working with an increased sense of confidence in their ability to use the operatic form as a vehicle for their artistic ambitions. Tippett's four operas have appeared at wide but regular intervals: *The Midsummer Marriage* was first performed in 1955, *King Priam* in 1962, *The Knot Garden* in 1970 and *The Ice Break*, which the composer himself announced would be the last of his operas, in 1977. Tippett's operas are full of his interest in symbols and metaphysical ideas, and, throughout, the search for a moral way of living is a central consideration. Isaiah Berlin, commenting on the great depth of Tippett's work, said of the composer, 'this most poetical, most serious, and very passionate composer is among the very few who have created worlds of their own, worlds any part of which is easily recognizable as uniquely theirs, from any distance'.

*The Midsummer Marriage*, the first of Tippett's operas, was originally given a very mixed welcome: it was ridiculed by certain sections of the popular press which did not even begin to understand the many levels of subtle thought that lay behind the work. One of the mocking headlines that greeted the work – 'Tree Takes a Bow' – says it all. But there were others who saw the great worth of the piece, and following works (as well as a very successful re-staging of *The Midsummer Marriage*) were treated with greater care. Tippett has been especially fortunate in being championed by the conductor Colin Davis, a modern example of the many positive benefits to be gained from a close working relationship between composer and conductor.

Tippett's mind turned to the ancient world for his second opera, *King*

*Priam*, where he saw the Trojan War through Trojan eyes; in *The Knot Garden*, his third opera, he examined human relationships in the modern world; and in his last opera, *The Ice Break*, Tippett developed, among other things, his long-standing and great interest in contemporary life and culture in the United States of America. (Americans have had a mutual curiosity and admiration for Michael Tippett, and his works have gone down well there: his Fourth Symphony was given its world première in Chicago by Georg Solti with the Chicago Symphony Orchestra who had commissioned it.) Other works have shared the great bursts of creative energy from which Tippett's operas came – parerga such as the *Songs for Achilles*, after his second opera, and *Songs for Dov*, after his third. He has also written various other choral pieces, including a highly effective piece for baritone solo, chorus and orchestra on the mystical vision of St Augustine.

Tippett is, to date, the composer of four symphonies and four string quartets. He has always felt able to work with traditional forms and his deep interest and admiration for the work of Beethoven has been of life-long importance to him. Professional musicians have the very highest opinion of Tippett as a composer of instrumental music and one day his power as a symphonist is sure to be widely considered one of his greatest achievements. But it is as a composer for voices that Tippett's reputation was established and has so far been sustained. From an early stage in his career a deep concern for setting English words has been important to him, as it has to so many of the English composers of the musical renaissance. A setting of 1942 of Gerard Manley Hopkins's 'The Wind-hover' shows, for example, Tippett's care in matching the sprung rhythm of the poet's lines:

I CAUGHT this morning morning's minion, king-
    dom of daylight's dauphin, dapple-dawn-drawn Falcon, in
        his riding
    Of the rolling level underneath him steady air, and striding
High there, how he rung upon the rein of a wimpling wing
In his ecstasy! . . .

Tippett has written about his and Britten's enthusiasm for the music of Purcell and they were especially keen to study and learn from Purcell's use of the English language – 'the carry and freedom of his vocal line', as Tippett put it. In this the composers were taking up a lead that had proved to be so fruitful for other recent English composers. Tippett and

Britten, however, made important advances of their own with the music of Purcell; and this was in some part due to the appearance of Alfred Deller, whose pure counter-tenor voice came as such a revelation to his generation, and who enabled Tippett and others to hear Purcell in the proper way.

Tippett has written of how his 'first problem came through language; how to set English'. He knew above all that 'the language which is set to music does affect the prosody of that music'. And while he was never a follower of the conventional folk-song school of English music that does not mean that he was not interested in it or immune from its influences. Some of Tippett's best-known and much loved earlier pieces show how well he was able to use typical English song-like material and he has spoken of the richness of the folk-song heritage of the British Isles: 'The people of these islands had indeed always been that "nest of singing birds" noted since the time of Dunstable.' But he also held the view that, 'I have never myself been of the opinion of Vaughan Williams that a narrowly national music should or could be founded on these tunes.' Tippett took what he needed for himself, and although we can note many obvious differences between him and Vaughan Williams, there are also intriguing similarities. Both composers had a deep wish to draw on what they considered to be the best lessons from English music of past times. Both men were patient with their music and knew that their full powers could only be reached through considerable effort – they were aware of the limitations of their tradition as well as its possibilities. Both invited their friends to playthroughs of their works before their final form was decided upon. Both also possessed a deep visionary sense and a firm moral strength of purpose. As has been seen over the matter of Tippett's pacifist views there were many areas where the two men did not see eye to eye but as two English country gentlemen of music they came out of moulds not wholly dissimilar.

Tippett's early use of folk-song was, in some part, due to his search for a musical language that would appeal to a wide audience. We are told that his early ballad opera *Robin Hood* was based on folk-tunes and in *A Child of Our Time* he used Negro spirituals to similar effect in order to give a vernacular appeal to his work. In later times Tippett's interest in the 'Blues' further extended his deliberate and fertile use of popular musical devices. But while some of his work has been deliberately created for a wide audience much of it also seems obscure, almost shut-in, to general listeners. The emphasis of many of Tippett's later works on the theme of *hortus inclusus*, the closed garden, should not, however, be taken to mean that Tippett completely lost interest in any music that was not of a private, visionary nature. Between 1965 and 1970, for example, he worked on *The Shires Suite* for the celebrated Leicestershire Schools Symphony Orchestra, a work that opens with a lively version of 'Summer is Icumen in', and there are plenty of other examples to show the continuing breadth of Tippett's view.

Tippett has said that as a child he had no conception of what being a composer meant. He explained to Murray Schafer how the experience of being a practising composer had worked for him. He said:

> I begin by first becoming aware of the overall length of the work, then of how it will divide itself into sections (perhaps movements), and then of the kind of texture or instruments that will perform it. I prefer not to look for the actual notes of the composition until this process has gone as far as possible.

The resulting music, coming from so deep inside Tippett, reflects the many and complicated parts of his personality. Tippett's music – especially in some of his later works – is not always easy to understand on first hearing, but there must be many who have been drawn further into his music by its evident qualities of seriousness of purpose and intelligence.

Tippett is a man who, both as writer and composer, has striven to keep in touch with his audience. When writing some years ago about the then new possibilities of interviewing composers on television, he quickly saw that this might sharpen and widen the impact of a living personality beyond anything sound radio could do. 'This kind of secondary contact between artist and public is not to be dismissed as unworthy.' Tippett's idea of how to reach the musical public is a large one, taking in the modern media as well as the traditional concert halls. On the other hand he has written that one should not think of the public as a consumer, free to dictate the market for music, and he has pointed out that a big public tends to be, by the nature of things, conservative in its tastes and expectations. Tippett noted in one of his essays that some of the great composers of the past – he instanced Haydn – had been in tune with the public (partly due, of course, to the fact that Haydn's public was not a mass public); other composers – here he used the example of J. S. Bach – had to face the dilemma of producing music that was not really what the public of the time desired to hear. This disconnection between the producer and consumer of music worried Tippett:

'The modern composer's dilemma is only Bach's dilemma writ large.'
Tippett was quite able to compose works for special commission - he
wrote an orchestral suite for one of Prince Charles's birthdays, for example - but his work, his passion 'to project into our mean world music
which is rich and generous', as he once put it, rejected mediocrity of
any sort. Tippett's view is that the artist should hope 'that his work of
art will belong in the great tradition' which, like Yeats, he called an
'activation of the Great Memory'.

It was not Tippett's way to restrict himself to a narrow audience: he
hoped he could appeal to as large a public as possible. Both in his work
as a practising musician and in his thoughts about music Tippett can be
seen as part of the strong British tradition of closeness between the
professional and amateur musician. He has written of the narrow world
of other modern composers - Schoenberg and Webern, for example -
and of how Stockhausen turned his back on the 'humanist tradition
Beethoven worked in', although, of course, he does not fault him on
that score. But this was not Tippett's own way. To him the artistically
chaotic period in which we live, 'without an agreed musical style, so
that composers must wrestle with their own language in a manner
unknown, say, to Mozart', as he has put it, can only be resolved indi-
vidually by each composer. His own contribution has been personal and
all the more important for that. But it is also a real response to his
potential audience, for such is the way of the great humanist tradition.

As a person Tippett has always held firmly to his own beliefs; the
humorous and almost self-mocking tone that he can adopt in public
interview never conceals for long that he is at heart a very serious man.
His well-publicized interest in the culture of American television - detective series, Westerns, soap-operas and the like - was reflected in his
latest opera *The Ice Break*, but this element should not deflect the listener
from getting at the deeper meaning of this work. Tippett's own
development as an artist was slow, painful and bereft of much public
attention. It is one of the great ironies of his life that he did not really
come into the forefront of public interest until the time of the complete
breakdown of the artistic traditions of past generations - in the 1960s.
One result of this was that Tippett was suddenly greeted as a tremen-
dously modern composer, and the deep roots that he had in the traditions
of composing in England were obscured. Tippett's central concern about
the reconciliation of a person's good and evil natures was very much in
vogue in the 1960s. Since that time, however, another change has taken

place. Now that we are beginning to see the decade of the 1960s in some sort of historical perspective Tippett is no longer regarded as one of the 'moderns' but, rather, as old-fashioned. Such has the fickle pendulum of favour swung for Tippett. But, in the end, changing fashions do not matter and the criticism sometimes heard nowadays, that much of Tippett's operatic work will soon look very dated, was answered by the composer himself: what may look dated today, he has observed, may well not do so in, say, a century's time. Like his heroes Goethe and Beethoven, Tippett's vision is very far-sighted, both as regards the nature of man and the future of his art. His latest major work, *The Mask of Time*, first performed in 1984, confirmed that, again like Beethoven, Tippett is truly to be thought of as a prophet of man.

When presenting an honorary doctorate of the University of Cambridge in 1964 the Public Orator well said of Michael Tippett that 'whatever this man touches he philosophizes'; and the composer himself has written of how as a student he felt that music needed relating to a considered system of thought. Tippett's system of thought is clearly revealed in the epigraph that he chose for *The Knot Garden* from *All's Well that Ends Well*: 'Simply the thing I am shall make me live.' By way of summary we can do no better than to turn to his extraordinarily evocative conclusion of the BBC TV programme in the 'One Pair of Eyes' series, called 'Poets in a Barren Age':

I have been writing music for forty years. During those years there have been huge and world-shattering events in which I have been inevitably caught up. Whether society has felt music valuable or needful I have gone on writing because I must. And I know that my true function within a society which embraces all of us, is to continue an age-old tradition, fundamental to our civilization, which goes back into pre-history and will go forward into the unknown future. This tradition is to create images from the depths of the imagination and to give them form whether visual, intellectual or musical. For it is only through images that the inner world communicates at all. Images of the past, shapes of the future. Images of vigour for a decadent period, images of calm for one too violent. Images of reconciliation for worlds torn by division. And in an age of mediocrity and shattered dreams, images of abounding, generous, exuberant beauty.

As we turn to the last portrait in this gallery of composers of the musical renaissance we make, by the standards of this survey, a major jump; for many of the composers looked at in the various chapters of this study were born within only a few years of each other. In this chapter, however, we have Tippett, who was born in 1905, and Britten, who was not born until 1913. Why is this? One of the main reasons is that Tippett developed slowly while the precocious Britten came into his own very swiftly, and their full development as composers came at roughly the same time.

Britten's musical gifts came to early maturity. It was in 1934, that year when Elgar, Delius and Holst all died, that Benjamin Britten, having passed his examinations at the Royal College of Music, stepped out into his own musical career. Thus as the last strains of the music of Edwardian England finally died away Britten stood on the threshold of his great career in music; and he was to be the man who took modern English music to a pinnacle previously undreamt of, except in the case of Elgar. These two men, indeed, stand as the highest points at either end of this period of exceptional fertility for English music, and although the differences between them are legion their points of similarity are none the less instructive.

What Parry had said about Elgar – that the English public could only recognize one native composer at a time – had retained a certain truth over the years. On the passing of Elgar the position of 'England's composer' became slightly less clear-cut than before: Vaughan Williams was obviously the senior figure in English music but Walton came to have a strong claim also. Britten, as a young man, had an amusing and neatly expressed entry in his diary for 1937 on this theme. He had lunched with William Walton at Sloane Square: 'He is charming, but I feel always the school relationship with him – he is so obviously the head prefect of English music, whereas I'm the promising young new boy. Soon of course he'll leave & return as a member of the staff – [Vaughan] Williams being of course the Headmaster. Elgar was never *that* – but a member of the Governing Board.' Britten, however, was to outstrip both Vaughan Williams and Walton, joining Elgar on the governing board, and take Parry's title as England's composer without serious rival. Britten was, indeed, honoured in his lifetime as no English composer had ever been before. The royal commission of an opera – *Gloriana*, in 1953 – was a unique tribute; as Vaughan Williams reminded the readers of *The Times*, it was 'the first time in history the Sovereign has commanded an opera by a composer from these islands for a great occasion'. Britten went on to collect various state honours, culminating in a peerage, the prize that Elgar so desired but was denied. The only English composer peer was, however, a very different man from Elgar, and this was clearly seen when *Gloriana* reached its first night. Many in the audience at Covent Garden had probably expected something essentially 'patriotic', in keeping with the prevailing mood of the New Elizabethans; but they were given something which was, rather, essentially musical, and they did not really know what to make of it. Britten was never the writer of widely popular serious music like Elgar; the audience which he reached was a much more restricted one than Elgar's, and while this was in some part due to great and fundamental changes in the world of music, it was also a reflection of the differences between Elgar and Britten themselves.

But there is much that bears comparison in the careers of the two composers. Neither man was the creation of the great musical establishment of their day, and both suffered to a degree thereby (Elgar, of course, for a much longer period than Britten). Both emerged, however, the stronger for these early difficulties and both were recognized, in their time, as leaders of the modern musical movement in England. This implied, in each case, that they were ahead of the field and that they started out and developed as strong individuals in their own right; and it was perhaps this, above all, that carried them so far into the popular imagination. Both men had such a clear and personal musical voice that the public could be relied upon to recognize their general style, and even deliberate parodies of their music could draw a wide response.

Benjamin Britten's strong musical interests and abilities date from the earliest period of his life. He was born in 1913, appropriately enough on St Cecilia's Day. His father was a successful dental surgeon and his childhood home was a place where his musical talents, obvious from an early age, were encouraged. His early attempts at composing were conventional enough: great architectural collections of notes that looked magnificent on manuscript paper – 'the result looked rather like the Forth Bridge', he later admitted – elaborate tone poems (lasting about twenty seconds), and a setting of Longfellow's 'Beware!'. But even at an early stage marked characteristics which were to remain with him for life could be seen. Britten was already a meticulous composer, taking great care to make precisely the effect he desired, indicating he already knew clearly what he wanted. It may well have been very important that Britten's father was not in favour of having a gramophone or radio at home; Imogen Holst tells us that it was felt that this would impair real music making. Britten must belong to the very last generation of composers brought up without the aid, or the hindrance, of these devices.

Music making in the Britten home was conventional for the period

but when Britten heard Frank Bridge's 'modern' work *The Sea* at the
1924 Norwich Festival he was, in his own words, 'knocked sideways'.
Three years later Britten became a pupil of Bridge, an arrangement that
was to be vital for him. It was, as we have seen, Bridge who taught him
to insist on 'the absolutely clear relationship of what was in my mind to
what was on the paper', and who gave the younger man 'a sense of
technical ambition'. Britten left his preparatory school in 1928 where he
had obviously led an active life, having been *Victor Ludorum* (one of his
life-long interests was playing tennis); he went on to Gresham's School
in Holt. Here he stayed only two years and in 1930 was admitted to the
Royal College of Music before his seventeenth birthday. A revealing
anecdote told by John Ireland, one of the three adjudicators at the Royal
College entrance interview, has one of the other adjudicators saying,
when faced with the young Britten and his works, 'What is an English
public schoolboy doing writing music of this kind?' Britten was out of
line with his college from the start: he later said of this period, 'When
you are immensely full of energy and ideas you don't want to waste
your time being taken through elementary exercises in dictation.' Britten's interests were much wider than those considered proper by the
College. His desire to go to study with Berg in Vienna met with a cool
response. The College apparently convinced his mother that such a trip
would not be good for him. Recalling this incident in 1963 Britten said,
'there was at that time an almost moral prejudice against serial music.
... I think also that there was some confusion in my parents' minds –
thinking that "not a good influence" meant morally, not musically.'
Here was the other side of the view of music and morality valued so
highly by Parry and his contempories. As a result of not being able to
study with Berg Britten felt that he had to climb over gates which
otherwise would have opened for him. The Royal College completely
failed to recognize the talent that it had within its walls and while he
was a student only one of Britten's works was heard there. In 1934, at
the age of twenty, he left the College and, determined to be a composer,
set about earning his living.

   The period from 1934 until 1941 was to be an exciting one for the
young Britten, a period that was recently well covered in a book by his
official biographer, Donald Mitchell, drawing on the composer's diaries
for the period. These diaries are not in themselves a profound source but
they do bring alive in a remarkable way how the young composer lived
and worked in the later part of the thirties; and they especially illuminate

Britten's collaboration with W.H. Auden on *Our Hunting Fathers* in 1936, his 'real Opus 1', as he felt. As Scott Goddard pointed out in *British Music of Our Time*, the performance of *Our Hunting Fathers* at the Norwich Festival in 1936, 'amused the sophisticated, scandalized those among the gentry who caught Auden's words, and left musicians dazzled at so much talent'. Britten became a part of the new artistic world, which centred around such figures as Auden, Christopher Isherwood, the producer Basil Wright, and the painter William Coldstream. Their experiments at this time with new art-forms were especially fruitful in drama and in film: Auden and Britten's work on the short film *Night Mail* is only the most celebrated example of this.

> This is the night mail crossing the border,
> Bringing the cheque and the postal order,
> Letters for the rich, letters for the poor,
> The shop at the corner and the girl next door . . .

Britten acquired a reputation at this period of his life for composing highly effective incidental music for films and plays. (Throughout his life Britten always took a highly professional attitude to his work. Peter Pears once noted that what Britten wanted to hear most of all in other composers' music was 'magic and efficiency. The magic cannot be explained; the efficiency is something any good composer should have.') His collaboration with Auden covered a number of projects, culminating in an operetta, *Paul Bunyan*, which was staged at Columbia University in New York in 1941. Auden was a very important liberating influence on the younger man's contact with the literary lions of the time, and taught Britten much about the world around him and his place in it. This was his most outwardly political period. While Britten's work in England was very successful he had, however, acquired in musical circles a reputation as a 'clever young man' – too clever for his own good, some thought. He was characterized as a brilliant musical pamphleteer, a purveyor of 'undergraduate music' (whatever that might mean – and this was ironic in that Britten never went to university), and as a composer of music that was thought 'cold', probably because it was 'clever'. It is a reputation that Britten has never entirely escaped. He was, however, doing well at this time with a wider European audience, especially with the ISCM; in 1936 he went to Barcelona to hear his Suite for Violin and Piano, and in the following year to Salzburg for his *Variations on a Theme of Frank Bridge*, which was then played often all over Europe.

For many reasons Britten was not happy in England, and he decided
to go to the United States. Years later he recalled this time when, 'I was
a discouraged young composer – muddled, fed up and looking for work,
longing to be used.' Britten's stay in the United States was immensely
productive. Here he produced *Les Illuminations*, a work for voice and
strings to verses by Rimbaud, and the *Seven Sonnets of Michelangelo* for
tenor and piano, works which he told Murray Schafer, 'were necessary
for me in order to shed the bad influence of the Royal College. With
both the French and the Italian [texts] I was perhaps responding to
Nietzsche's call to "mediterraneanize music".' This period also marks
the beginning of the vitally important partnership with Peter Pears, for
whom Britten wrote much of his greatest music. Unlike Auden, however, whom he had deliberately followed across the ocean, Britten came
to realize that his future lay in the island of his birth, and in 1941 an
article he read in the *Listener* by E.M. Forster on the poet George Crabbe
had an enormous influence on him. Forster wrote:

> To talk about Crabbe is to talk about England. He never left our shores....
> He did not go to London much, but lived in villages and small country towns.
> [He] was born at Aldeburgh, on the coast of Suffolk. It is a bleak little place,
> not beautiful. It huddles round a flint-towered church and sprawls down to the
> North Sea – and what a wallop the sea makes as it pounds at the shingle! Near
> by is a quay at the side of an estuary, and here the scenery becomes melancholy
> and flat; expanses of mud, saltish commons, the marsh-birds crying. Crabbe
> heard that sound and saw that melancholy, and they got into his verse.

Britten and Pears turned to Crabbe's work and there began the idea that
a few years later was to become *Peter Grimes*. But first they knew that
they had to return to England, a country that had been at war for two
years. As pacifists this situation would not be an easy one but, unlike
Auden, they came to see that they should be in England at this time: 'I
suddenly realized where I belonged and what I lacked', Britten later
recalled, adding, 'I had become without roots.' He was now, however,
ready to put his roots down and he knew where and how to do it. And
this greatly affected his music and musical language. Pears has written of
the time in America, 'It was not for three years that he was to realize
that his roots (and his language) were English.'

Britten and Pears came back to Britain in 1942 and were exempted
from military service on condition that they gave recitals for the Council
for the Encouragement of Music and the Arts. This was the period when
they worked most closely with Michael Tippett; Tippett's *Boyhood End*

was, for instance, written for them at this time. (Tippett was later to pay
Britten the highest compliment when he described him as 'the most
purely musical person I have ever met'.) Britten wrote much useful
music at this time: the *Hymn to St Cecilia*, *A Ceremony of Carols*, the
*Serenade* for tenor, horn and strings for the celebrated horn-player
Dennis Brain, and *The Ballad of Little Musgrave and Lady Barnard* for the
prisoners of war of OFLAG VII B. He was also working on *Peter Grimes*.

Based now in Aldeburgh, Britten produced a number of major works
in the post-war years; but first and foremost was *Peter Grimes* which, at
its initial performance in June 1945, put the seal on all that had gone
before in his career and really established him as a major musical figure
in his country. There followed *The Rape of Lucretia*, *Albert Herring*, *Billy
Budd*, *Gloriana*, *The Turn of the Screw*, *A Midsummer Night's Dream*,
*Curlew River*, *Owen Wingrave*, *Death in Venice* and much more besides.
The output was continuous, impressive and always looked forward to
by the general musical public. Britten now became something of a
national institution, and it was the success of *Peter Grimes* that really
turned the corner for the composer in the public's eye, for the opera was
greeted with approval such as had met no comparable English work
since the time of Elgar. The quest for an English operatic opportunity
had finally found a solution.

The traditional form of English opera – as we have seen, essentially
an amateur tradition – was something that Britten could not tolerate.
Thus, among the enormous range of activities that he undertook in these
years, the composer caused a reliable, professional body of singers to be
formed who would be able to produce fine performances of his own
works, as well as those of other composers. What others had dreamt of
– setting up a really first-class body of operatic performers – Britten put
into effect. At first in conjunction with Glyndebourne, and then on its
own – the Byzantine politics of the affair need not detain us – the English
Opera Group became Britten's vehicle of excellence. The composer also
surrounded himself with the very best talent in staging and directing
operas. Britten's seemingly ceaseless energy also established annual festivals at Aldeburgh, an affair that grew from modest beginnings to major
proportions. Britten was where he wanted to be and he wanted to bring
music not just to his friends but also to the local people. As he himself
said in 1964:

I belong at home – there – in Aldeburgh. I have tried to bring music *to* it in
the shape of our local Festival; and all the music I write comes *from* it. I believe

in roots, associations, in backgrounds, in personal relationships.... I do not
write for posterity.... I write music, now, in Aldeburgh, for people living
there, and further afield, indeed for anyone who cares to play it or listen to it.

The impetus to write a new work almost always came from outside
Britten. He was not a man who wanted to explore himself or his music
in a steady stream of symphonies but, rather, he preferred to act upon
a given stimulus, which could perhaps be a direct commission, or the
desire to write a piece for a specific performer: like, for example, the
works that he wrote for the cellist Mstislav Rostropovich.

Britten's desire to compose grew out of his specific wish to communicate with other people. In a speech that he made when he was given
the freedom of Lowestoft in 1951 he said, 'as an artist, I want to serve
the community. In other days, artists were the servants of institutions
like the Church, or of private patrons. Today it is the community that
orders the artist about, and it is not a bad thing to try to serve all sorts
of different people, and to have to work to order.' Britten's desire to
bring music to as wide a general public as possible sometimes led him
to say things that may seem a little naïve to his successors but his point
was clear and deeply sincere. Many of Britten's works were written for
young or for amateur musicians to play and his involvement of the
audience in his musical pieces is well known. In another speech some
years later, this time replying to being granted the freedom of Aldeburgh, Britten returned to this theme: 'I believe that an artist should be
part of his community.' How similar this sounds in retrospect to some
of the things said by, among others, Rutland Boughton, Holst, Vaughan
Williams and even Parry. Britten felt that the work of an artist without
an audience or with only a high-brow one tended to become 'ivory
tower, without focus'. Britten went on, 'this has made a great deal of
modern work obscure and impractical'. The composer stressed that it
was not that he was against all 'new and strange ideas' but that he was
against experiment for experiment's sake. 'It's necessary to say this
because there are audiences who are not discriminating about it. They
think that everything new is good; that if it is shocking it must be
important.' Britten's beliefs drew him, rather, to the people who performed music themselves.

Britten had a very moral view of the world around him. Peter Pears
has said that Britten 'thought people should behave properly and not
betray one another'. He was a complicated man. When young he had
felt a deep sense of insecurity: he was very much the youngest member

of the Auden gang and his diary entries reveal just how acutely he felt this. Auden believed that Britten was in need of a 'passionate affair', and other friends of the time wondered about Britten's sexuality. The break with Auden, whose 'bossiness', as he put it, Britten had begun to find overbearing, and the return to England in the war marked a new personal strength in Britten, however, and over the years at Aldeburgh he grew greatly in confidence. Various complicated traits have been seen in his music. One of his friends and musical collaborators, Hans Keller, has pointed to a 'homosexual tension' in his music, and others have written about a streak of near-cruelty that can be seen and heard in places in his operas. Peter Pears has perhaps best summed up all these various observations with the remark that Britten had a 'craving for lost innocence brought on by his increasing disillusionment with man'.

Some of Britten's friends recalled after his death that he could be harshly critical of bad performance. (It is interesting to note in this context that Britten was never really a teacher.) Partly this reflects Britten's own character but it was also a constant theme of many of the composers of the musical renaissance. And they were absolutely right to insist on the highest standards of performance: accepting something rather less than the best has long been one of the worst diseases in the body of English music. Britten's sometimes rather unbending determination that the music he made should be of the highest standards led him, on occasion, to be extremely demanding of other people; but of nobody did he demand more than himself. He was often greatly stretched by the amount of work which he undertook. He continued to work throughout his life as a performer, especially as Peter Pears's pianist. He also travelled widely both as a performer and as a conductor. Moreover he was responsible for much of the detailed planning of the festivals at Aldeburgh, spending his energy on a vast range of projects. His boyish energy was remarkable until the illness that brought his life to such a sad and early close in 1976. Britten was a man who, as we can see from many published memoirs of him, achieved an almost holy aura at Aldeburgh; a man the demands of whose work brought some of his friends 'in' favour while others were 'out'; and yet he was also obviously a man of great charm – able to get on well with the local people, the fishermen, the workmen who helped build his concert hall, and able to communicate especially clearly with children.

Britten was as demanding a composer as he was a performer. In working on his operas he would ceaselessly discuss points of the finest detail with his librettists, and would need to know in his mind exactly how a scene was played before he could settle the music. Describing his technique as a composer to Murray Schafer, Britten said, 'usually I have the music complete in my mind before putting pencil to paper. That doesn't mean that every note has been composed, perhaps not one has, but I have worked out questions of form, texture, character, and so forth, in a very precise way so that I know exactly what effects I want and how I am going to achieve them.'

Frank Bridge's lessons had paid full dividends. Britten went on to describe the strict routine to which he adhered while he was working. He would work in the morning, walk in the afternoon and work again in the evening, going to bed early in order to start the procedure again the next day. Because so many of his works were specific commissions Britten usually worked to a deadline, and this he clearly found helpful.

Britten believed that a composer should not lose touch with his audience. 'I think there is a snobbery of enormous pretensions connected with the most recent trends in music', he told Schafer. He believed that there was still much that could be done within the wide bounds of conventional tonality. He also made the valuable point that as the contemporary music of the time was often so extremely difficult to perform it was sometimes almost impossible to get right. Talking of his performance with Peter Pears of songs by Webern, Britten said, 'we die a thousand deaths trying to get them exactly right and it is still nearly impossible'.

Britten was very much his own man when it came to his compositions: he was never close to any group of composers – although he did once collaborate with Lennox Berkeley on *Mont Juic*. He did, however, give considerable support to many of his contemporary and younger English composers throughout his career. Past English composers had a strong influence on Britten and, in particular, he shared with Michael Tippett a great love of the music of Purcell. Britten worked on performing editions of Purcell's music and used a Purcell theme for one of his best-known works – *The Young Person's Guide to the Orchestra*. The vital key that Purcell provided for Britten was the successful setting of English words to music. Of his Purcell realizations he wrote, 'it has been the constant endeavour of the arranger to apply to these realizations something of that mixture of clarity, brilliance, tenderness and strangeness which shines out in all Purcell's music'. As we have already seen, Tippett also remarked about himself and Britten that they responded to the 'carry and freedom' of Purcell's vocal line. Furthermore, Peter Pears noticed of his friend that 'there blows in his vocal music ... a strong revitalizing south-east wind which has rid English music of much accumulated dust and cobwebs, and he renewed the vigour of the sung word with Purcellian attack'. Having begun to develop a way of setting English, Britten searched out suitable texts for his artistic purposes. Talking of texts for opera, Britten once said that what he required were 'memorable and thrilling phrases'. Few settings of contemporary poets were being made in the 1930s, but Britten learnt a lot from his early collaboration with Auden, and his settings of Auden's verse were a great success. Many new influences were to come into the world of English music through Britten's ability to look forward in this way.

In musical terms Schubert – among others – was a very important influence on Britten; Pears and Britten became especially well known for their performances of his songs. And this was revealing. The musical scholar H.F. Redlich felt that Britten shared with Schubert one basically important characteristic, 'that his music receives its specific shape and its general inspiration from the poetic word'; and there can be little doubt that choice of words – if not always entirely successful – was vital to Britten's music. Late in his life he turned to a setting of 'The Death of Saint Narcissus' by T.S. Eliot and made the revealing comment that he had done so for 'the clarity and security of his language'. In his music Britten also aimed at nothing so much as clarity. 'Music for me is clarification; I try to clarify, to refine', he told Murray Schafer. 'My technique is to tear all the waste away; to achieve perfect clarity of expression, that is my aim.'

There is always a tendency to regard the most recent great composer as somehow divorced from the tradition, and in Britten's case that is a view that has been commonly held. But Britten was not always looked at in such isolation nor will he be thus regarded in the future. Many people now recognize the particularly English qualities in Britten's music and although he was a very different person and wrote a different kind of music from those English composers who came before him it is possible to place him within a general revival of composition in England. At a very early stage in his career the point was made that Britten seemed to be the least 'national' composer, in what was then the conventional sense; but when a study of Britten's works was published in 1952 much was made of what was called Britten's 'Englishry'. Donald Mitchell declared that 'Britten's Englishry is of the profoundest significance for the musical culture of Europe and ourselves', and while, of

course, stressing Britten's European outlook and the remarkable reception that his work had received overseas, the strong impression of an
English composer remained. Mitchell began an analysis of what consti-
tuted the English qualities of Britten's work and reached the conclusion
that 'Britten has created an Englishry of his own'. One suspects that the
word 'Englishry' was used in this context to suggest just this: that while
Britten was manifestly a composer with strong English musical characteristics of his own he was not marked at all with the 'Englishness' of
the Shropshire Lad – or any other – 'school' of English composers. The
new generation of music writers was staking out its own interpretation
of English music; as had so many of the immediately preceding generations.

As Britten's life went on the dominant features of his 'Englishry'
became much clearer. His choice of fine English texts, his concern for
the setting of words, his festival in its splendid Suffolk setting, the group
of friends he surrounded himself with, all testified in different ways to
his very specific English qualities, qualities that also permeate his works.
While Britten eschewed the folk-song tradition of Vaughan Williams,
as composers of his generation had to, it did not mean that he turned his
back on folk-songs themselves. Britten was particularly taken by the
folk-song arrangements of Percy Grainger: in 1933 he had written of
'two brilliant folk-song arrangements of Percy Grainger ... knocking all
the V. Williams and R.O. Morris arrangements into a cocked-hat'. (Indeed, some of the last pieces that Britten finished before his death were
eight folk-song arrangements for harp or piano.) In many other ways
also Britten made something new out of the best traditions of English
music. He discarded, for example, a prevailing churchiness that was a
feature of much of the religious music of the time and brought in a
profound – yet still very English – sense of religion of his own. He said
once, when addressing an audience in the Soviet Union, that he realized
that music develops along national lines and that the music of one
country may not always be immediately recognizable to another. He
also felt that the physical settings where his pieces were put on were
important: he said, for example, that the *War Requiem* was 'perfectly in
place in Coventry Cathedral but pointless in Cairo or Peking'.

The appearance of Britten's post-war works was the signal for a new
wave of discussion about a musical renaissance in England. Imogen Holst
tells us that Britten himself wrote of it in 1943 – 'that "something" in
the air which heralds a renaissance' – and it was not long before many

writers revived the theme, and this has continued to the present day. At the time of the new edition (1983) of his book on Britten and his operas, the composer's friend Eric Walter White, for instance, wrote of 'those of us who took part in the renaissance of English music which occurred during Britten's lifetime'; but it was both this and more. Benjamin Britten was also part of a great succession of composers seen in England from the time of Edward Elgar, who together had created and sustained a major renaissance in English music.

# Postscript

All periods of artistic history are constructions; and we can best see the English musical renaissance as an astronomer construes the constellations of the night sky – from a distance. And while, from our viewpoint, we can make some shape and sense of the points of light that make up the constellation of the musical renaissance, we also know that, like stars, the individual composers are fixed in their own quite independent positions.

It was not practicable in the opening chapter of this book to try to pin down an exact moment when the musical renaissance began, and it is equally profitless now to search for one when it might be said to have ended. But looking back from our present-day perspective we can get a rough idea of when the main characteristics of the renaissance ceased to have real meaning and we can now usefully seek out the causes and the character of the major changes that came into music in England.

The overall decline in amateur music making was one of the major changes. For this there were many reasons, and one of the chief of them was music losing the high position it had previously held in the minds of people throughout the country. The shift away from the popular belief that music should be educational towards a view that it should be entertainment – a movement that was greatly accelerated during the two world wars, especially the second, when the 'mobilization' of popular music became an important part of the war effort – was of fundamental importance. And if music was to be seen as an entertainment it followed that it came into competition with other forms of entertainment in people's minds. Taking a serious interest in music slipped down the list of desirable personal attainments as other, more enticing, diversions presented themselves. That music should have a moral or an educational role became a decidedly unpopular view. The effects of this shift in opinion were considerable and there was a great decline in amateur music making in general. Music was now beginning to be thought of much more as a 'professional' activity. This was reflected in many ways. The music publishing business, for instance, underwent a considerable recession as music making at home declined. This had the effect of forcing up the price of music relative to other sorts of personal expenditure. And there were many other similar instances. The complex and interdependent parts of the music world that had been set in motion by the late Victorians and which had served England well for the best part of a century began to come unravelled.

The most potent force of change was, however, the newly developed means of mass-communication that grew up during the period: recordings of music on gramophone records, radio, film and television have meant a vast increase in the amount of music actually made. But more has meant worse. Music has become appallingly popular, as Constant Lambert put it. Over the years many hopes as well as fears were expressed about the use of the new means of mass-communication, but, overall, the interest in serious music greatly declined. To hear music is not necessarily to listen to it, and the radio makes few demands on its listeners – even when it is switched on. What serious music there is in people's homes nowadays is most often second-hand music: the piano in the parlour has given way to the radio – active participation to passive.

Benjamin Britten once remarked, 'If I say that the loudspeaker is the principal enemy of music, I don't mean that I am not grateful to it as a means of education or study, or as an evoker of memories. But it is not part of true musical *experience*.' True musical experience to Britten, as to Elgar or Vaughan Williams or any of the other composers we have looked at in this book, was something where musical people were essentially active, not passive. Although Britten passionately believed in professionalism in all that he did he also knew that amateurs had always been 'an important force in the shaping of our musical tradition'. And pieces of Britten's music which need professionals to perform them still speak to ordinary music-lovers in a language that they can follow. 'It is insulting to address anyone in a language which they do not understand', Britten believed. Further, he was appalled, Imogen Holst tells us, at the thought of young composers 'writing more and more for machines, in conditions dictated by machines'.

And this was another important element in the great changes that had come into music, for the composer and his audience were losing touch with each other, and an enormous snobbery was growing up around modern music; this was clearly seen by Britten in his own day. Gone also was that close understanding and mutual respect that had existed between the 'serious' and the 'light' composers. And the creation of 'superstar' performers and conductors, who seem to restrict themselves to performing, in the main, only a relatively limited number of well-known works, has meant that less familiar composers and their works are not often nowadays heard. In all these ways the contemporary musical world has built up barriers for itself.

The 1950s and 1960s saw many younger composers completely departing from the previous musical tradition – even a tradition of rebellion – and going off on their own radical path; and their failure to try to take the musical public with them further seriously damaged the fabric of musical life in Great Britain. The view that music is some kind of subtle international language, only to be understood by the few, has flourished again in the refined air of the 'serious' side of the modern media and the professional 'musicological' world that effectively controls the output of such media. The musical language adopted by these younger composers was deliberately obscure, and the move away from a language of music that was basically melodic meant that all forms of singing groups except professional ones were, in practice, excluded from participation. Equally, little music was written for solo instruments or chamber groups that the average amateur music maker could perform. This struck deep at the very heart of the greatest strength of the English tradition.

The position of the composers themselves also underwent great change, especially in respect to their financial basis. The former reliance on a private income or on personal patronage had left many composers free to develop their art at their own speed. Those composers who came from poor backgrounds were at least able to earn some sort of living working in the wide and active musical world that existed in most of the period considered in this book. The severe and extensive contraction of much amateur music making and teaching has, ironically, made it far more difficult in our wealthier times for an aspiring composer from a poor background to support himself by working in the general musical world, as did many composers looked at in this book. And the modern great patrons of music – central and local government authorities, big business corporations, universities and so on – are much less successful in this respect than their predecessors, who would often completely support an artist. The idea of paying a composer a salary simply to exist and write his music is one that has often been discussed in recent years but it has not been made a reality: the idea of a 'composer in residence' is about as far as this has gone and even this places constraints on the artist, who knows that he will be supported for only a brief period. Much competition takes place for the funds available and one of the results of this is that composers often now see their immediate audience as those professional musicologists who tend to administer such schemes; and this too has further helped to restrict their horizons. Many composers have found it expedient to develop two styles of music: one for 'popular' consumption and another, in a private language of utter introspection which most will find completely obscure, for the specialist few. We have experienced some years of this unwelcome polarity in music now and, if nothing else is clear, we know that this is the wrong way to go forward if we are to have a widely-based living musical culture, one in which individual genius can flourish.

And a living musical culture was, above all, what the composers looked at in this book belonged to. They all understood that music needs to be seen in its social context. They shared a basic language and sense of the purpose of music that was deeply rooted in both their minds and those of their audiences. Theirs was a serious view: some were religious in a conventional sense, some were closer to spiritualism, some held firm political views, others, in a spirit of humanism, affirmed a deep belief in human dignity and life. Together they sought through their music to bring order and understanding into the fractured world in which they lived. They freed themselves from domination by the great musical traditions of the Continent, turning, rather, to earlier English music, to the almost endlessly rich and varied music of the English Church, to the folk-song of their own country, and to the abundant fount of English verse for their inspiration. And these men were true to their tradition in one respect above all others, and that was the strength of their individuality. They formed a tradition of independence; equally heirs and rebels, rebels and heirs. And within the living musical world in which they worked and had their being they were the music makers.

# Bibliography

This bibliography concentrates on the major works on the composers considered in this book: only a few general works are included and many standard, well-known texts - above all the incomparable *New Grove* and its predecessors - are omitted, allowing the limited space available to be used for lesser-known books about specific composers.

## GENERAL BOOKS

Bacharach, A.L. (ed.), *British Music of Our Time*, Penguin, 1946 (new edn 1951).

Blom, Eric, *Music in England*, Penguin, 1942.

Dickinson, Peter (ed.), *Twenty British Composers*, Chester Music, 1975.

Frank, Alan, *Modern British Composers*, Dennis Dobson, 1953.

Hadow, W.H., *English Music*, Longman Green, 1931.

Howes, Frank, *The English Musical Renaissance*, Secker & Warburg, 1966.

Leach, Gerald, *British Composer Profiles*, British Music Society, 1980.

Mackerness, E.D., *A Social History of English Music*, Routledge & Kegan Paul, 1964.

Peacock, Alan and Weir, Ronald, *The Composer in the Market Place*, Faber Music, 1975.

Pirie, Peter J., *The English Musical Renaissance: Twentieth Century British Composers and Their Works*, Victor Gollancz, 1979.

Raynor, Henry, *Music in England*, Robert Hale, 1980.

Routh, Francis, *Contemporary British Music*, Macdonald, 1972.

Schafer, Murray, *British Composers in Interview*, Faber & Faber, 1963.

Scholes, Percy A., *The Mirror of Music 1844-1944: A Century of Musical Life in Britain as reflected in the pages of The Musical Times*, 2 vols, Novello with Oxford University Press, 1947.

White, Eric Walter, *A History of English Opera*, Faber & Faber, 1983.

## ELGAR

For a general survey of the main books on Elgar – with reliable, short evaluations – see Alan Webb's 'Elgar Bibliography' in *The Elgar Society Newsletter*, September 1976.

#### LETTERS, LECTURES AND PHOTOGRAPHS

Moore, Jerrold Northrop (compiled by), *Elgar: A Life in Photographs*, Oxford University Press, 1972.
Young, Percy M. (ed.), *A Future for English Music and other Lectures*, Dennis Dobson, 1968.
Young, Percy M. (ed.), *Letters of Edward Elgar and other Writings*, Geoffrey Bliss, 1956.
Young, Percy M. (ed.), *Letters to Nimrod*, Dennis Dobson, 1965.

#### MEMOIRS

Atkins, E. Wulstan, *The Elgar-Atkins Friendship*, David & Charles, 1984.
Burley, Rosa, and Carruthers, Frank C., *Edward Elgar: The Record of a Friendship*, Barrie & Jenkins, 1972.
Powell, Dora M. (Mrs Richard Powell), *Edward Elgar: Memories of a Variation*, Oxford University Press, 1937 (2nd edn, 1947; reprinted Remploy, 1979).
Reed, William H., *Elgar as I Knew Him*, Victor Gollancz, 1936 (reissued, 1973).

#### RECENT BIOGRAPHIES, ETC.

Kennedy, Michael, *Portrait of Elgar*, Oxford University Press, 2nd edn, 1982.
McVeagh, Diana M., *Edward Elgar: His Life and Music*, Dent, 1955.
Moore, Jerrold Northrop, *Edward Elgar: A Creative Life*, Oxford University Press, 1984.
Parrott, Ian, *Elgar*, the Master Musicians Series, Dent, 1971.
Redwood, Christopher, *An Elgar Companion*, Sequoia/Moorland, 1982.
Young, Percy M., *Alice Elgar: Enigma of a Victorian Lady*, Dennis Dobson, 1978.
Young, Percy M., *Elgar O.M.*, revised edn, White Lion, 1973 (first published Collins, 1955).

## DELIUS

Beecham, Thomas, *Frederick Delius*, revised edn, Severn House, 1975 (first published Hutchinson, 1959).
Carley, Lionel, *Delius: A Life in Letters, 1862–1908*, Scolar Press, 1983.
Carley, Lionel, *Delius: the Paris Years*, Triad Press, 1975.

Carley, Lionel, and Threlfall, Robert, *Delius: A Life in Pictures*, Oxford University Press, 1977.

Delius, Clare, *Frederick Delius: Memories of my Brother*, Ivor Nicholson & Watson, 1935.

Fenby, Eric, *Delius*, the Great Composers Series, Faber & Faber, 1971.

Fenby, Eric, *Delius as I Knew Him*, revised edn, Faber & Faber, 1981 (first published G. Bell, 1936).

Hutchings, Arthur, *Delius*, Macmillan, 1948.

Jefferson, Allan, *Delius*, the Master Musicians Series, Dent, 1972.

Palmer, Christopher, *Delius: Portrait of a Cosmopolitan*, Duckworth, 1976.

Redwood, Christopher (ed.), *A Delius Companion*, revised edn, John Calder, 1980.

Warlock, Peter (Philip Heseltine), *Frederick Delius*, revised edn, The Bodley Head, 1952 (first published as by 'Philip Heseltine', The Bodley Head, 1923).

*see also:*

Gray, Cecil, *Peter Warlock: A Memoir of Philip Heseltine*, Jonathan Cape, 1934.

Tomlinson, Fred, *Warlock and Delius*, Thames Publishing, 1976.


HURLSTONE

Hurlstone, Katherine (ed.), *William Hurlstone, Musician: Memories and Records by His Friends*, Cary, 1949.


COLERIDGE-TAYLOR

Coleridge-Taylor, Avril, *The Heritage of Samuel Coleridge-Taylor*, Dennis Dobson, 1979.

Coleridge-Taylor, Jessie, *Coleridge-Taylor: A Memory Sketch or Personal Reminiscences of My Husband, Genius and Musician*, privately printed, 1943.

Sayers, W.C. Berwick, *Samuel Coleridge-Taylor: His Life and Letters*, 2nd edn, Augener, 1927 (first published Cassell, 1915).

Tortolano, William, *Samuel Coleridge-Taylor: Anglo-Black Composer 1875-1912*, The Scarecrow Press, New Jersey, 1977.


BOUGHTON

Hurd, Michael, *Immortal Hour: The Life and Period of Rutland Boughton*, Routledge & Kegan Paul, 1962.

## HOLBROOKE

Holbrooke, Josef, *Contemporary British Composers*, Cecil Palmer, 1925.
*Josef Holbrooke: Various Appreciations by Many Authors*, Rudall Carte and the Holbrooke Society, 1937.
Lowe, George, *Joseph Holbrooke and His Work*, Kegan Paul, Trench, Trubner, 1920.

## BANTOCK

Anderton, H. Orsmond, *Granville Bantock*, The Bodley Head, 1915.
Bantock, Myrrha, *Granville Bantock: A Personal Portrait*, Dent, 1972.

## HAVERGAL BRIAN

Eastaugh, Kenneth, *Havergal Brian: The Making of a Composer*, Harrap, 1976.
Foreman, Lewis, *Havergal Brian and the Performance of his Orchestral Music*, Thames Publishing, 1976.
Nettel, Reginald, *Havergal Brian and his Music*, Dennis Dobson, 1976.
Rapoport, Paul, *Opus Est: Six Composers from Northern Europe*, Kahn & Averill, 1978.

## WALFORD DAVIES

Colles, H.C., *Walford Davies: A Biography*, Oxford University Press, 1942.

## ETHEL SMYTH

St John, Christopher, *Ethel Smyth: A Biography*, Longman, 1959.

## VAUGHAN WILLIAMS

Day, James, *Vaughan Williams*, the Master Musicians Series, 3rd edn, Dent, 1974.
Douglas, Roy, *Working with R.V.W.*, Oxford University Press, 1972.
Kennedy, Michael, *The Works of Ralph Vaughan Williams*, new edn, Oxford University Press, 1980 (originally published as a companion volume to Ursula Vaughan Williams's biography in 1964).
Ottaway, Hugh, *Vaughan Williams Symphonies*, BBC, 1972.
Vaughan Williams, Ralph, *National Music and Other Essays*, Oxford University Press, 1963.
Vaughan Williams, Ralph and Holst, Gustav, *Heirs and Rebels: Letters written to*

*each other and occasional writings on music* (ed. Ursula Vaughan Williams and Imogen Holst), Oxford University Press, 1959.

Vaughan Williams, Ursula, *R.V.W.: A Biography of Ralph Vaughan Williams*, Oxford University Press, 1964.

Vaughan Williams, Ursula and Lunn, J.E., *Ralph Vaughan Williams: A Pictorial Biography*, Oxford University Press, 1971.

## HOLST

Holst, Gustav, *Letters to W.G. Whittaker* (ed. Michael Short), University of Glasgow Press, 1974.

Holst, Imogen, *Gustav Holst: A Biography,* 2nd edn, Oxford University Press, 1969.

Holst, Imogen, *Holst*, the Great Composers Series, 2nd edn, Faber & Faber, 1981.

Holst, Imogen, *The Music of Gustav Holst,* 2nd edn, Oxford University Press, 1968.

Rubbra, Edmund, *Collected Essays on Gustav Holst*, Triad Press, 1974.

Short, Michael, *Gustav Holst: A Centenary Documentation*, White Lion, 1974.

Vaughan Williams, Ralph, and Holst, Gustav, *Heirs and Rebels*, see above.

## BUTTERWORTH

A volume of letters, memoirs etc. was privately printed in 1918: a copy is in the British Library.

## BAX

Bax, Arnold, *Farewell my Youth*, Longman Green, 1943.

O'Byrne, Dermot, *Poems by Arnold Bax* (ed. Lewis Foreman), Thames Publishing, 1979.

Foreman, Lewis, *Bax: A Composer and His Times*, Scolar Press, 1983.

Scott-Sutherland, Colin, *Arnold Bax*, Dent, 1973.

## IRELAND

Longmire, John, *John Ireland: Portrait of a Friend*, John Baker, 1969.

Scott-Sutherland, Colin, *John Ireland*, Triad Press, 1980.

Searle, Muriel V., *John Ireland: The Man and his Music*, Midas Books, 1979.

## BRIDGE

Payne, Anthony, Foreman, Lewis, and Bishop, John, *The Music of Frank Bridge*, Thames Publishing, 1976.
Pirie, Peter J., *Frank Bridge*, Triad Press, 1971.

## O'NEILL

Hudson, Derek, *Norman O'Neill: A Life of Music*, Quality Press, 1945.

## QUILTER

Hold, Trevor, *The Walled-In Garden: A Study of the Songs of Roger Quilter (1877-1953)*, Triad Press, 1978.

## SCOTT

Hull, A. Eaglefield, *Cyril Scott: Composer, Poet and Philosopher*, Kegan Paul, Trench, Trubner, 1918.
Scott, Cyril, *Bone of Contention: Life Story and Confessions*, The Aquarian Press, 1969.
Scott, Cyril, *My Years of Indiscretion*, Mills & Boon, 1924.

## GRAINGER

Bird, John, *Percy Grainger*, revised edn, Faber & Faber, 1982 (first published Paul Elek, 1976).
Foreman, Lewis (ed.), *The Percy Grainger Companion*, Thames Publishing, 1981.

## BLISS

Bliss, Arthur, *As I Remember*, Faber & Faber, 1970.
Foreman, Lewis, *Arthur Bliss: Catalogue of Complete Works*, Novello, 1980.
Palmer, Christopher, *Bliss*, Novello, 1976.

## WALTON

Howes, Frank, *The Music of William Walton*, 2nd edn, Oxford University Press, 1974.
Craggs, Stewart R. (with a critical appreciation by Michael Kennedy), *William Walton: A Thematic Catalogue of his Musical Works*, Oxford University Press, 1977.

## LAMBERT

Lambert, Constant, *Music Ho! A Study of Music in Decline*, 3rd edn, Faber & Faber, 1966 (first published, 1934).
Shead, Richard (with a memoir by Anthony Powell), *Constant Lambert*, Simon Publications, 1973.

## WARLOCK

Copley, I.A., *The Music of Peter Warlock: A Critical Survey*, Denis Dobson, 1979.
Gray, Cecil, *Peter Warlock: A Memoir of Philip Heseltine*, Jonathan Cape, 1934.
Tomlinson, Fred, *A Peter Warlock Handbook*, 2 vols, Triad Press, 1974, 1977.

## MOERAN

Wild, Stephen, *E.J. Moeran*, Triad Press, 1973.

## GURNEY

Gurney, Ivor, *Collected Poems* (ed. P.J. Kavanagh), Oxford University Press, 1982.
Gurney, Ivor, *War Letters: A Selection* (ed. R.K.R. Thornton), Mid Northumberland Arts Group and Carcanet New Press, 1983.
Hurd, Michael, *The Ordeal of Ivor Gurney*, Oxford University Press, 1978.

## HOWELLS

Palmer, Christopher, *Herbert Howells: A Study*, Novello, 1978.

## BUSH

*Tribute to Alan Bush on His Fiftieth Birthday: A Symposium*, Workers Music Association, 1980.
Bush, Alan, *In My Eighth Decade and Other Essays*, Kahn & Averill, 1980.

## RUBBRA

Foreman, Lewis (ed.), *Edmund Rubbra*, Triad Press, 1977.
Ottaway, Hugh, *Edmund Rubbra: An Appreciation*, Alfred Lengnick, 1981.

## TIPPETT

Bowen, Meirion, *Michael Tippett*, Robson Books, 1982.

Hurd, Michael, *Tippett*, Novello, 1978.

Kemp, Ian (ed.), *Michael Tippett: A Symposium on His 60th Birthday*, Faber & Faber, 1965.

Matthews, David, *Michael Tippett: An Introductory Study*, Faber & Faber, 1980.

Tippett, Michael, *Moving into Aquarius*, enlarged edn, Paladin Books, 1974 (first published Routledge & Kegan Paul, 1959).

Tippett, Michael, *Music of the Angels: Essays and Sketchbooks of Michael Tippett* (ed. Meirion Bowen), Eulenberg Books, 1980.

White, Eric Walter, *Tippett and His Operas*, Barrie & Jenkins, 1979.

Whittall, Arnold, *The Music of Britten and Tippett: Studies in Themes and Techniques*, Cambridge University Press, 1982.

## BRITTEN

Blyth, Alan (ed.), *Remembering Britten*, Hutchinson, 1981.

Britten, Benjamin, *On Receiving the First Aspen Award*, 2nd impression, Faber Music, 1978.

Evans, Peter, *The Music of Benjamin Britten*, Dent, 1979.

Gishford, Anthony (ed.), *Tribute to Benjamin Britten on his Fiftieth Birthday*, Faber & Faber, 1963.

Holst, Imogen, *Britten*, the Great Composers Series, 3rd edn, Faber & Faber, 1980.

Kennedy, Michael, *Britten*, the Master Musicians Series, Dent, 1981.

Mitchell, Donald (ed.), *Britten and Auden in the Thirties: The Year 1936*, Faber & Faber, 1981.

Mitchell, Donald, and Evans, John, *Benjamin Britten: Pictures from a Life 1913–76*, Faber & Faber, 1978.

Mitchell, Donald and Keller, Hans (eds.), *Benjamin Britten: A Commentary on his Works by a Group of Specialists*, Rockliffe, 1952.

Palmer, Christopher (ed.), *The Britten Companion*, Faber & Faber, 1984.

White, Eric Walter, *Benjamin Britten: His Life and Operas*, new edn, Faber & Faber, 1983.

Whittall, Arnold, *The Music of Britten and Tippett*, see above.

# Index

Elgar, Sir Edward (*cont.*)

about music, 23, 25, 33; private life and
interests, 23–4; occasional pieces, 24, 32;
as progressive, 25; delineates people in
music, 26; composing method, 26;
moods, 26; lectures and teaching,
27–30; dominance, 30, 79, 230–1;
supports English music and musicians,
30–1; and folk music, 31; later years,
31–3; accused of vulgarity, 33; death
and burial, 33; visit to Delius, 34–5; on
flying, 34; dislike of ballet, 44; on
Coleridge-Taylor, 51, 53–4; earnings,
55; rejects Buckley's poems, 63;
supports Boughton's Glastonbury
project, 65; in provinces, 78–9;
friendship with Bantock, 79, 81;
Cumberland attacks, 79, 83;
recommends Walford Davies, 92;
studies abroad, 98; Vaughan Williams
seeks to study with, 98; and symphonic
form, 102; late muturity, 109; and
Musical League, 123; and John Ireland,
135; on Cyril Scott, 147; and Bliss,
157, 158, 162; Walton admires, 172;
Lambert on, 178–9
MUSICAL WORKS: *The Apostles*, 22, 27,
73; *Caractarus*, 25; Cello Concerto, 22;
*Cockaigne*, 22, 158; *The Dream of
Gerontius*, 22, 25, 29, 53, 55; 'The
Empire March', 32; *Falstaff*, 22, 35,
172; 'For the Fallen', 88; *Introduction
and Allegro for Strings*, 22, 35; *The
Kingdom*, 22; *King Olaf*, 84; 'Land of
Hope and Glory', 32; *The Music
Makers*, 22, 31; *The Spirit of England*,
22, 24, 33; *Variations on an Original
Theme* ('Enigma'), 18, 22–3, 26, 108;
Violin Concerto, 34; *Wand of Youth*,
170
Eliot, T.S., 223, 239; *The Waste Land*,
178
Ellington, Duke, 152–3
Ellis, Bevis, 117–18, 123
Elwes, Gervase, 144
*English Hymnal, The*, 96, 101

English Opera Group, 235
Epstein, Jacob, 161
Ernst, Max, 174

Farrow, Ernest, 214
Fenby, Eric: on Elgar's music, 25; on
Elgar's visit to Delius, 34; describes
Delius, 35–6, 41; on Delius's
composing, 39; as Delius's amanuensis,
41; and Delius on 'English music', 42;
on Delius's reading, 43; and Delius's
view of Beethoven, 44; on O'Neill,
143; on Grainger, 154; on Heseltine's
*The Curlew*, 192; *Delius As I Knew
Him*, 35
Festival of Britain, 1951, 209, 219
festivals, music, 12, 71, 81; *see also*
individual festivals
Fickenscher, Arthur, 153
Finzi, Gerald: friendship with Vaughan
Williams, 104; champions Gurney, 196,
204, 214; life and career, **214–16**;
marriage, 214; illness and death, 214;
song settings, 216
MUSICAL WORKS: *Dies Natalis*, 215; *In
Terra Pax*, 215; *Intimations of
Immortality*, 216; *Severn Rhapsody*, 215
Finzi, Joyce (*née* Black; wife of GF), 196,
214
Fisher, H.A.L., 96
folk music: Vaughan Williams and, 9,
99–101, 110; Holst and, 109–10, 116;
Butterworth and, 116, 118–19;
Grainger and, 150–1, 240; Lambert
disparages, 177–8; Moeran and, 193;
Britten and, 240
Foreman, Lewis, 123
Forster, E.M., 234
Foss, Hubert, 3, 60, 105, 179
Frankfurt Gang, **139–55**
Fraser, Marjory Kennedy *see* Kennedy-
Fraser, Marjory
'Free Music' (Grainger's), 153
*Freeman's Journal* (Dublin), 124
Fry, Christopher, 220
Fyfe, Hamilton, 70

INDEX